A GUIDE T

TEF Study Guides

This series was first sponsored and subsidized by the Theological Education Fund of the WCC in response to requests from Africa, Asia, the Caribbean, and the Pacific. The books are prepared by and in consultation with theological teachers in those areas. Special attention is given to problems of interpretation and application arising there as well as in the west, and to the particular needs of students using English as a second language.

General Editors: Daphne Terry and Nicholas Beddow

ALREADY PUBLISHED

IN PREPARATION

TEF Study Guide 21

A GUIDE TO ISAIAH 1—39

Jack Partain and
Richard Deutsch

First published in 1986
SPCK
Holy Trinity Church
Marylebone Road
London NW1 4DU

Unless otherwise stated the Scripture quotations in this publication are from the Revised Standard Version of the Bible (Ecumenical Edition), copyrighted 1973 by the Division of Christian Education of the National Council of the Churches of Christ in the USA.

The photographs are reproduced by courtesy of Camera Press Ltd, E. D. Terry (p. 28 top), and Dr Marietta Gesquiere-Peitz (p. 69).

British Library Cataloguing in Publication Data

Partain, Jack
   A guide to Isaiah 1–39.—(TEF study guides; 21)
   1. Bible. O.T. Isaiah I–XXXIX—Commentaries
   I. Title   II. Deutsch, Richard   III. Series
   224′.107   BS1515.3

Printed in Great Britain by the
University Press, Cambridge.

ISBN 0 281 04182 2 (net edition)
ISBN 0 281 04183 0 (non-net edition for Africa, Asia,
                    S. Pacific, and Caribbean)

Contents

CONTENTS

Editor's Note – Using this Guide

This book must be called the product of two part-authors, rather than of joint authorship. Dr Jack Partain, then at the Baptist Seminary of East Africa, was already working on an introduction to First Isaiah in Swahili when originally commissioned to prepare the Guide. But he had only got as far as chapter 12 when a motor accident in which he and his wife were both severely injured made it impossible for him to continue. We were fortunate, however, in persuading Dr Richard Deutsch of the Basle Mission, who was teaching at Chung Chi College in the Chinese University of Hong Kong, to take up the mantle. He has not only been responsible for chapters 13—39 and the Introduction and Special Notes, but has generously given invaluable help in the final editorial work on chapters 1—12, thus bringing some unity to the whole. We have not, however, attempted to impose a single style or approach on the two parts of the book, and readers may notice some differences of standpoint between the two authors, and in the way in which they have tackled their task.

The plan of the Guide follows much the same pattern as other biblical Guides in the series.

The general *Introduction* gives an outline of the historical situation in Palestine and the Near East at the time when Isaiah of Jerusalem was at work; a glance at the position of the prophets in society and their own conception of their role as interpreters of God's will for His people; and a very brief summary of the Book of Isaiah as a whole, the probable stages of its compilation, and its importance within the overall canon of Scripture.

Study of the Bible text itself has been divided into shorter or longer sections according to continuity or otherwise of subject-matter. Some cover relatively short passages where important themes are discussed in detail. Others deal in a more summary way with whole chapters, or even groups of chapters whose content overlaps with that of other sections. The treatment in each section normally consists of:

1. An *Outline* of the passage summarizing its main theme(s), prefaced where necessary by an *Introduction* explaining the literary context of the passage or the probable occasion of its composition.
2. *Notes* on particular words and points of possible difficulty, especially as relating to the historical background and to comparable passages and references in other parts of the Bible, and an *Interpretation* of the prophet's message as it applied to the people to whom it was

addressed, and as we should understand it and apply its teaching in our lives at the present time.

SPECIAL NOTES

Three separate Special Notes deal in greater detail with (1) the *historical context* of the Book of Isaiah as a whole, (2) the *literary questions* raised by the book as a whole, and more especially how and why Isaiah 1—39 was put together, (3) *prophets and their function*, both in the world of the Old Testament and today. These Notes are positioned at points where they may help to give a fuller understanding of the Bible text under study. As noted above, the general Introduction provides some background information on these subjects, and readers with limited time need not regard the Special Notes as essential to their study of Isaiah. Others may wish to read them through even before starting their study of the Bible text, rather than at the points where they are placed in the Guide.

GUIDELINES FOR BIBLE READING AND STUDY

The Guidelines following the general Introduction show how a close study of the language and structure of a passage can help to clarify its meaning. They are chiefly intended for students who are able to spend some time in textual analysis. Those who need to work through the book more quickly will find it useful to apply them as closely as they have time for, or perhaps to do so in detail for any passage which proves particularly difficult or confusing. All readers, however, are urged to read them through at least once before starting their study.

STUDY SUGGESTIONS AND QUESTIONS

Suggestions for further study and review are included at the end of each section. Besides enabling students who are working alone to check their own progress, they provide subjects for individual and group research, and topics for discussion. In most cases they are divided into four main sorts:

1. *Word Study:* to help readers check and deepen their understanding of important words and phrases.
2. *Review of Content:* to enable readers to ensure that they have fully grasped the ideas and points of teaching studied.
3. *Bible Study:* to show how the ideas and teaching in each passage studied relate to those in other parts of the Bible, and how the work and words of the prophet were understood and passed on by writers of the New Testament as well as the Old Testament.
4. *Application, Opinion, and Research:* chiefly to help readers clarify their own ideas and beliefs and relate the prophet's message to their own lives as Christians and to the work of the Church today.

The best way to use these Study Suggestions is: first, re-read the Bible passage; second, re-read the appropriate section of the Guide once or twice, carefully following up any cross-references given; and then do the work suggested, either in writing or in group discussion, without looking at the Guide again except where instructed to do so.

The *Key to Study Suggestions* at the end of the Guide will enable you to check your work on those questions which can be checked in this way. In most cases the Key does not give the answer to a question: it shows where an answer is to be found.

Please note that all these are only *suggestions*. Some readers may not wish to use them. Some teachers may wish to select only those which are most relevant to the needs of their particular students, or to substitute questions of their own.

INDEX

The Index includes only the more important names of people and places and the main subjects which appear in Isaiah 1—39 or are discussed in the Guide. Bold-type references are however provided in the Index to indicate the pages or sections where particular themes or subjects are discussed in detail.

BIBLE VERSION

The English translation of the Bible used in the Guide is the *Revised Standard Version of the Bible (Ecumenical Edition)* (RSV). Reference is also made to the *New English Bible* (NEB), the *Jerusalem Bible* (JB), and the *Good News Bible* (GNB) where these help to show the meaning more clearly, and in one or two instances to the *Authorized* (King James) *Version* (AV) and the *New International Version* (NIV).

AUTHORS' NOTE

We would like to express our deep appreciation of the work of Daphne Terry in the editing of this book. She has given considerable help and encouragement to us, and without her untiring and patient editorial work this volume would never have come to fruition.

RICHARD DEUTSCH
JACK PARTAIN

Further Reading

INTRODUCTORY BOOKS

John A. Sawyer, *Isaiah I* (Daily Study Bible). St Andrew's Press, Edinburgh.

A. S. Herbert, *Isaiah 1–39* (Cambridge Bible Commentary on the NEB). Cambridge University Press.

Ronald E. Clements, *Isaiah 1–39* (New Century Bible). Eerdmans, Grand Rapids and Marshall, Morgan and Scott.

Joseph Jensen OSB, *Isaiah 1–39*. Michael Glazier, Wilmington Delaware.

Introductory articles in The Interpreter's Bible Old Testament, Interpreter's One-Volume Commentary and Peake's One-Volume Commentary.

OLD TESTAMENT BACKGROUND BOOKS

Ronald E. Clements, *Old Testament Theology*. Marshall, Morgan and Scott.

John Drane, *The Old Testament Story: An Illustrated Documentary*. Lion Publishing, Tring.

William Neil, *Can we Trust the Old Testament?* Mowbrays.

MORE ADVANCED BOOKS

E. W. Heaton, *The Hebrew Kingdoms* (New Clarendon Bible). Oxford University Press.

P. R. Ackroyd, *Israel under Babylonia and Persia* (New Clarendon Bible). Oxford University Press.

J. Lindblom, *Prophecy in Ancient Israel*. Blackwell, Oxford.

John Bright, *A History of Israel*. SCM Press.

Introduction
The Prophet Isaiah and the Book of Isaiah

THE MAN

Very little is known about Isaiah's personal background, apart from the name of his father, Amoz, and the fact that he was married with at least two sons (1.1; 7.3; 8.3). His whole life seems to have been spent in Jerusalem. He is generally thought to have been of good family, perhaps even a member of the court and regular adviser to the kings, but scholars today are less certain of this. The suggestion that he held an official position in the Temple is also questioned.

We do know, however, that Isaiah lived and worked in Judah during the second half of the 8th century BC, when the Israelite people had separated into the two kingdoms of Israel to the North and Judah to the South.

The exact chronology of the period, that is, the order of events with the dates on which they occurred, is difficult to work out. Although the historical reference to 'the year that King Uzziah died' (6.1) seems clear enough, the dates which scholars suggest for the death of Uzziah (sometimes called Azariah) vary from 742 to 735 BC. There is also uncertainty about the dates of Uzziah's successors in Judah, Kings Jotham, Ahaz, and Hezekiah, during whose reigns Isaiah spoke. If we take it that God's call came to Isaiah about the year 740, then presumably he was born at least twenty years earlier, at the time when the prophet Amos was preaching in the Northern Kingdom.

THE NATIONS

At the time when Isaiah received the call to be a prophet (6.1) the two Israelite kingdoms were prosperous and at peace (2 Kings 14.23—15.7), though it seems that the prosperity was enjoyed chiefly by the wealthy landowners and merchants and corrupt officials.

The kings of the time had long reigns: Jeroboam II of Israel 41 years, from about 786–746 BC and Uzziah (Azariah) of Judah probably 42 years, from about 783–742 BC (see Special Note 1).

The international situation in the Near East was fairly peaceful too during the first half of the 8th century. The Assyrians, who ruled over most of the Near East at that time, except for Egypt, had difficulties with their north-eastern neighbour, Urartu, and Assyria's own kings were weak. This allowed the smaller states in Palestine and Syria to recover from earlier Assyrian attacks.

1

But when Tiglath-pileser III became king in Assyria (745–727 BC), the situation changed. He reorganized the administration of the army, and once again subdued Assyria's smaller neighbours. Most of his successors were strong rulers too, and this resulted in more than 100 years of undisputed Assyrian domination, until about 630 BC.

From words which the prophet Isaiah probably spoke during the earlier of these periods, we can see that he knew the peace would not last (see 7.1—8.10). None of the other Near Eastern nations were strong enough to stop Assyria from regaining control over the smaller states.

When King Ahaz decided, against Isaiah's advice, to request Assyrian support, Tiglath-pileser was probably already deciding to subdue Syria and Israel once again (see 7.3–9; 2 Kings 16.5–9). So when Ahaz became Assyria's vassal of his own free will, this was certainly welcome to Tiglath-pileser. But it was also exactly what Isaiah had wanted to prevent, because being a vassal state meant that the people had to worship the gods of the overlord (2 Kings 16.10–16). Hezekiah's rebellion against Assyria a little later on was at least one of the reasons why he removed all idols from the Temple in Jerusalem, and from the 'high places' where they were worshipped, as these idols would have included Assyrian 'gods'.

The reference to the Syro-Ephraimitic war in chapter 7 is the only definite mention of Israel in that part of the Book of Isaiah which relates to the lifetime of Isaiah himself. But it is possible that he was referring to Israel as well as Judah in some of his general accusations (e.g. 1.3; 5.7).

Isaiah clearly recognized Assyria as God's tool for the punishment of Judah: 'Ah, Assyria, the rod of my anger, the staff of my fury! against a godless nation I send him...to tread them down like the mire of the streets' (10.5, 6). He was also expressing this view in 7.18–20 and 8.4–8.'

Egypt he saw as continually tempting the Judean kings to rely on Egyptian military help and rebel against Assyria as a means of escaping God's wrath, instead of mending their ways and turning back to God (20.1–6; 30.1–7; 31.1–3).

Of the other nations in Palestine, Moab was seen as a 'fellow-sufferer' under alien rule, who needed and should receive support (15.1–8; 16.1, 3–5). Chapter 23, too, can perhaps be understood as a sort of lament for Tyre. But chapter 34 is an outright attack on Edom, Judah's traditional enemy. These passages, however, seem to belong to a later time than that of the prophet Isaiah himself.

THE PROPHETS

All of the prophets who spoke in Israel and Judah were deeply concerned with the political situation of each nation.

However, there is a difference between the ideas of the prophets before the destruction of Jerusalem by the Babylonians in 587/586 BC and those after this date. Isaiah of Jerusalem saw foreign powers as a tool of God's wrath (10.5). But later on these powers were seen by some as agents of God's grace (44.28; 45.1–3), and by others (such as Nahum, Habakkuk, and Zephaniah) as the enemies of God and His people. The reason for this change of opinion was the change in the historical situation of Israel and Judah. During the Exile the people desperately needed to believe that God would bring them out of suffering into a better future. And after the Exile the Israelite kingdoms no longer existed as independent nations, except during the brief period of Maccabean rule (see Special Note 1).

Many passages in the New Testament suggest that the early Christians in the first few centuries AD read the words of the prophets as 'predictions'. It seemed to them that such texts as Isaiah 7.10–17, chapters 52 and 53, and Ps. 22 foretold not only the coming of a Messiah (Christ), but also what happened to Jesus during his Passion and in his Resurrection (compare Matt. chapters 26—28; Mark 14—16; Luke 24). Today, too, many Christians read the Old Testament, and particularly the words of the prophets, in this way.

We can usefully look at this question from two viewpoints:

1. The viewpoint of faith: Early Christians were convinced that Jesus of Nazareth was the Messiah, the Christ whom God had sent to lead not only the Jews, but all human beings, back to Him; and

2. The viewpoint of the prophets: The prophets had to speak to their people in very concrete political situations, to make known to them God's will on the moral and religious problems of the time.

To look at it in this way may help us to solve some common misunderstandings.

As we have seen above, Isaiah was trying to advise the kings of his time what they should do. It seems clear that in his message to King Ahaz (chapter 7), he was talking about the immediate situation, rather than predicting events which would occur in the faraway future, 700 years ahead. The same is true for chapters 9 and 11: Isaiah was chiefly concerned with the problems of his own time, and spoke of events that would take place then and there, in the very immediate future. So it seems that the 'young woman' (7.14) was probably someone known to Ahaz (some scholars suggest one of the princesses, or perhaps Isaiah's wife). We should note that only the Septuagint (the first Greek translation of the Jewish Scriptures), and thus also early Christian translations, use the word 'virgin' in this verse. And the message which the verse carries seems to have been not a promise, but a threat.

The messages in 9.1–6 and 11.1–9 (and some other passages), however, are of a very different kind, as we shall see when we come to study them in detail. In general their writers made use of two traditional beliefs which the people held at that time:

1. The expectation of an ideal king, often described as 'David's descendant', who would come to reign in the future;

2. The return of paradise.

Both these traditional expectations or hopes were frequently expressed in later Jewish writings of the sort called 'apocalyptic' (see Introduction to chapters 24—27), and there are several examples of them in the Book of Isaiah, e.g. 2.2–4 (compare Micah 4.1–4); parts of chapters 24—27; 30.19–26; parts of 33; and 35 (see also chapters 60—62; 65; 66). Similar passages can be found in the Book of Zechariah, and in non-Biblical apocalyptic writings such as Enoch and the Testaments of the Twelve Patriarchs.

From this brief survey we can see that at different times people were concerned with different matters. When times were bad for the Jews they thought and wrote a lot about the salvation they hoped for. This was part of their faith in God. So we can also understand that the prophets, and particularly the prophet Isaiah, were concerned with what was going on in their own times.

When we come to study these same texts from the viewpoint of the faith of the early Church, however, everything looks very different. For the early Christians, the belief that Jesus was the Messiah or Christ sent by God was the first and most important matter. When they read the Scriptures they were not so much interested in what the problems had been at the time when Isaiah or other prophets were actually speaking or writing. They found in the Scriptures many things which reminded them of what they believed in, i.e. God's purpose for human beings, peace and safety, God's great love, the life and work of Jesus. So they often used the words of the earlier writers to describe their own faith, and what God's saving act in Jesus the Christ meant to them.

We can also now see that a variety of texts from different times are contained in the present Book of Isaiah.

THE BOOK

In ancient times, moreover, people were less concerned than we are today to know about questions of authorship, or whether a particular passage was spoken by Isaiah or by someone else. They were mainly interested in the meaning of the message itself.

At a certain time, perhaps during or after the Exile, Jewish scholars and religious leaders put the words of the prophets together for a specific purpose: to be read in the worship services of the Jewish community. These texts were to illustrate, and to help the people to understand, the teachings of the Law as recorded in the *Torah*, i.e. the so-called 'Five Books of Moses': Genesis to Deuteronomy, as they stand in our Bibles.

The words of the prophets had already been collected earlier by their friends and disciples. We can tell this from certain groups of passages, such as Isaiah 6—8; 5 and 9; and 10, which have common features. Chapters 24—27; 32—35; and 36—39 also belong among these passages, though they were actually written at a later time. So we can speak of several 'stages' in the development and compilation of the Book of Isaiah. The so-called 'historical appendix', chapters 36—39, seems to suggest that chapters 1—39 may possibly have been collected into a 'Book of Isaiah' some time before chapters 40—45 and the later chapters 56—66 were added (though there is no direct evidence for this).

But the whole Book must nevertheless be seen as a unit. It leads from the time of sin, punishment, and struggle (chapters 1—39), through to the time of exultation and comfort (chapters 40—55), and finally to the time of the eventual fulfillment of God's promises (chapters 56—66).

From all this we can see that the messages in the Book of Isaiah are linked to historical events which took place over a period of more than 200 years, and that this period, and hence the Book itself, falls into three main parts, of which a brief summary may be useful at this point:

1. Following the call of Isaiah himself in about 740 BC, as recorded in 6.1, the prophet's warnings to the kings who reigned in the second part of the 8th century BC and in the 7th century foreshadowed the disasters described in the rest of chapters 1—39. These were the disasters experienced by the Israelites throughout the 7th century at the hands of the Assyrians, first in the Northern Kingdom and then in Judah, until the capture of Jerusalem by the Chaldean forces of Babylon and the final deportation of the people in 587.

2. Chapters 40—55 relate to the period of Babylonian power which followed the collapse of Assyria, leading up to the fall of Babylon to Cyrus the Persian in 539 BC. The prophet addresses the exiled Jews in Babylon, comforting them and promising their liberation and return to Judah/Jerusalem. But only on one condition: they must 'return' to their God with renewed trust and faith.

3. Chapters 56—60 relate to the people's return to their own country, and their efforts to rebuild Jerusalem and re-establish the true worship of Yahweh in a new Temple which was finally completed in 515 BC.

In spite of the differences between the three parts of the Book, many similarities can be found between a number of the earlier passages and certain passages in later chapters. For this reason, some biblical scholars still hold the traditional view that the whole Book was the work of Isaiah himself, working in the 8th century BC and foretelling with great exactness the events of later centuries, even naming the political leaders who would take part in them.

The differences between the different parts of the Book are, however, very much greater than the similarities, and this is true not only of the historical background, but also of the general tone and literary style. Most biblical scholars today, therefore, regard the Book of Isaiah as a sort of 'basin', in which many prophetic oracles or messages from God are collected together, although, as we have seen, they did not all come from Isaiah of Jerusalem himself.

One reason for this may have been the high respect many later people had for this prophet. So it seems that when any of his admirers made a collection of the words he had spoken or written, they would include other oracles which they thought important and worth preserving. And because these oracles were put together by those responsible for the people's worship, the compilers probably did not hesitate to add words and ideas of their own, or of others whom they knew and respected as spiritual leaders of the people.

In still later times, books were often written or compiled and named after important people of the past in order to give them authority. The later Books of Daniel, Enoch, the Wisdom of Solomon, the Testaments of the Twelve Patriarchs, and several books with the name 'Ezra' other than the one in our Bible, are examples of books named after famous people of earlier times. All of this was in accordance with common practice and it was done in good faith for valid religious and theological reasons. The intention of the writers or compilers was not to 'cheat', but to show the nature of the writings and to emphasize their importance. This practice may be compared with the way in which many writers or artists use pseudonyms or 'pen names' today.

As we have seen, Isaiah's own messages were concerned directly with the situation in Judah in the latter part of the 8th century BC, and with the consequences to be expected from the short-comings of both the leaders and the people at that time. But there is much that we today can learn from his teaching about the nature of God, and about the demands God makes upon His people, and the salvation He promises. Christian writers have always regarded Isaiah as specially important among the Old Testament prophets.

STUDY SUGGESTIONS

1. Approximately when did Isaiah receive the call to be a prophet of God, and where did he work?
2. What was the political situation in Palestine generally during Isaiah's lifetime?
3. Why did Isaiah advise King Ahaz against asking for Assyrian support and protection when the Northern Kingdom joined Syria in plotting against Judah?

4. What was Isaiah's opinion of Egypt, and why?
5. What was the difference between the ideas about foreign powers which the prophets of God held before 587/586 BC and their ideas after that date, and what was the event which changed them?
6. (a) For what chief purpose were the traditional expectations about the coming of an ideal king, and about the return of paradise, made use of by the prophets and writers whose words are contained in Isaiah 1—39?
   (b) What did the early Christians and writers of the New Testament understand from the prophets' use of those traditional beliefs and expectations?
   (c) What do Christians today understand from (i) the prophets', and (ii) the New Testament writers', use of those beliefs?
7. The book of Isaiah as a whole falls into three parts: chapters 1—39, 40—55, and 56—66. What period does each of these parts cover, and what are the main subjects or themes of each?
8. What are the most important differences between the different parts of the Book of Isaiah, which lead most biblical scholars today to believe that Isaiah of Jerusalem was not himself the 'author' of the Book as a whole?
9. What are some of the chief lessons which Christians today can learn from the study of Isaiah?

General Guidelines
for Bible Reading and Study

As with anything we read, a careful study of the language and structure of the Bible text as we work through it can help to clarify its meaning. The guidelines below are specially intended for students of the Book of Isaiah who are able to spend some time in detailed textual analysis. But even those who wish to work through the book more quickly will find it useful to follow them as closely as they have time for.

1. Before you begin work on each section or 'lesson' in this Guide, read the Bible passage straight through so as to get a general idea of its meaning. Then read it again once or twice very carefully, if possible in more than one translation, and of course in your own language first of all, if this is not English. (Students who can do so should also read the original Hebrew.)

As you read, note any natural breaks or divisions in the passage. To do this, you should look out for changes in the subject or style: Is it written in the first, second, or third person? Is it in the singular or plural? Look also for changes in the sort of writing: Is the passage a statement, a dialogue, a narrative? Is it prose or poetry, prayer, etc.? In some Bible versions those passages which are in verse, i.e. poems, poetic narratives, or hymns to be used in worship, are set out in a different way from those which are in prose.

2. Put all your findings down on a sheet of paper, leaving enough space to allow you to add to it as you study the passage more deeply.

3. Beside each unit or division of the text, with your reasons for separating it from the rest, put down any key words, or give it a title, showing what it is about.

4. By now you should be able to decide what the literary structure of the passage is. Is it an introduction, the development or discussion of a theme, an explanation, a summary, a conclusion, or perhaps just a link with the preceding or following passage of text? Does it consist of a collection of small units, or is it a single complete unit in itself?

5. During this preliminary study you will probably find yourself asking certain questions: Who is or are the speaker(s)? What was the occasion of speaking? What was the reason for speaking or writing? What political, social, or cultural situation can you see or deduce from the passage, and what details enable you to do this? To whom was the passage addressed? You will probably not be able to answer all of these

questions straight away. The Notes and Interpretation in each section, together with your answers to the Study Suggestions, will help you to do so.

6. For some questions you may need to consult a reference book. A *Concordance*, for example, will enable you to find out how any difficult or particularly important words are used in other passages in Isaiah or in other parts of the bible, and so help you to discover their meaning or understand it more fully. A *Bible Dictionary* will help you to discover more about historical, political, cultural, and other background details. A *Bible Atlas* should help you to understand more clearly the implications of any geographical details.

7. Try also to understand the place, function, and purpose of the passage within its literary context. i.e. in relation to the preceding and following passages, and beyond this, perhaps, to the Book of Isaiah as a whole.

8. If the passage reminds you of other Bible passages you are familiar with, read those through carefully and notice the points of similarity and difference.

9. As you do all this, try to be objective, i.e. avoid drawing on the ideas you already have about this or other passages. Don't assume that you already know all about it. Try to compare what you are able to find out with what you already knew, or thought you knew, beforehand.

1.1–9
Rebellious Sons

OUTLINE

The Book of Isaiah begins with what could be called 'typical messages' from the prophet.

V. 1: A descriptive heading or title for these messages.

Vv. 2–4: The prophet calls the whole universe to witness in God's case against the amazing and stubborn rebellion of His people.

Vv. 5–9: Judah has been invaded and Jerusalem has barely escaped. The country lies desolate, like a wounded man near to death.

NOTES AND INTERPRETATION

1.1: The vision of Isaiah...which he saw...in the days of Uzziah...: Compare 6.1: 'In the year that King Uzziah died I saw the Lord...'. The reference to Isaiah as 'he' in 1.1 clearly shows that this verse is the heading or title which a later editor gave to the collection of Isaiah's messages which follows. It is the first of two introductions, the other being 2.1. Here in 1.1 what the prophet has to say is called a 'vision', and 2.1 also refers to the word which Isaiah 'saw'. But we do not know exactly how Isaiah received the message which God revealed.

This title verse does however tell us three things:

(a) *Who spoke the prophecy:* It tells us the names of the prophet and his father Amoz (not the same as the prophet Amos).

(b) *When Isaiah lived:* The kings named ruled in Judah from about 783–687 BC. But from 6.1 we learn that Isaiah was not called to be a prophet until the last year of King Uzziah's life, that is, about 742 BC or a little later.

(c) *Who the message was for:* that is, the people of Jerusalem and Judah. This title verse was probably first meant only for a collection of Isaiah's messages concerning Judah and Jerusalem. However, it now seems to stand as an introduction for the Book as a whole, which includes prophecies concerning many other peoples, and, as most biblical scholars now believe, by other prophets as well.

1.2: Hear...and give ear...reared and brought up: We should notice that in many of Isaiah's messages he said the same thing twice, but in different words. This use of 'doublets', or twin-words which *mean* the same, is characteristic of Hebrew poetry, just as rhyme (words which *sound* the same) is characteristic of some poetry in English and other languages today. Many of the prophets used poetic language rather than prose to make their messages clearer and more striking and memorable. In the RSV and most modern Bibles the poetic passages are set out in a series of long and short lines, unlike prose, to show the rhythm or metre in which they would be spoken or sung (see e.g. the books of Jeremiah, Hosea, Amos, Micah, parts of Ezekiel, etc.).

O heavens...O earth: to understand this passage we need to imagine the scene in a law-court. God is the King and Judge who presides over the court, and heaven and earth, that is, the whole of His creation, is summoned to give witness. God's people, the Israelites, are in the dock, and the words which begin in v. 3b are the Judge's charge or accusation against them.

1.4: Ah, sinful nation...they have forsaken the LORD: These seem to be the words of a witness against Judah. In vv. 5–8 someone else, perhaps the prophet, speaks directly to the accused. And finally, in v. 9, the accused themselves are speaking.

Sons: The very first word of God's charge against His people emphasized the closeness of their relationship to Him, and thus the seriousness of their act of rebellion against Him.

The Holy One of Israel: The prophet often used this title as a way of reminding people what God is like. (In fact it appears more often in the Book of Isaiah than in all the rest of the Bible together.) When Isaiah received his call he was made very much aware of God's holiness (see notes on 6.3 and Interpretation p. 67). To say that God is the 'Holy One' is not only to emphasize His perfection or His power and glory. It is also a reminder that God and man are separated by sin. Because of sin human beings must be in awe before God. Our sense of God's holiness reflects the sense of our own sin and lack of holiness, and the awe we feel when we are aware of God's presence (see note on 6.5).

The prophet Isaiah himself (in Isa. 1—39) used this title, and the idea of God's holiness, to emphasize the justice of God in His judgement and punishment of Judah. By contrast the prophet of the Exile (in Isa. 40—55) used it to comfort the Israelites in captivity: God's 'holiness' is also the guarantee of mercy and salvation.

1.5: Why will you still be smitten...continue to rebel? The message in vv. 5–8 is addressed to the whole people. Isaiah speaks of the nation as he would speak of one person, just as today we often use the singular pronoun 'she' to mean a whole country or state. Judah had been 'smitten' like a man wounded in battle, but still the people failed to understand that this was a direct consequence of their own disobedience and estrangement from God. They simply continued in their evil ways.

1.7: Your country lies desolate...overthrown by aliens: We cannot be certain which war Isaiah was referring to. But Judah had clearly been overrun by a foreign army, probably that of the Assyrian overlords in

'Imagine the scene in a law-court. God is the Judge, the whole creation is to give witness, God's people are in the dock' (p. 11).

In this court in Malaya, the charge against the accused was murder.

What was the accusation against God's people, according to Isaiah, and what sort of witness could 'the whole creation' give?

701 BC, when all the fortified cities except Jerusalem itself were destroyed as a punishment for King Hezekiah's rebellion, or perhaps earlier during the Syro-Ephraimitic war (2 Kings 18.5–9; but see also Isa. 7.1, 2). Isaiah poignantly describes the sadness and loneliness of defeat.

1.8: The daughter of Zion is left: 'Zion' was the small ridge or 'mount' on which the original town of Jerusalem had been built, and on which the Temple stood. 'Daughter of Zion' was a poetic way of saying 'the people of Jerusalem'. Only Jerusalem, where Hezekiah was forced to surrender, had been spared from destruction (see 2 Kings 18.13–16).

A booth...a lodge: These were small temporary shelters used by the watchmen who guarded the harvest from birds, animals, or thieves.

1.9: The LORD of hosts: Many Old Testament writers, and especially the prophets, used the title 'LORD of hosts' (i.e. of armies) to show that God acts with power in the lives of nations as well as individuals. See notes on 6.3 and 24.21.

A few survivors: The AV and some other English Bible versions translate this as 'remnant', but the Hebrew word is not the one Isaiah used elsewhere for the 'remnant' of Israel whom God would justify and preserve. Here he was not so much giving the people a promise of salvation, as a stern last warning that, unless they turned back to God while there was still time, they would share the fate of the 'lost cities' Sodom and Gomorrah: all, or almost all, the inhabitants would be destroyed (see Gen. 19.24–28).

Chapter 1 has been described as 'a brilliant introduction to the entire message of Isaiah'. That message had two main themes:

1. *The reaffirmation of God's promises to David:* 'I the LORD will be their God, and my servant David shall be prince over them' (Ezek. 34.24 and see 2 Kings 8.19). This in turn reflected God's promise to Moses: 'I will deliver you...and I will take you for my people, and I will be your God' (Exod. 6.6, 7). And it was coupled with the hope of a 'coming king' (Messiah) under whose righteous rule God's people would live in peace and safety 'forever' (see 32.16–18).

2. *The denunciation of the people's disobedience* in having forsaken the ways of life God had shown them, and stern warnings of the disasters which would inevitably follow.

GOD'S CASE AGAINST HIS PEOPLE

Since the days of Abraham God had treated the Israelites as a father treats his children. He had given them a special homeland and established a special relationship with them. For many centuries they had experienced His steadfast love and care. But sometimes people disregard or even despise those who care most for them, who help them most. The Israelites despised God (3.4) and rebelled against Him, going their own way and refusing to behave as good sons should.

Isaiah's many accusations against Israel help us to understand the seriousness of sin. Here he compares it to the 'rebellion' of children who know very well what their relationship with their parents ought to be. To 'know' God (v. 3) as one knows a parent is no small matter. Such knowledge goes far deeper than mere information about God and about God's will. It is – or should be – intimate, emotional, revealing, and demanding. Some other Old Testament writers even compared such a relationship with God to that of a wife and husband. Rebellion or separation from someone we know in this way is a terrible thing, even in a purely human relationship. The Israelites' rebellion, and their failure to accept and preserve the special covenant relationship God had granted to them, was a terrible sin. Sin is nothing else but separation from God; and the defeat and disaster they were suffering was the 'punishment' for that sin.

In Isaiah's time most of the nations were governed by kings, many of whom had powers over the vassal nations whom they had defeated in battle. Usually these powers were defined by some sort of agreement or covenant. Then if there was rebellion or uprising among the vassal nations a Council would be called to witness against the troublemakers, and pass sentence according to the seriousness of the accusation. Prophets often used the idea of such a Council or lawcourt, with the Lord as King and Judge, to convey their accusations against the leaders and people of Israel. Isaiah certainly had such a picture in his mind here (and also in 1.18 and 3.13–15).

THE RESULTS OF REBELLION

Isaiah made it very clear that the troubles which had come upon Israel and Judah were the direct result of their disobedience. Instead of living as God had taught them, and trusting Him to help them as He had in the past, they had allowed corruption and injustice to undermine their society. They had despised God's protection and relied on military alliances instead, as when Ahaz asked the King of Assyria for help against the Syrians (2 Kings 16.7). The result was military defeat and disaster, cities were burned, foreign armies 'devoured the land'. No wonder Isaiah felt compelled to rebuke his people and challenge them to return to their former faith and obedience. But Ahaz said 'I will not...' (Isa. 7.12), and so later on did Hezekiah and his ministers. And as Isaiah had warned, God's judgement was inescapable: He left His people to suffer the consequences of their rebellion – a fate which was very nearly as bad as that of Sodom and Gomorrah, the cities whose false worship is described in the next part of the chapter.

Some readers may ask whether Isaiah's words mean that the leaders of Christian nations today ought not to enter into alliances with other nations for purposes of defence. But we have to remember that Isaiah was speaking in particular circumstances at a particular time; he was not making pronouncements about military strategy as such. But his message certainly carries a meaning which remains true for all time, which is that the peace and prosperity of any people depends more on their relationship with God and the way they use His gifts, than on the military power or material wealth they may possess.

STUDY SUGGESTIONS

WORD STUDY

1. The words printed in italics below have special meanings in this passage. For each of these words choose *one* of the three words which follow it, which has a similar meaning. (You may find it helpful to look up the words in a dictionary before making your choice.)
   (a) *estranged:* separated from   orderly   peculiar
   (b) *know or knows:* be acquainted with   be closely related to   be full of learning
   (c) *smitten:* judged   beaten   attracted
   (d) *despised:* disregarded   pitied   hated
   (e) *aliens:* insects   enemies   foreigners
2. 'The vision of Isaiah...which he saw concerning Judah and Jerusalem' (v. 1).
   (a) Explain what is meant by the word 'vision' as used in this verse.
   (b) Use a Concordance to find other passages in the Bible where the word 'vision' is used with the same meaning as in v. 1, and list some of the doublets or twin-words which were used with 'vision' in those passages.

REVIEW OF CONTENT

3. 'In the days of Uzziah, Jotham, Ahaz, Hezekiah'. Approximately when did these kings reign?
4. For what reasons did Isaiah call on the 'heavens' and the 'earth' to hear his message?
5. Who were the 'sons' mentioned in v. 2, and in what way had the Lord 'reared them' and 'brought them up'?
6. The 'whole head...whole heart...sole of the foot'. Whose body was Isaiah describing in this way?
7. What is meant by 'daughter of Zion', (3.8), and why was she compared to a 'booth' and a 'lodge'?

BIBLE STUDY

8. Use a Concordance to find other instances of the title 'Holy One of Israel' in the Book of Isaiah. What important differences do you find between the way this title is used in chapters 1–31, and the way it is used in chapters 40—45?

9. 'Israel does not know me.' The prophets frequently complained that the people did not 'know' God. Read Amos 3.2 and Hosea 4.1,6, and compare the way the word 'know' is used in those passages with the way it is used in the phrase 'to know me is to do my will'. Would better education have given the Israelites the sort of knowledge of God they lacked?

Notice the statements about 'knowing' in John 14.7 and 17.3, and in 2 Timothy 1.12. What is the Christian view?

10. (a) Use a Concordance to discover which of the prophets, if any, actually refer to the heavenly court in which God is Judge, as a 'Council'.

(b) For each of the following passages say (i) what it adds to our understanding about the heavenly Council, and (ii) which characteristic parts of the Covenant lawsuit it refers to.
(a) 1 Kings 22.19–28 (b) Jer. 2.1–37 (c) Jer. 23.18–22 Hos. 2.2–15
(d) Hos. 4.1–10 (e) Amos 3.1–15 (f) Amos 4.1–3 (g) Micah 6.1–15

APPLICATION, OPINION, AND RESEARCH

11. To whom and in what situation did Isaiah speak? In what ways does knowing who Isaiah's listeners were, help us today to know how we should apply his words? Who are 'God's people' today? In what ways, if any, could we apply Isaiah's words to any nation which has been destroyed by war?

12. Read the story of the destruction of Sodom and Gomorrah in Genesis 18.16—19.28. Isaiah referred to these cities as examples or warnings. What are they examples of?

13. Isaiah recognized God's hand in a war against his country. Can Christians today rightly say that any particular war is approved, or led, or used by God? Can they *know* whether it is?

14. If Isaiah was living in your country today, what message or messages do you think he would have for the leaders of the nation? For the people as a whole?

1.10–20
False Standards of Worship

OUTLINE

V. 10: Introductory verse linking a separate oracle to Vv. 1–9 by a sarcastic repetition of the reference to Sodom and Gomorrah.

Vv. 11–15: The prophet denounces the double standards prevailing in Judah's religion. Splendid ritual and costly sacrifices would not blind the Lord to injustice and oppression.

Vv. 16, 17: These verses continue the 'judgement' theme. The prophet challenges the people to put an end to the exploitation of the poor and weak.

Vv. 18–20. The accused are offered a choice – if they will only return to obedience and the covenant relationship with God, their rebellion will be forgiven. If not, they must take the consequences.

NOTES AND INTERPRETATION

1.10: Hear the word of the LORD ... the teaching of our God: Again Isaiah saw himself in God's royal court of justice. We still use the word 'court' for the place where justice is dispensed, because traditionally kings were not only the rulers, but also the judges of their people. Notice that the words of this verse are not enclosed in quotation marks: they are the words of the court crier announcing that the case is to begin. The Hebrew word '*Torah*', here translated 'teaching' is usually translated as 'Law', meaning all the revelation and guidance which God gave His people through the words of the prophets since the time of Moses. The rest of the passage is a statement of God's case or accusation against His people.

You rulers of Sodom ... of Gomorrah: A continuation of the comparison in v. 9, where Isaiah used the two cities as examples of total destruction. Here in v. 10 he calls the Israelite leaders '*rulers* of Sodom and Gomorrah' to emphasize their total badness. Once again he was warning the Israelites that unless they changed their ways they would come to a bad end. Because of their badness God was permitting their destruction instead of protecting them. Thus their sin would necessarily bring its own punishment – *unless* they would 'give ear and repent'.

1.11–15: The multitude of your sacrifices ... burnt offerings ... vain offerings; incense ... solemn assembly ... appointed feasts ... many prayers: In these verses we get a vivid picture of what the worship services were like in Isaiah's time. Although some parts of the animals offered in sacrifice ('fat'…'blood', v. 11), and also some cereal offerings, were burnt on the altar (see Lev. 2.1–3; 3.1–5), 'sacrifice' is the general word for the gifts which the people brought to God. Some offerings were shared out among those who brought them and the priests, and were eaten as 'community sacrifices' (see 1. Sam. 1.3–5; 2.13,14; Amos 5.22).

Many of these offerings were of great value, and many no doubt were offered in great hope. But they were unacceptable to God, as was all the rest of the Temple worship, and therefore 'vain', worthless, when the people offering them were doing evil instead of good. More than that, such sacrifices were an 'abomination' (v. 13 – the word mostly used to describe worship of idols – see Prov. 21.27).

1.12: When you appear before me: The Hebrew words actually mean 'when you come to see my face'. Clearly the people believed that God was specially present at the Temple in Jerusalem and other places of worship, just as many Christians feel (rightly or wrongly) that God is somehow specially present in church buildings. But in v. 12 there is another reference to the idea of judgement by the heavenly 'Council', and Isaiah was not implying that worshippers would see God face to face.

The ordinary people did not actually enter the Temple building at Jerusalem. Only the priests were allowed inside. Worship took place in the large outer space or courtyard – the 'court' of God who was both King and Judge. It seems that the people thought they could please God by the number of times they visited the Temple on the set days for worship, and by the number of sacrifices they offered, rather than by sincerely trusting in Him and trying to live according to His law. Instead, of course, the opposite was true: instead of pleasing God, such artificial worship was a 'burden' to Him (v. 14).

1.13: I cannot endure iniquity and solemn assembly: Many readers have been puzzled by this verse, which some take as a suggestion that religious festivals are wrong in themselves. But this can hardly have been Isaiah's view, and it seems more likely to have been a protest against the hypocritical combination of wickedness and worship. However, even the early translators failed to understand this, as the ancient Greek version differs from the Hebrew, and modern translations vary considerably.

1.15: When you spread forth your hands: It was the custom at that time to pray standing up, looking upwards, and with hands outstretched and open as if to receive (see 1 Kings 8.22).

Your hands are full of blood is picture-language, not a reference to the actual blood of the sacrifices. Isaiah was not opposed to sacrifice as such, and the words of the following verse: 'wash yourselves…remove the evil of your doings', show that he was speaking figuratively. He was accusing the people of exploiting and destroying their fellows. To say 'your hands are full of blood' is the same as saying 'you murderer!'

1.16: Make yourselves clean: Ceremonial washing was a normal part of Temple worship, but God required a cleanness which no outward ceremony would bring. God's people must cease to do evil both inwardly and outwardly in their daily lives.

1.17: Seek justice: In this verse God as Judge pronounces the ruling of the court. Notice the commands to action: 'Learn, seek, correct, defend, plead', which sum up the positive steps His people are ordered to take, especially in their own administration of justice. These are a direct reminder of the commandments which God gave to His people through Moses many centuries earlier (see Exod. 20.1–20).

1.18: Let us reason together: In the original Hebrew this is a legal phrase relating to the judgement of the court. The accused are finally offered a choice: to do as the court rules and forsake their sins, or to be destroyed.

Scarlet...crimson: The colour reference seems to link the 'court ruling' in vv. 18–20 with the warning in v. 11 that God has no use for the prayers or sacrifices of people who have 'blood on their hands' (v. 15b). Some interpreters think the words of this verse are meant to be sarcastic, reflecting the people's own self-righteous opinion of themselves as pious and dutiful worshippers fulfilling all their religious obligations to the letter. Others regard them simply as a promise that because the Israelites were *God's* people, He would in the end acquit them and overlook their sins. It seems, however, that the key to understanding v. 18 is to be found in the next verse:

1.19: If you are willing and obedient you shall eat the good of the land: that is, 'if you are willing and obedient, your sins, however "scarlet", will be washed away'. But only *if* the people turned from their evil ways. If, on the other hand, they continued in their unjust, corrupt, and oppressive behaviour they would be 'devoured by the sword' (v. 20), no matter how regularly they attended the religious festivals and offered sacrifices and prayers.

1.20: The mouth of the LORD has spoken: Isaiah would not have expected his hearers to take these words literally. The phrase 'mouth of the Lord' was used symbolically by many of the prophets to mean God's voice or a word or message of revelation received from Him.

TRUE AND FALSE RELIGION

Isaiah's chief concern in this whole oracle was to show that there is a big difference between the outward show of religion, or 'religiosity', and true religion which springs from a deep inward faith. The people to whom he spoke were very religious. They were very proud of being God's people, and were anxious to win His favour by their strictness in keeping all the set rules for the worship services, and by giving generously for the upkeep of the Temple and for its sacrifices. But at the same time they were guilty of dishonesty, corruption, and injustice, and were piling up wealth for themselves instead of helping the poor and needy. We could say that not only were they giving and accepting bribes in their daily lives; by their outward show of worship they were trying to bribe God!

But God is not to be bribed. His grace is not for sale. Isaiah was saying that trying to win favours from God by religious observance is as useless as the pagan Canaanites' practice of offering sacrifices to the 'gods' whose idols they worshipped (see e.g. 1 Kings 11.7,8). This may have been why he called the people's incense an 'abomination' (see note on v. 13), and why he made such a pointed reference to the practice of fixing religious festivals according to the moon, as pagan moon-worshippers did.

It is true that the Israelites did continue many Canaanite customs, and combined many originally pagan ideas about worship with the ideas underlying their own worship of Yahweh. This was a serious problem for many centuries. But in this oracle it was not for their worship of pagan gods that Isaiah was rebuking the people, though he did so elsewhere. He was not condemning their religious activity itself as described in vv. 11–15. He was accusing the leaders and people of *using* religion in a wrong and dangerous way, without real faith or trust in God. Instead of being an expression of sorrow for their sins, of gratitude for God's goodness to them, and of faith and trust in His continuing love and care, their worship had become a mere mechanical performance, a display of virtue, and, much worse, a way of trying to buy God's favour and protection. It was no longer true worship but hypocrisy.

THE DANGER OF HYPOCRISY

So the lesson we today can learn from this oracle is that any sort of religious observance can be offensive to God, rather than pleasing, if the worshippers are not striving to be obedient to Him in their lives. There is a danger that this will happen in almost any 'organized' religion. Jesus accused the religious leaders of His time of just this same sort of false worship (see Matt. 23.1–7 and 23—28: 'You are like whitewashed tombs...you outwardly appear righteous but within you are full of hypocrisy and injustice'). And though Paul was not thinking only about the rules for religious observance, he was teaching the Corinthian Christians the same truth when he stressed the difference between trusting in God's power and love and trusting in ourselves, or as he put it the other way round, between the 'written code' or letter of the law which 'kills' and the Spirit which 'gives life' (2 Cor. 3.6).

Isaiah's message to Judah was that the people's hypocritical worship would not save them from the consequences of their sin, that is, the destruction of their city and for themselves death by the sword of the enemy. His message to us is that our worship is acceptable to God only if we worship Him for the right reasons, and if we are living a morally 'clean' life. This means that we must be treating our fellow human beings as brothers and sisters. Dishonesty, injustice, and bad human relationships make true worship impossible.

NOTE: In this Guide we have used the word 'pagan' as a convenient way of distinguishing (a) the religions of the ancient peoples of the Near East and (b) the official religions of the Greek and Roman Empires, in all of which many gods were worshipped, from (c) the religion of God's people, both the Jews and later the Christians, who worship Him alone. Although today 'pagan' is sometimes used in a rather contemptuous way, it actually comes from a Latin word which simply means 'civilian'. It was first given a religious meaning when the early Christians began to call themselves 'soldiers of Christ', and adopted the ordinary term for anyone not in military service to describe anyone who was not a Christian.

STUDY SUGGESTIONS

WORD STUDY

1. Explain in your own words the meaning of each of the following phrases as used in 1.10–20.
   (a) appear before God   (b) spread your hands
   (c) reason together   (d) devoured by the sword
' 2. Which *three* of the following words are nearest in meaning to 'an abomination' as used in this passage?
   a curse   idolatry   a trial   detestable   abhorrent
   contestable   an abstraction

REVIEW OF CONTENT

3. (a) Why did the prophet call his hearers 'rulers of Sodom' and 'people of Gomorrah' (v. 10)?
   (b) Why did he say that God could not endure the worship they were offering Him?
4. What is the meaning of 'fed beasts' (v. 11)?
5. Describe one important difference between the ideas of the pagan Canaanites and those of the Israelites about 'burnt offerings'.
6. 'Your hands are full of blood' was not a reference to the actual blood of the sacrifices (v. 10).
   (a) What was it a reference to?
   (b) What connection, if any do you find between the reference to 'blood' in v. 15 and the words of v. 18?

7. (a) What did the prophet mean by 'new moon(s)' in vv. 13 and 14?
   (b) In what way(s) had such occasions become a 'burden' to God?
8. What is meant by the phrase 'the mouth of the LORD' (v. 20)?

BIBLE STUDY

9. Many of the prophets spoke of what God requires from those who wish to worship Him truly.
   (i) Read the following passages and say in each case what the prophet listed as the requirements for true worship of God.
   (a) 1 Sam. 15.22   (b) Hos. 6.6   (c) Amos 5.21–24   (d) Micah 6.6–8
   (ii) Read the following passages and say in each case what Jesus said was required for true worship of God.
   (a) Mark 7.6–8   (b) John 4.19–24   (c) Matt. 6.1–17
   (iii) What chief differences, if any, do you find between the teaching of the prophets about true worship, and the teaching of Jesus on the subject?
10. Read Psalm 50. vv. 7–23. In what ways do the theme and message of this passage match or differ from the theme and message of Isaiah 1.10–20?

APPLICATION, OPINION, AND RESEARCH

11. A student reading 1.13 said: 'But surely we read in the Books of Exodus and Leviticus that it was God Himself who required such religious practices. How then could He say that He could not bear them?' What is your opinion?
12. 'Any sort of religious practice can be offensive to God.' What modern religious practices, if any, do you think may be offensive to God? Have you yourself followed any such practices? Why do you think they are offensive?
13. (a) Ministers today often rebuke people for not attending worship regularly, for not giving enough money, or for failing to say their daily prayers. In what ways does Isaiah's message confirm or conflict with this understanding of what God demands from His people?
    (b) Church members who lapse from their commitment to Christ often say 'I went to church regularly, I gave generous offerings, I prayed often. But God never blessed me, so what profit is there in being a Christian?' In what ways does Isaiah's message provide the answer to their question?
14. Read again vv. 19, 20. Do these verses mean that if Christians are 'willing and obedient', and sincerely strive to do good, God will always accept their worship and save them from 'the sword'? If so, why is it that so many willing and obedient Christians have died by the sword? If not, what do they mean?

1.21—2.5
Jerusalem: Present Corruption – Future Perfection

OUTLINE

In the remainder of chapter 1 and the beginning of chapter 2 a number of short passages have been brought together, in all of which the prophet was speaking to the people of Jerusalem, his own home city.

1.1–23: A lament or elegy bewailing the spiritual corruption which had become widespread in Jerusalem, and especially in the lawcourts where it was impossible for the ordinary people to obtain justice.

1.24–26: An oracle warning that God would purge the city, burning away its impurity, and restoring it to its earlier state of righteousness and justice.

1.27, 28: A short fragment, probably of a later date, promising Zion's redemption and the destruction of those who continued to rebel.

1.29–31: Another fragment, possibly not by Isaiah, describing the fate of those who join in pagan worship.

2.1: Introduces the passage which follows as a vision: 'The word which Isaiah...saw'.

2.2–4: This much-quoted passage, ascribed by some interpreters to a later date, also appears in almost exactly the same form in Micah 4.1–3. It describes Jerusalem as the 'mountain of the LORD', a place where God would chiefly make His presence known to His people, and thus the most important place in the world. The people of all nations would come there to accept God's perfect rule, so bringing war between the nations to an end forever.

2.5: The prophet invites his hearers to 'walk in the light of the LORD', that is to repent and forsake their present sinful ways.

NOTES AND INTERPRETATION

1.21: The faithful city...a harlot: 'Harlot' is an old-fashioned word for a whore or prostitute. In using this term to describe Israel's faithlessness and breaking of the covenant relationship with God, Isaiah may have had in mind the pagan custom of ritual prostitution. But in these verses he was not specifically accusing the people of taking part in pagan worship. His accusation here seems to cover the whole life of society generally in Jerusalem at that time.

Murderers should not be taken literally, but as meaning that in the city whose people had once prided themselves on their obedience and close relationship to God, that relationship, and all trusting relationships of the people one with another, had been destroyed (see note on 1.15 and compare 'bloodshed' in 5.7).

1.22: Silver become dross and **wine mixed with water** refer not only to dishonesty and greed in trade and business relationships, but to the lowering of standards of behaviour generally. The people's moral principles had become diluted or 'watered down'.

1.23: Princes... every one loves a bribe: Members of the ruling family and court, who were also judges and government officials, were only concerned to enrich themselves by accepting bribes. They connived with criminals to defraud the very people, the widows and orphans, whom they had a special responsibility under the covenant to look after. As magistrates they refused even to hear the cases of the poor and weak who could not pay.

1.24: Therefore the Lord says, the LORD of Hosts, the Mighty One of Israel...: Isaiah seemingly added title upon title to emphasize God's greatness and the seriousness of the warning of punishment to follow. **Vent my wrath on my enemies... avenge myself:** Some interpreters have read this as a reference to the eventual defeat and punishment of the Assyrians. But in this context it seems clear that it was the faithless and disobedient people themselves who had become God's 'enemies', so that the term corresponds with 'harlot' in v. 21.

1.25: I will turn my hand against you: The words 'hand [or 'arm'] of God' usually symbolize His authority and His protective power. But clearly God's hand can punish as well as protect. (See notes on 9.12 and 11.11.)

Smelt away your dross: In this case God's hand would be turned against His people to purify them, as metal is purified by the fire which burns away the base elements and impurities from the ore. The words 'smelt', 'dross', 'lye', and 'alloy' in this verse all belong to the metal-working trade.

1.26: I will restore your judges as at the first... councillors as at the beginning: This verse is not easy to understand. Some interpreters have suggested that since the oracle was concerned with Jerusalem, the prophet was referring to the time when King David first made it his capital city. But David's government was not particularly righteous or just, and others think that Isaiah meant a more ancient tradition about Jerusalem and Melchizedek the ideal righteous king. In either case the good character of the councillors was a very important matter, and to 'restore' must mean to return to the former state, with the people's relationship with Yahweh again as it should be, corruption eliminated, and just government re-established. Then the people of Jerusalem would once again deserve to be called 'righteous' and 'faithful'.

1.27,28: Zion shall be redeemed by justice, and those in her who repent,

by righteousness: The message in these verses echoes the promise and warning in 1.19, 20. The city will be redeemed, not by God's grace alone in the way that a Christian is forgiven his sins, but in the way that the people of a city infected by disease can be saved by the introduction of preventive medicine and proper methods of hygiene.

Those...who repent are those of the inhabitants who 'turn around' or 'convert', i.e. they turn back to God and change and cleanse their ways of living.

1.29: The oaks in which you delighted...the gardens you have chosen: Some translations have 'terebinths' instead of 'oaks', but the sort of tree is not important. The prophet was clearly warning people against joining in the traditional Canaanite worship of idols which took place under sacred trees and in garden-shrines (see NEB). Those who did so would not only be ashamed, but would 'wither' and die as trees do for lack of water in the dry season (or, as the Canaanite worshippers believed, as the god of life and fertility dies in a time of drought). Even the strong and powerful among the people would come to grief as the result of their idolatrous worship. In the end idolatry does destroy those who practise it.

2.1: The word which Isaiah...saw: These words are clearly another introductory 'title' for a further message or messages (see note on 1.1). It states that Isaiah 'saw' the word, showing that the Hebrew for 'word' can mean more than merely something spoken. It can carry the idea of a 'thing', a real object, an event or happening. This 'reality' is described in 2.2–5.

2.2: It shall come to pass: That is, it *will* happen.

The poem in 2.2–5 appears in almost exactly the same terms in Micah 4.1–4. Why should this be so? There are several possible answers:

1. Isaiah and Micah both lived in Judah and at almost the same time in history. So perhaps they were both inspired by the same idea or event, or God gave the same revelation to each. Even so, that both should use almost exactly the same words seems rather too much of a coincidence!

2. Perhaps one was simply quoting words first preached by the other. Micah includes an additional verse, and also ends with the words 'the mouth of the Lord has spoken', which appear frequently in the Book of Isaiah (see note on 1.20) but nowhere else in the Bible. This could mean that Micah quoted or borrowed a poem first preached or written by Isaiah, adding some words of his own.

3. Perhaps both prophets were quoting a poem by some other person – a well-known poem, say, or a popular hymn – which expressed what each wanted to say, and which would have been familiar to their hearers.

This third possibility seems the most likely, as many of the prophets quoted common sayings, proverbs, stories, legends, and songs. And it would explain why the poem was included in the collected works of each of them. Or of course it could simply have been added to both books by a later editor who thought it matched or emphasized what each prophet was saying.

Whoever in fact was the author, these verses are great poetry. They express most beautifully one of the deepest of human hopes: that a time will come when wars are ended and all peoples live together in peace under the holy rule of God.

2.2: The latter days: This may simply mean some time in the future. However, as we shall see in chapters 24—27, this phrase, or the similar 'last days', came later on to mean a special time, at the end of human history, when God would defeat all evil and bring peace and justice for Israel.

The mountain of the house of the LORD...highest of the mountains: Taken with v. 3 this clearly means the hill of Zion (see note on 1.8), which had traditionally been regarded as the dwelling-place of God, and on which the Temple was built. Many of the prophets used this and similar phrases to mean Jerusalem (see Isa. 27.13; Ezek. 20.40; 28.16; Zech. 8.3). 'Highest' must not be taken literally. The poet was not making geographical predictions; he did not expect Mount Zion to become as high as Mount Everest. For him, Zion was the most important of all mountains because it was in the Temple that the teaching and 'word of the LORD' (v. 3) were made known to the people. It was a symbol of God's presence and power (compare 'high and lifted up' in 6.1).

2.2,3: All the nations...many peoples: In many parts of the Old Testament these terms are used in a bad sense, to mean Israel's enemies. Here the people of 'all the nations' come to God because they are looking for guidance. They 'flow' to Jerusalem like a great river, so that God may teach them His 'ways'. His teaching ('law') flows 'out of Zion' to them so that all may live as His people. This *Torah* may be a new word from God spoken by a priest or prophet. But mostly it is the revelation and guidance contained in the various books of the law which eventually came to form the Old Testament as we have it today. To live in accordance with the teaching of God is often called a 'way'. The earliest Christians were called the people of 'The Way' (see Acts 19.23). We may also compare this with *Tao*, one of the religious systems first established in China, which is both 'teaching' and 'way'. See also 35.8–10.

2.4: He shall judge: God acts as ruler of the nations, and under His perfect rule, that is, in the Kingdom of God, there is perfect justice.

They shall beat their swords into ploughshares: The common weapons of war in those times become the common farming tools on which people depend for their life and livelihood.

Shall not lift up sword...neither shall they learn war: To 'lift up sword' means 'to make war'. Individual people – and even children – fight only too readily. But warfare between nations is something which the young men and women of the armed services have to *learn*, for which they need to be trained. God's rule does away with the need for such education.

In the poem as it appears in Micah, a final stanza is added, describing a future in which people enjoy prosperity and freedom from fear:
'They shall sit every man under his vine
and under his fig tree;
and none shall make them afraid.
For the mouth of the LORD of Hosts has spoken.'

2.3,5: House of the God of Jacob...house of Jacob: 'Jacob' in both verses means Jacob the son of Isaac and grandson of Abraham, that is, the forefather of the nation of Israel, God's people. Thus 'house of the God of Jacob' means the Temple of the One true God whom Israel worshipped. But 'house of Jacob' does not mean a building; it means the clan or descendants of Jacob, that is, the Israelite people themselves.

RELIGION IN LIFE

We shall find the message of this passage repeated again and again as we work through the Book of Isaiah: God is not concerned only with 'religious' affairs, nor with people as individuals in their home and 'Church' life only. He is equally concerned with the life of society as a whole; with the groups to which we belong as clans, tribes, nations. He is concerned with the structure and working of society in cities and villages, schools and universities, farms, factories, offices, political parties, co-operatives, sports teams – in everything we are and do.

The many laws God laid down for His people show that His guidance touches every area of life. We could say that *all* life is equally religious. There is to be no division of life into 'sacred' on one hand and 'secular' on the other. No-one is outside God's rule. And under that rule the highest government official or Church leader and the poorest peasant or worker are of equal value, and have equal rights. We can be obedient to God in *all* we do, not merely by strict religious observance. God's concern is not that we should be more religious, but that we should be more truly human as He created us to be 'at the beginning'.

For these reasons the prophets insisted that corruption in society was a sign that the people had rebelled against God and forsaken His ways. Just as fever is a sign of sickness in the body, so corruption is a sign of sickness in society – a sickness caused by the people's failure to put their trust in God. Honest voting practices, diligent teaching in schools, loving care of the sick and needy – all these are rooted in the ways of obedience to God's will. Without these roots the plant of faith cannot grow.

'Sabbaths and the calling of assemblies I cannot endure...your appointed feasts my soul hates' (1.13, 14). 'Religious observance can be offensive to God if the worshippers are not obedient to Him in their lives...God is not concerned only with "religious" affairs' (pp. 20 and 27).

Sunday worshippers gather at a country church in Botswana, and the Christmas festival is celebrated in a German Cathedral.

What sort of religious observance best helps people to be obedient to God in their lives?

THE CITY OF RIGHTEOUSNESS

Since the first cities were established, people have had two opposite feelings about them. Cities represent the highest achievements of human civilization and culture, but they also hold some of humanity's worst evils. Many of the Bible writers used the great cities as symbols of evil: Sodom and Gomorrah, Babylon, Nineveh, Rome. But not Jerusalem. Jerusalem is described *both* as Zion the Holy City, 'mountain of the house of the Lord', *and* as the 'harlot', full of corruption, murderers, rebels, and sinners.

From the time of David, Jerusalem was capital city, first of the undivided Israelite kingdom, then of Judah (see 2 Sam. 5.6–10; 1 Kings 2.11). It was the largest city, the economic and cultural centre of the region, and even more important, the religious centre. The Ark of the Covenant, a symbol of God's salvation, was kept in the Temple there; and because of David's successful rule the people believed that God had chosen Jerusalem as the place where He was specially present.

By the time of Isaiah, however, society in Jerusalem had become corrupt. As happens in many growing cities, a great gap had developed between the rich and arrogant ruling classes and the poor whom they exploited, the unskilled workers who were easy prey to debt, crime, violence, prostitution, and drunkenness. Even so, Jerusalem kept its special status in the people's minds and feelings. Isaiah seems to have preached only to the people of the city. Jesus himself longed for Jerusalem's redemption (see Luke 13.22–35).

Jerusalem has kept this special status as a symbol of the Kingdom of God through the centuries, right down to the present time. Indeed we could say that part of the promise in the poem of Isaiah 2.2–4 is already being fulfilled by the great numbers of Jews and Christians, and people of other faiths from all parts of the world, who flock to the Holy Land and visit Jerusalem the Holy City each year.

Not all these people go to Jerusalem in order that God may 'teach them His ways', and many people still feel that city life is full of dangers and temptations which make it difficult to live there in ways that are pleasing to God. But we should remember that the earliest Churches began in the great cities around the eastern Mediterranean, and that although Isaiah called Jerusalem a harlot, it was not the city itself, but the wrongdoings of its citizens, that he condemned.

PEACE MADE PERFECT

No biblical promise is more treasured by God's people than the promise of 'peace on earth'. But no promise seems further from fulfillment. God's will is that all people should live together in harmony and peace. War seems like a curse upon mankind, disrupting all the normal

29

patterns of life, and appealing to our worst emotions – hatred, greed, and fear.

Some passages in the Old Testament seem to suggest that God approves of war and fights on the side of His people (e.g. 2 Chron. 26.1–8), even that He uses war to carry out His purposes (Isa. 10.5, 6). And this has led many people, including many Christians, to believe in the idea of what has come to be called the 'just war', in which one side at least (and sometimes both!) believe that they are fighting for a cause which God approves. Perhaps they are fulfilling a promise to defend a small nation attacked by a more powerful neighbour, or they are fighting to put down a tyrannical regime. And almost all of the Christian nations today believe they have the right to defend themselves against attack. So the production of armaments has become big business. New weapons are invented every year, and already the super-powers have piled up enough nuclear armaments to destroy each other many times over, even perhaps to destroy the planet Earth.

So the search for peace has become more urgent than ever before. Organizations to keep the peace, like the League of Nations after World War I and the United Nations after World War II, have done their best, but lasting agreement between the nations still seems almost impossible to achieve. And until human beings admit that war is the result of their own sin there is unlikely to be lasting peace on earth.

The reason why we cannot live peaceably with one another is because we are estranged from God. This is the message of Genesis 1—11. But peace is not something we can gain by pursuing it for its own sake. Like happiness, peace is the *result* of living in a certain way – God's way.

The prophet's vision described in Isaiah 2.1–4 is of peace made perfect only when nations turn to God and accept His rule, instead of seeking to increase their own strength by exploiting and dehumanizing those weaker than themselves. Nevertheless the message is one of high hope and promise. Fighting and killing *will* come to an end: 'It shall come to pass' if and when all peoples respond to the call 'come, let us walk in the light of the LORD'.

STUDY SUGGESTIONS

WORD STUDY

1. Who were (a) the 'murderers' and (b) the 'princes' whom Isaiah was accusing in 1.21 and 1.23?
2. The term 'my enemies' (as used in 1.24), corresponds to 'harlot' in 1.21. Explain what Isaiah meant when he used these two terms to describe the people of Jerusalem.

3. Which *two* of the following words are closest in meaning to 'redeemed' as used in 1.27?
restored   ransomed   pardoned   rescued   reformed
revived   renewed

REVIEW OF CONTENT

4. (a) What did the prophet mean when he said that Jerusalem had once been full of 'justice' and 'righteousness' (1.21)?
(b) In what chief ways had the people of Jerusalem become corrupt?
5. To what historical event was the prophet referring when he described the coming 'purification' of the people (1.24–26)?
6. In 1.28–31 the prophet spoke of 'oaks' (or 'terebinths') and 'gardens'. Was he scolding the people about their methods of forestry and horticulture? If not, what was he talking about, and why did he use those terms?
7. What explanation(s) can be given for the fact that the poem in Isa. 2.2–4 appears also in almost identical words in Micah 4.1–4?
8. (a) What important promise is the subject of Isa. 2.2–4?
(b) What has to happen in order that this promise can be fulfilled?

BIBLE STUDY

9. What difference(s) are there between the meaning(s) of 'word' as used in Isa. 2.1 and 2.3 and its meaning as used in John 1.1? Why is it spelt with a capital W in John 1.1?
10. Read the following passages and say in each case what connection you find with Isa. 1.21–25. What do you think is the explanation of that connection?
(a) Zech. 8.3   (b) Ps. 68.15–16   (c) Jer. 31.6.
11. Read Exod. 22.21—23.29. Which of God's 'laws' listed in that passage were the leaders and people of Jerusalem guilty of breaking, according to Isa. 1.21–31? Give detailed references in each case.

APPLICATION, OPINION, AND RESEARCH

12. Does the sort of 'corruption described in 1.21–23 exist in your country today? If so, what are the government or religious authorities doing to prevent it? What more could they do? Do you think those responsible for such corruption today are ever 'punished' by God, and if so, how?
13. Some politicians say, 'The only way to achieve a just society is to destroy the corrupt one we have now, even if that leads to chaos.' Do you think it is ever right to act in ways that will lead to social chaos? Give your reasons.

31

14. (a) 'Jesus answered..."You will hear of wars and rumours of war...this must take place"' (Matt. 24.4–6). Some people think this means that it is useless to try to prevent war. What is your opinion?
   (b) 'Neither shall they learn war any more' (2.4). What is the policy of your country about military training? Do you think wars would end if all nations gave up military training and the maintenance of armies in peace-time? Give your reasons.
15. 'In the end, idolatry destroys those who practise it' (p. 25). Is the worship of 'idols' common in your country? If so, what sort of idols are they, and what effect is such worship actually having on those who practise it?
16. The prophet called on his hearers to 'walk in the light of the LORD'. We find a similar call to Christians in Eph. 5.8, 9: 'Walk as children of light...learn what is pleasing to the Lord'. What are some of the ways in which we today can 'learn what is pleasing to the Lord'?

2.6–22
'The Lord Alone will be Exalted'

OUTLINE

A single theme runs through this passage: God's judgement against those who put their trust in their own strength rather than in His power and protection.

Vv. 6–8: The Lord has rejected His people. They are full of superstition, subject to foreign influences, and more concerned with wealth, armaments, and idolatry than with obeying God's laws.

Vv. 9–11: A day is coming when the proud will be humbled and God alone will be exalted.

Vv. 12–17: On that day the Lord will bring low all the symbols of human greatness.

Vv. 18–22: Then the people will reject their useless idols and hide in terror from God's majesty.

NOTES AND INTERPRETATION

2.6: House of Jacob: See note on 2.3,5.

Diviners...soothsayers like the Philistines: The exact meaning of the Hebrew text of v. 6 is not very clear. The phrase translated 'diviners' as word-twin of 'soothsayers' actually means 'of the east'. It shows that 'wisdom' or 'secret knowledge' was traditionally associated with countries to the east of Palestine (see 1 Kings 4.30). Diviners and soothsayers are the 'wise men' or sorcerers who use magic to try to discover the causes behind what happens in the world and to foretell what will happen in the future.

Strike hands with foreigners: This too is unclear. The words may be a reference to foreign trade; they may mean 'to be haughty and arrogant' (compare Job 34.37 and Ezek. 25.6), or to follow foreign customs and take part in foreign (i.e. pagan) worship. These 'foreigners' (and also the Philistines from the coastal regions to the south-west) would probably have been practising the Canaanite religion.

2.7: Silver, gold...treasures...horses...chariots: All these seem to symbolize Judah's prosperity and military strength. The description suggests that this passage dates from fairly early in Isaiah's ministry, before the Assyrian attacks had disrupted the country's trade and agriculture. Notice the emphatic style Isaiah used to strenghen his warning that the people were too much concerned with material things.

2.8: Filled with idols: From the time when they first settled in Palestine the Israelites had followed some of the Canaanite religious practices, including the use of idols. Some of these idols were believed to represent the Lord, but mostly they were simply part of the pagan cult at the local shrines (see notes on 1.11–15).

2.9,10: So man is humbled...brought low before the terror of the LORD...the glory of his majesty: The first of two repeated themes or refrains which recur in this passage, suggesting that perhaps two poems have been woven into one. But they are not merely choruses; the order of the repeated phrases changes each time, and the repetition makes the prophet's warning seem increasingly serious and dangerous as the poem proceeds. Readers using more than one Bible version will notice that the translations differ greatly in certain verses. This is because there are differences between the various early manuscript versions of the passage, some of which, as the RSV footnotes show, lack certain words or even whole verses altogether.

Forgive them not: These words seem out of place. They may have been added by an early scribe or translator to make sense of a puzzling phrase (see previous note). The NEB translates them 'and how can they raise themselves?'

2.11: Men shall be brought low...humbled...the LORD alone will be exalted: This verse states more fully the recurring theme which is developed in vv. 9, 10, further developed in vv. 12–16, and stated again in v. 17. That is, the coming time of judgement, when the proud and arrogant will be punished and shown that all their strength is as nothing beside the glorious power and majesty of God.

In that day: Like so many of the Old Testament writers, Isaiah used the word 'day' to mean not 24 hours but the time when a particular event would take place at some undefined date in the future (see note on 2.2). Such a 'day' might be short or long. It might even fall outside time, or rather at the end of time as we know it. Isaiah described the sort of 'day' he had in mind in v. 12 (and see 13.9).

THE 'DAY OF THE LORD'

The great prophets of Israel often spoke of 'the day of the LORD' (e.g. Ezek. 30.3; Joel 1.15; Amos 5.18–20), and beliefs about this 'day' had been common among the people for a long time. They felt that the strength and prosperity they had enjoyed under the rule of Kings David and Solomon were only the beginning of the good which God had in store for Israel.

In fact the divided little kingdom was not always strong and prosperous, but disappointment gave birth to hope. God was strong and holy. His people believed that He would not always allow them to be trampled by invading armies. A time would come when He would set things right. Just as God had fought for His people in the past, so He would fight for them again. He would destroy their enemies (who were His own enemies), and restore His people to their rightful place in the world. The Israelites prayed that God would bring this day soon, and many of the psalms and hymns they used in worship expressed this hope, thanking and praising God for the future joy they expected (see e.g. 4.2–6; 12.1–5).

This hope was built upon certain truths. Other religions of the time were based on the belief that time is a never-ending cycle, repeating itself season after season and year after year. But the Israelites knew well that time flows, that it moves towards a goal, and they understood that God directs the lives of all human beings towards that goal. He is Lord of time and history, as well as creator of the natural world. This insight is one of the most fundamental in the Bible.

The prophets agreed that God is moving everything towards a goal. They believed that human decisions and actions helped to shape that goal, but that God himself will one day bring everything into a meaningful whole. In that 'day', God's day, He alone will be important.

A TIME OF JUDGEMENT

The Israelites mistakenly thought that because they were God's people, the day of the Lord would necessarily be a day of victory and happiness for them. Not so, said Isaiah (compare Amos 5.18–20). That day would be the day *of the Lord*, when He would subject His people to judgement. Those who did not trust and obey God's law, and live as His covenant people, could not expect to share in His victory. For God's stubbornly rebellious sons the day would not be a day of light as they expected, but a day of judgement and dark gloom (see 8.21, 22; 9.2).

Isaiah suggested, too, that on that day God would judge *all* peoples and nations, not just Israel and her enemies. From the 8th century onwards the 'day of the LORD' became a more and more important theme in prophetic preaching (see e.g. Zech. 1—3).

Moreover, the phrase 'day of the LORD' was not limited to a single occasion. It was used to describe a number of different occasions, for example the destruction of Jerusalem in 587 BC (see Lam. 1.21; Ezek. 34.12).

Later writers began to apply the idea of God's great 'day' exclusively to the final end of time, when God would bring all human history to a close. Prophetic writers began to explain in great detail what might happen then. They called this end goal the *eschaton* (from the Greek for 'last'), from which the term 'eschatology', i.e. teachings about the 'last things', is derived.

The New Testament writers also used the phrase 'day of the Lord' to mean the Day of Judgement, but they thought of it as the 'day of Christ', that is the expected time of His Second Coming, when He would judge both the living and the dead.

2.12–14: Against all that is proud and lofty...lifted up and high...cedars of Lebanon...oaks of Bashan...mountains...hills: In many languages, words such as 'lofty' and 'high' are used to describe things which people regard as important and of which they are proud. The things so described in vv. 13–16 were a source of pride to Judah, and the people probably boasted about them instead of thanking God for them. Like the people of Babel they thought to build themselves up to the point where they would no longer have need of God's help (see Gen. 11.1–9 and note on Isa. 2.2: 'highest of the mountains').

2.18: The idols shall utterly pass away: The people's last resort, trust in the power of idols, would be proved useless, so that in the end the people themselves would reject them (see v. 20), and recognize that 'the LORD alone would be exalted'.

2.19: Men shall enter the caves...from before the terror...the glory of his majesty: By contrast with the heights to which the people mistakenly believed they had risen by their own power, the prophet warned of the depths to which those who rebel against God will eventually fall as a result of their sin. 'Terror' is what they will experience as they come to recognize their own nothingness beside the 'glory' of God's majesty. These words echo the description of what God's people had felt on another 'day of the LORD', when He had rescued them from Egypt. See Exod. 16.6, 7, 10; 19.16; 20.18–20; also compare Isaiah's own reactions to his encounter with God at the time of his call (Isa. 6.1–5 and see note on 6.3).

2.22: Turn away from man: This verse clearly does not belong to the rest of the poem. It does not appear in the Septuagint, and seems to be a prayer probably added by a later reader or copyist. We find the same sentiments (which are not very usual among Old Testament writers) expressed, for example, in Psalm 144.3, 4.

In this whole poem Isaiah was describing more fully one sort of sin which the Lord would judge the people of Judah to be guilty of. As we have seen, they had become estranged from God, and the prophet pointed to three chief ways in which they thought they could make themselves safe without God's help: (1) through sorcery and witchcraft, (2) through material prosperity and military strength, and (3) through the worship of idols. It seems that all three were partly the result of foreign influences in Judah, but all three also reflect the temptation which all human beings experience: to trust in their own strength and cleverness rather than accept their dependence on God.

THE SIN OF IDOLATRY

People who are not confident of God's rule in history and nature find it difficult to see any pattern in their lives. Nothing seems so uncertain as the future, and they tend to be full of fear about what may happen to them. So they seek to control events, and thus to reduce this fear, by trying to look into the future by means of sorcery and divination. Even in our own scientific and technological societies, thousands of people order their daily lives according to the predictions of astrologers, numerologists, and other so-called 'prophets' of the future.

Materialism too is probably more widespread in our present secular age than at any other time in history. In Isaiah's time Judah, like many countries today, had lately experienced a period of material growth. Agriculture, trade, education, government, and the army had developed rapidly under Uzziah's rule. The people not only prided themselves on the greatness of the natural wonders and resources of their country, they also drew a sense of security from their material wealth, impressive buildings and fortifications, their ocean-going ships, and the trade and military agreements with other nations which these made possible. Today the richer nations of the world pile up wealth and multiply their armaments, and most of the poorer nations try to do the same.

In trying to make life less uncertain in these ways, human beings build 'defences' for themselves, and then put their trust in what they have made. This is no less idolatry than the worship of 'graven images' practised in the Caananite religion and followed, as we have seen, by many of the Israelites also. And it is far more dangerous to true security than the uncertainties and dangers it is supposed to guard against.

Through idolatry people seek to control God, rather than accepting the fact that He controls all things, themselves included. They imagine that they can persuade God to do what they wish, that they can make God serve human beings rather than serving Him themselves. They deceive themselves into thinking they can 'get God on their side'.

THE SIN OF PRIDE

Isaiah's message was a very specific one, warning that God's judgement would certainly come upon His people. But it applies equally to people of all times who set themselves up against God. Judah's sin was the sin of pride, but a special sort of pride – the pride of people who imagine they can manage everything for themselves in the world. This sort of pride was the sin of Adam and Eve as well as the people of Babel. It was the sin of the Assyrians whom God used to 'bring low' the people of Judah and then punished in the same way. It was the sin of the Jewish religious leaders whom Jesus accused of receiving 'glory from one another' and failing to seek 'the glory that comes from the only God' (see John 5.43, 44). And it is this sort of pride that we can only too easily fall into today, when the sum of human knowledge and achievement seems to be increasing so rapidly.

But it is a pride which 'shall be brought low'. Isaiah described the angry disappointment of the people who thought they could do without God. When trouble and defeat came they fled in panic to the hills and broke the idols which had no power to help them. In warning against such pride, however, Isaiah did not mean that the people were to do nothing for themselves. The call to 'repent' (1.27) is a call to do things in a different way. The meaning of his message for us is not that we should sit passively waiting for God to do everything for us. It means that we should confidently obey the laws which God has given for the good government of the world, and put our trust in Him who alone will be exalted, and who alone controls the future.

STUDY SUGGESTIONS

WORD STUDY

1. Explain very briefly what is meant by the word 'day' in v. 12.

REVIEW OF CONTENT

2. For what reason has it been suggested that Isaiah 2.6–22 may consist of two poems woven into one?
3. Read again the first two sections of the general Introduction, pp. 1, 2. Then give a brief account in your own words of the history of Judah during the lifetime of Isaiah. At what time were the people experiencing the sort of conditions described in Isaiah 2.6–22?

4. What particular facts about the strength and prosperity of Judah can we learn from vv. 7,15, and 16 in this passage?
5. In what three chief ways were the people of Judah relying on their own strength rather than on God, according to this passage?
6. What sorts of 'terror' was Isaiah warning the people of, which would make them 'enter the caves of the rocks and the holes of the ground'?

BIBLE STUDY

7. In what ways does the picture of sin in each of the following passages in the Book of Genesis resemble that in Isaiah 2.6–22? In what way does it differ?
   (a) 3.1–7   (b) 4.3–9   (c) 4.23,24   (d) 6.1–5   (e) 11.1–9
8. The following passages illustrate a problem for students of the Bible which arises also in Isaiah 2.6–22. What is the problem, and how did it arise? What difference, if any, does it make to our understanding of the passage in each case?
   (a) Mark 16.9–20   (b) John 7.53—8.11   (c) Acts 8.37
   (d) Acts 24.6–8

APPLICATION, OPINION, AND RESEARCH

9. Compare the description of the 'day of the LORD' in this passage with that of 'the latter days' in 2.1–4. Do the two descriptions seem to refer to the same event or to two different events? Give reasons for your answer.
10. Do many people in your country try to find out the future by consulting 'diviners and soothsayers' or other sorts of fortune-teller? What is your own attitude to such fortune-tellers? Do you believe they really can foretell what will happen in the future?
11. Many of the Bible writers give God the title 'LORD of hosts', i.e. of armies. Does this mean that God 'approves' of war? If not, what does it mean?
12. In this passage Isaiah repeatedly referred to the 'terror of the Lord' which the people of Judah would experience. In what ways, if any, is God a 'terror' to Christians?
13. Join with some of your friends in making a list of things which people in your country take great pride in, or which cause them to feel safe. Then try to 'translate' 2.12–16, substituting such common symbols of security among your own people for those listed by Isaiah (e.g. for 'ships of Tarshish' you might substitute 'nuclear-powered submarines'). To what extent do you think such things really make people safe?

3.1—4.1
Social break-down

OUTLINE

There are two main themes in chapter 3. Verses 1–15 threaten the collapse of society in Judah as an outcome of God's judgement. Verses 16–26 plus 4.1 describe more specifically the fate awaiting the women of Jerusalem.

3.1–7: A direct threat that as Judah's leaders have failed to rule the country properly, so God will open the doors to violence and anarchy, followed by the prediction that the social order will break down in confusion and fear.

3.8–12: The real cause of this chaos is Judah's refusal to accept God's rule.

3.13–15: A scene of judgement: The Lord presses His case against the leaders who use their status to cheat the powerless poor.

3.16–26 and 4.1: Additional threats against the noble women of Jerusalem, whose extravagant luxury and vanities matched the greed and corruption of the men. When God's judgement comes they will be stripped of their finery, their men will be killed in battle, and they will be left to mourn.

NOTES AND INTERPRETATION

3.1: the Lord, the LORD of hosts: Readers may wonder why the words 'Lord', which occurs many times in this chapter, and 'God' are sometimes set as 'LORD' and 'GOD' all in capital letters in the RSV, and sometimes not. The explanation is that where all capitals are used, the word translates the Divine Name for God which in Hebrew is spelt with the consonents YHWH (sometimes put into English versions with the necessary vowels as YAHWEH, and sometimes translated as Jehovah). This name was considered too sacred to be spoken. So wherever it occurred in the Hebrew Scriptures the vowel sounds for Adonai (Lord) or Elohim (God) were inserted, to indicate that one or other of these titles should be substituted for YHWH when the Scriptures were read aloud in worship services. Accordingly, in the RSV (as in a number of other English translations), LORD or GOD in capitals are similarly substituted for YAHWEH. Where the actual words Adonai and Elohim occur in the Hebrew they are translated 'Lord' and 'God' set with lower case letters.

The Lord...is taking away...stay and staff: The meaning of 'stay and staff' becomes clear as we read the list of different people in vv. 2, 3. These are the important people, the leaders who are like 'props and stays' helping to hold the country together. The 'mighty man' probably means a military leader, and the 'captain' too could be a military rank or perhaps a provincial official. Isaiah had already warned that people would be punished for relying on 'diviners' (2.6), and these and the 'magicians' were probably the official advisers whom the leaders consulted when deciding government policy, and whom the people too could consult by paying a fee. The 'expert in charms' was probably the equivalent of a sorcerer, or a gypsy who sells love-potions. Because all these 'pillars of society' had proved both corrupt and oppressive, their power would be swept away. With no-one left to hold the balance, the people would oppress one another, and traditional relationships within society would be turned upside-down (v. 5).

The 'whole stay of bread...whole stay of water': These two lines, suggesting famine and drought, seem to differ from Isaiah's theme in the passage as a whole. They may be a later addition or comment on the disruption of food supplies and break-down of irrigation systems which would have occurred after the Assyrians carried away Judah's leading citizens and skilled craftsmen into captivity, leaving the direction of affairs in the hands of inexperienced and incompetent 'boys' and 'babes' (v. 4).

3.6,7: You have a mantle, you shall be our leader...I will not be a healer: Lacking qualified leaders, the people will look to any citizen of substance to take charge. But things will be so bad that no-one will want to take on the responsibility of trying to 'heal' the situation.

3.8: Against the LORD, defying his glorious presence: Isaiah makes it plain *why* the social order would collapse in this way. It was not simply that the leaders were incompetent or failed to weigh up the economic situation, but because in all they did – 'their speech and their deed' (v. 8) – and in spite of Jerusalem's special position, they purposely ignored God's presence among them and defied His law.

3.9(a): Their partiality witnesses against them: Another verse where the Hebrew is unclear and translations differ, but the general meaning seems plain enough.

3.9(b)–11: Woe...the righteous...the wicked: Compare with similar parallels in 1.19,20 and in 1.27,28, and see notes on those verses. The style here echoes that of the 'wisdom' writers (see e.g. Proverbs 11.8). Perhaps Isaiah was quoting from their sayings, or perhaps these verses are a wisdom saying inserted as comment by a later compiler.

3.12: Children are their oppressors...women rule...leaders mislead...and confuse: A further warning that normal social structures will be overturned. As distinct from v. 4, however, vv 9 and 12 may point to the historical reality of Isaiah's own time: see 2 Kings 21.1–6; 'Manasseh was 12 years old when he began to reign...his mother's name was Hephzibah. And he did what was evil.'

3.13: The LORD has taken his place to contend...stands to judge...enters into judgement: Again the prophet uses the language of the courts, and this time God is not only the judge, but also the prosecutor who accuses the 'elders and princes', and the defending counsel for the wronged party: 'what do you mean by crushing my people?'

3.14: You have devoured the vineyard, the spoil of the poor is in your houses: Israel was often thought of as God's 'vineyard' (see e.g. 5.1–7; and compare 5.10 and Jer. 12.10). Obviously the gardener's work is to tend the vines, not to eat the grapes! But the leaders had enriched themselves by despoiling those whom they were supposed to 'tend' ('spoil' has the same meaning as 'loot'). The prophet Amos made the same accusation even more directly (see Amos 2.6–8 and 5.11, 12).

3.15: Grinding the face of the poor: We can feel the prophet's own anger against the unjust leaders in the vivid picture-language he used to describe the harsh way they treated those whom they ought rather to help and serve.

3.16,17: Daughters of Zion: That is, the women of Jerusalem; or rather, it was the rich and idle ones whom Isaiah was condemning, for their arrogance and their vanity. His word-picture of the way they paraded through the streets with their noses in the air, ogling the men and showing off their expensive clothes and jewellery, is especially striking because of its position between the stark description of the oppressed and exploited poor (in v. 15), and that of the punishment the women will suffer (in v. 17). The Hebrew does not make clear what disease it was that would make their hair fall out and disfigure their faces (see v. 24). Some translators substitute 'forehead' for 'secret parts' in v. 17.

3.18: The finery...: There is no other list of women's clothes and ornaments in ancient writings comparable to that in the prose passage vv. 18–23, so we cannot be sure what some of the Hebrew words mean. 'Mincing along, feet tinkling' is probably a reference to anklets linked by a chain, so that the wearer could only take very short steps.

3.26: Her gates shall lament: It was near to the city gates that the elders and counsellors sat to judge disputes and advise the people (see vv. 2,3). After the city's defeat these leaders would be taken into captivity, and there would be no-one left to carry out their functions.

4.1: Seven women shall take hold of one man...saying...'take away our reproach'. In Hebrew custom it was considered shameful for a woman to be unmarried or childless. When the Lord punished the women for their pride and vanity, so that the ugliness of their inner lives was displayed instead of their surface beauty, great numbers of the men would be killed in the battles to come. The women would not only be

'They will oppress one another...crushing
my people...grinding the face of the poor'
(3.5, 15). 'Isaiah condemned the rich and
arrogant women for their haughtiness and
pride' (p. 43).

Indian women carry crushing loads all day
but still cannot earn enough to feed their
families properly. In Togo the country's
economy is run by wealthy women traders
Here they were congratulating the first
President after helping to finance his
election campaign.

How do these women compare with those
in Judah? How does their position compare
with that of women in your country today?

left mourning and desolate, they would be so desperate that they would give up the right of a wife to receive food and clothing, and would endure any humiliation in order to find a home and a husband.

Like Amos, Isaiah condemned the rich and arrogant women of the city with bitter sarcasm. (Amos was even less polite. He called the women of Samaria 'cows of Bashan' – a district famous for its fat cattle!)

Some readers assume that Isaiah was condemning the women for their wealth, and for living the 'high life' in the city. But the sort of punishment he promised them shows the sort of sin he was condemning them for. They would be humiliated: this showed that their chief sin was haughtiness and pride.

Rich people everywhere are tempted to be arrogant. Especially when they have become rich through their own efforts, they put on airs and despise those poorer than themselves, regarding them as too lazy or stupid to gain wealth for themselves. They judge others to be good or bad according to how much wealth they possess. Some poor people make the same mistake of judging people's worth according to the extent of their material possessions. But to God *all* people are equally valuable. He values them as *persons*, and in no other way.

Great wealth can also make people 'morally blind'. They fail to see that some ways of gaining and keeping their riches are wrong. They oppress others without realizing that they are doing so.

We may also ask why Isaiah singled out the women for special condemnation. He spoke sternly to the men too, but he seems to have regarded the women's pride and vanity as a specially bad influence among God's people. Although by custom women are often made to feel that they are second-class human beings, yet as wives and mothers they do have great influence. It is they who chiefly teach children and young people what is good or bad, important or unimportant, acceptable or unacceptable. And these women of Jerusalem, who cared for nothing but clothes and jewellery and thought themselves better than anyone else, were the complete opposite of the 'good wife' praised in Proverbs 31 as one 'who fears the Lord', and is hardworking, prudent, kind, dignified, and generous to the poor and needy. The Jerusalem women were also the opposite of what Paul told Timothy and Titus Christian women should be like: sensible and modest, 'not with braided hair or gold or pearls or costly attire', continuing in 'faith and love and holiness' to 'teach what is good' (see 1 Tim. 2.9–15; 3.11; Titus 2.3–5).

Women can often prevent the sort of decay which was ruining Judah, but if they themselves are a source of corruption, then there is little hope for the nation they belong to.

STUDY SUGGESTIONS

WORD STUDY

1. Which *three* of the following terms are nearest in meaning to the phrase 'stay and staff' as used in 3.1?
   remainder support sustenance shaft personnel stick visitation provision manpower

2. Explain what is meant by each of the following:
   (a) 'partiality' (v. 9) (b) 'spoil' (v. 14) (c) 'gates' (v. 26)

REVIEW OF CONTENT

3. What event led to a situation in Judah such as that described in 3.1–7?

4. Why would no-one want to become a 'healer' or 'leader' of the people as described in 3.6,7?

5. What was the prophet chiefly accusing the leaders of in 3.14,15?

6. Who were the 'daughters of Zion' and what did Isaiah chiefly accuse them of?

7. In the RSV (and some other English Bible versions) we sometimes find the word 'Lord' set all in capital letters: 'LORD'. What does this tell us about the original Hebrew word which is translated 'LORD' in these Bibles?

BIBLE STUDY

8. Read Isaiah 32.9–12; Jeremiah 44.15–30; Amos 4.1–3. How would you answer someone who said that these passages show that the prophets were anti-feminist, that is, against women?

9. In what chief ways do verses 3.13–15 resemble 1.18–20 and 2.2–4?

APPLICATION, OPINION, AND RESEARCH

10. In 3.2,3 Isaiah listed the 'pillars of society' whose supporting presence would be 'taken away' as a result of the coming invasion by the Assyrians. Who are the comparable 'pillars of society' in your country, and in what ways would their presence be missed today?

11. Make lists of the good qualities and bad qualities of the leaders in (a) your nation, (b) your neighbourhood, and (c) your Church, and discuss these lists with friends or fellow students. Do the leaders behave in ways which could be described as 'grinding the face of the poor'? What steps can be taken to ensure that leaders have no opportunities to oppress those poorer than themselves?

12. (a) Some people say that the rich are rich because they have cheated

others, and prevented them from getting their rightful share of the world's wealth. What is your opinion?

(b) Others say that the poor are poor because they are lazy or stupid or both, and that anyone who uses their intelligence and works hard can prosper in the world. Again, what is your opinion?

13. Isaiah preached *to* the wealthy ruling élite in Jerusalem, not *about* them to others. Many Christian pastors today have only poor people in their congregations. What dangers, if any, may arise if a pastor uses Isaiah's words in preaching to the poor *about* the rich élite?

14. What happens in a country when the social order 'breaks down' as described in 3.4,5? What are the three chief results which Isaiah mentions? Would these be the chief results if such social chaos or 'anarchy' occurred in your country? If not, what would the chief results be?

15. An English poet wrote: 'the hand that rocks the cradle is the hand that rules the world'. Do women really have so much influence on society? Do you think they *ought* to have such influence? In what chief ways do women exert their influence in your country?

16. What are some of the ways in which people who are rich and important can overcome the temptation to think themselves better than other people?

4.2—5.7
The Zion of the Future and God's Vineyard

OUTLINE

Two quite separate and contrasting messages follow.

4.2–6: A beautiful word-picture of what survives in Jerusalem after its destruction. The city has been cleansed, and God now glorifies and protects it with His presence. Most scholars consider this prose passage to be by a later writer, not Isaiah. Others think there is insufficient evidence either way, and suggest that it may belong to the later years of Isaiah's ministry. In either case an editor probably positioned it here because the reference to 'daughters of Zion' seems to link it to 3.16—4.1.

5.1–7: A poetic oracle by Isaiah in the form of a bitter-sweet parable describing how God's vineyard, Israel, has failed to bear fruit.

NOTES AND INTERPRETATION

THE CLEANSING OF JERUSALEM

Although 4.2–6 are in prose they contain many of the characteristics of Hebrew poetry (see note on 1.2), and may originally have been in poetic form.

4.2: In that day: See note on 2.11, 'The Day of the Lord'. Here the phrase clearly has an eschatological meaning. It is the 'day' when God's purposes are fulfilled and the salvation of His people is completed.

The branch of the LORD: Old Testament writers sometimes used this word 'branch' for the Messiah King for whom the Israelites waited (see 9.6,7). Here the Hebrew word is not the same as that used in Isaiah 11.1, but later prophets certainly used it to mean the 'coming King' (see Jer. 23.5; Zech. 6.12,13), and in such passages the 'branch' means the 'descendant of David', whether or not it has a messianic meaning. In this passage, even if it simply relates, as some scholars think, to the crops from which the 'fruit of the land' will be harvested, this fruit too is one of the signs of the Messiah and the salvation He will bring (see Isa. 32.1,16; 35.1,2; Ezek. 23—27).

4.2,3: The survivors...he who is left will be called holy...everyone who has been recorded for life: See notes on 1.9 and 1.24–26. This reference to a faithful and purified 'remnant', which is an important theme throughout the Book of Isaiah, is the key to the whole passage. The words 'called holy' and 'recorded' (NEB has 'enrolled in the book of life') relate to God's special act of grace in preserving the 'remnant' who survive the time of punishment. And the 'life' of this remnant has a special quality. It symbolizes God's new care for Jerusalem and the Jews, and the whole passage is concerned with the hope of salvation. Looked at in this way all the other details fall into place: the cleansing, God's 'spirit of judgement', and the renewed glory of His presence (v. 5) which is also a refuge and a shelter for His people. See also note on 10.20–22 and interpretation pp. 47 and 103.

4.4: The filth of the daughters of Zion...the bloodstains of Jerusalem: Clearly the editor who arranged the contents of Isaiah 1—39 in its present order saw in this verse a reference to 3.16,17,24 (and also perhaps to 1.15). He probably regarded the whole passage 4.2–6 as a direct sequel to the oracle in 3.16–26.

A spirit of judgement and a spirit of burning: See notes on 1.7, 1.25, and 2.10. Here again the idea that punishment for sin will take the form of destruction by fire gives way to the idea that the effect of the burning will be cleansing and purification.

4.5,6: Then the LORD will create over Mount Zion a cloud by day...and a flaming fire by night...over all the glory a canopy and a pavilion: The surviving remnant of God's people will experience the fullness of His promised presence and protection (see 1 Kings 8.10–11; Exod. 40.34–36; also Isa. 11.9; 4.5; and 60.19–21; and compare with 7.15,16; and 21.3,4, 22–27).

Most of the messages which we know to be Isaiah's own are accusations against sin, or warnings and threats of God's judgement and wrath to come. But a later writer makes it clear that Isaiah's emphasis can be misunderstood, and reminds us that God's final purpose is not to destroy but to save and restore His people. God 'will not keep his anger for ever' (Ps. 103.9). In Isaiah 4.2–6 we can find three aspects of this 'restoration'.

1. Human beings can fully enjoy and use the 'fruit of the land' – all the natural resources of the world which God has provided – only when their relationships with Him and with each other are what He intends them to be. The story of the 'fall' in Genesis makes this quite clear. The pollution and destruction we cause by our disobedience – our ignorance, our greedy and thoughtless exploitation of nature and of each other, and our continual warfare – is obvious, and some of the damage is beyond our power to repair. We do also restore and develop the land, turn deserts into farms and gardens, and harness the power of wind, water, and fire. We can undo *some* of the harm we have done. But the glory of God's restoration is far beyond any human achievement.

2. Human beings are also to some extent capable of cleansing themselves. We can repent and fight against the power of sin in our lives. Even a hardened criminal can 'turn over a new leaf'. But we still carry the marks and burden of our wrongdoing until God Himself cleanses and restores us by a radical act of salvation. 'I am the LORD', He says, 'and besides me there is no saviour...I have swept away your transgressions like a cloud, and your sins like mist; return to me, for I have redeemed you' (43.11; 44.22; and see also 45.22–25; Jer. 31.33; Ezek. 36.24–27). Christians see this cleansing as having been achieved once and for all through the death of Jesus on the cross, although, like the people of Jerusalem, we have to 'return' to God and repent in order to experience the restoration and the glory.

3. God makes Himself known and comes to live in and among the people whom He has 'restored'. For the people of Jerusalem this was a reaffirmation of God's promise to Moses that He would be present with them and protect them in all their journeying. So long as God's people were estranged from Him, His coming and His judgement were a threat and a danger to them. Now He makes them into 'holy people', 'in righteousness established', and under the protection of His glory (54.14; and see again 1.26,27 and Jer. 31.33,34). We should note, however, that even where God is present with His people and makes Himself known to them, He still remains hidden in mystery. In 4.5, 'a

cloud by day', the prophet seems partly to hide his meaning as well as to explain it.

GOD'S VINEYARD

5.1: Let me sing for my beloved a love-song concerning his vineyard: In 5.1–7 Isaiah chose to convey his message in a way not often found in the Old Testament. In the first place, this poem is in the form of a love-song or ballad with a refrain, like those commonly sung by roving singers among the crowds at great festivals. Secondly, the message itself is in the form of a parable or story, like the stories in the ballads and folksongs which are popular in every country.

To start by disguising in this way the stern accusation he was about to make would have been a good way for the prophet to secure the attention and interest of his listeners. Perhaps Isaiah actually sang it when the Feast of Tabernacles was being held to celebrate the grape harvest. Love-songs were especially popular at this wine festival. There are some comparable passages and vineyard references in the Song of Solomon, but the idea of a vineyard is used symbolically with several different meanings by Isaiah himself and by other prophets.

My beloved...his vineyard: As the poem proceeds, the prophet makes it quite clear that the owner of the vineyard is God, and the vineyard itself the people of Israel/Judah. We may find it surprising that Isaiah should refer to God in so intimate a way as 'my beloved', but this may simply have been a traditional way of beginning a love-song. In some English Bible versions the word is translated 'friend' instead.

5.2: He looked for it to yield grapes: Grapes are an important crop all round the Mediterranean, where the climate and soil are well suited to vineyards. But developing a new vineyard takes time and money, and a great deal of work. Isaiah describes step by step all the care and hard labour the owner invests in it, in the expectation of an abundant harvest of choice fruit.

But it yielded wild grapes – small and hard and sour.

5.3,4: Now, men of Judah, judge between me and my vineyard. What was there to do that I have not done? Like Jesus, who so often turned people's questions back at them to answer for themselves, Isaiah set a trap for his listeners. He asked them to advise the owner: What more could he have done? What should he do now?

5.5,6: Now I will tell you what I will do...remove its hedge...break down its wall...make it a waste: The judgement is clear. As the vineyard had not responded to the owner's care and protection, so that care and protection would be taken away. The vines which produced only wild grapes would be left to become a wasteland.

5.6: I will command the clouds that they rain no rain: Now the singer begins to reveal the truth of his message. The 'owner', who can 'command the clouds', can be no human friend.

48

5.6: The vineyard is the house of Israel: And the men of Judah are the carefully nurtured vines. As we have seen, vines and vineyards were so common and so important to everyone in Palestine that many of the Bible writers used them as examples in this way.

5.7: He looked for justice but behold bloodshed; for righteousness but behold a cry: The prophet not only gave extra force to the 'moral' of his message by making it the climax of his song, suddenly thundering out his accusation against the 'men of Judah' as the third and final refrain. To drive home the whole point of the song he emphasized the contrast between the expected 'harvest' and the actual fruit, by using a powerful play on Hebrew words which sound alike but have wholly opposite meanings:

He looked for *mishpat* (justice),
but behold, *mishpa* (bloodshed),
for *sedaqah* (righteousness),
but behold, *se'akah* (a cry).

Instead of the justice and righteousness which God could rightly expect of His covenant people, as fruit of the grace and protection He had bestowed on them, the 'harvest' they yielded was rebellion, leading to bloodshed in their relationships with other nations and the 'cry' of the poor and oppressed in their own land.

We have already studied some messages about God's judgement of His people, and the harsh punishment they could expect (see 1.7,8; 2.12–17; 3.1–5). And we have read of the painful 'cleansing' process they would have to undergo as a prelude to the salvation He had in store for them (4.2–6).

But the punishment described here is the severest and most frightening of all. God does not plan to chastise or destroy His people, but simply to withdraw His care and protection: to abandon them to the sin and evil they have chosen to follow instead of the way He has shown them. As St Paul put it in another context, they 'were without excuse, for although they knew God they did not honour him...therefore God gave them up' (Rom. 1.20,21,24).

ISAIAH'S METHOD AND STYLE

We study the Book of Isaiah firstly because of its message. We may also study it as an example of fine Hebrew literature. We miss some of the force of what Isaiah said if we give no attention to the *ways* in which he spoke. A great speaker or writer is usually an expert in the use of language, and uses words as a musician uses an instrument or as an artist or sculptor uses paint or wood or stone or clay. So the words are put together in ways intended to cause the hearers not merely to understand what is said, but to be angry, or happy, or sorry, or ambitious. The effect of *what* is said cannot be separated from the *way* it is said.

Isaiah's messages are fine examples of ancient Hebrew literature.

Some of the power of what he is saying is lost when the words are translated into other languages, e.g. the play on sounds and meanings in 5.7. But we can learn to appreciate much of their effect just as his original disciples did.

Most of Isaiah's 'sermons' were short, and most of them are poems with fixed rhythms and a pattern in which the meaning of one line matches that of another (see note on 1.2). His teaching was filled with word-pictures of familiar things that would stimulate his hearers' imagination, or prompt them to take action. To understand this 'picture-language' we need to use our own imagination.

Isaiah was also ready to take advantage of any occasion or use any teaching method which would help him to get a hearing for God's word. For example he used a signboard (8.1–4), a startling costume – or rather lack of costume (20.1–6), the naming of a child (7.3 and 8.3–5), an acted-out parable (38.21,22) – indeed, anything that would get the message across. In this passage, as we have seen, he not only seems to have seized the occasion of a festival to put his message across as a song, but also made the subject of the song into a parable, so that his hearers were led to condemn themselves for their wrongdoing.

Jesus Himself used the idea of the vineyard in many of His parables, and when He described Himself as the 'true vine' and His disciples as the branches (John 15.1–8) He knew that the idea would already be familiar to them from hearing Isaiah's words read aloud in the synagogue.

Christian writers and preachers today are not likely to be successful if they merely imitate the style and methods of the ancient prophets whose circumstances were quite different. But many Christians through the centuries, and today too, have chosen to proclaim their faith in songs and stories of a popular nature. And we cannot afford to be less skilful in our use of language and teaching method than the best poets, story-tellers, song-writers, and propagandists of our time. We should never let it be said of us that 'the sons of this world are more shrewd in dealing with their own generation than the sons of light' (Luke 16.8).

STUDY SUGGESTIONS

WORD STUDY

1. What is the meaning of the phrase 'branch of the LORD' (4.2)? Using a Concordance, find as many instances as you can of the use of the phrase in the Old Testament. What is its full meaning in each case?

2. What is meant by 'recorded for life' in v. 3?

REVIEW OF CONTENT

3. What did the editor who arranged the contents of the Book of Isaiah see in 4.2–6 which led him to place this passage immediately following the messages in chapter 3?

4. Whose 'spirit' was Isaiah talking about in v. 4?

5. What do we learn about the nature of God from 5.5,6? What do we *not* learn about God from these verses?

6. 'My beloved had a vineyard' (5.1). Who was the prophet's 'beloved'?

7. (a) 'This poem is in the form of a ballad or a love-song with a refrain' (p. 48). In which verses do we find the refrain, and what form does it take?
(b) 'The message itself is in the form of a parable' (p. 48). What is a parable?

BIBLE STUDY

8. Read 2 Samuel 12.1–7. In what ways is the method of telling that parable like or unlike the method used in Isaiah 5.1–7?

9. Compare and contrast the way in which the idea of vines and vineyard is used in each of the following passages, with the way it is used in Isaiah 5.1–7.
(a) Deut. 32.28–33   (b) Ps. 80.8–13   (c) Jer. 2.20–22
(d) Ezek. 19.10–14   (e) Matt. 21.33–43   (f) John 15.1–8.

APPLICATION, OPINION, AND RESEARCH

10. 'Washed away the filth...cleansed the bloodstains' (4.4). What do you think are the chief sorts of 'filth' and 'bloodstains' of which the Lord might cleanse (a) the world as a whole, and (b) your own country, in order to create the beauty and 'glory' described in 4.2–6?

11. 'A cloud by day and a smoke and a flaming fire by night' (4.5). Are these the signs by which people might recognize God's presence among them today? If not, what might be the shape of such signs?

12. If Isaiah had been preaching in your country today, what form do you think he would have used to communicate the subject matter of the 'vineyard' poem? Do any of the Churches in your country use such popular forms or media for the purpose of evangelism or teaching? Do any Christian individuals use such forms or media?

13. Rewrite the song of the vineyard in your own words, in the form of a short story such as might be broadcast on the radio. (You could add details to make the story live, but keep the same plot and message.)

14. Make a list of all the song lyrics you can discover which have a

religious theme. Say in each case what is the specifically religious message or teaching the song contains, and in the case of Christian songs, if it is linked to any particular Bible text give the appropriate reference for it.

5.8–23
Woe to the Oppressors

INTRODUCTION AND OUTLINE

This passage consists of a collection of 'woe words' prophesying punishments to come upon Judah. No doubt these messages were grouped here by an editor to follow on from the general accusation against the national leaders in 5.7, as they threaten particular punishments for some particular sorts of sin of which the leaders were guilty. Six different groups of people are mentioned, each message being introduced by the word 'woe'.

Vv. 8–10: Group 1. Those who use their position to grab land and houses from others; they will be cut off from the rest of society, and their estates will fall into decay.

Vv. 11–12: Group 2. Those who spend the whole of their time at drinking parties and forget what God demands of those who hold positions of authority. This section leads directly into...

Vv. 13–17: A description of some of the results of such irresponsible leadership, i.e. exile, death, and humiliation.

Vv. 18–19: Group 3. Those who can no longer loose themselves from their sins, but actually boast of their independence from God and mock at His judgement.

V. 20: Group 4. Those who are no longer able to distinguish right from wrong.

V. 21: Group 5. Those who think they know everything, and boast of their own wisdom and shrewdness.

Vv. 22,23: Group 6. Those who are brave and boastful when drunk, but cowardly and corrupt when it comes to standing up in court in defence of the truth and in defence of the innocent.

NOTES AND INTERPRETATION

5.8–10: Woe to those who join house to house, who add field to field: Many of the prophets used the word 'woe' in addressing their listeners. This word can be understood in three chief ways: (a) As a curse or warning, meaning 'beware of disaster to come'. (b) As a rebuke or scolding:

'shame on you!'. (c) As a lament: 'Alas! you are lost!' Poets often used the word in composing funeral songs, and Isaiah was so sure that Judah was doomed that he gave these messages in the form of a dirge for the nation.

The outright buying and selling of land was forbidden under the covenant law, and in earlier times the buying and selling of houses was strictly controlled (see Lev. 25.23–34). But most of the people in positions of power were simply ignoring these laws (see 1.4). It seems clear, too, that they were not only openly buying up land and buildings so as to enlarge their own property, but were also gaining possession of other people's land by trickery and corruption (see 3.14,15).

5.10: Ten acres of vineyard shall yield but one bath, and a homer of seed shall yield but an ephah: We cannot be sure what the present-day equivalents of the ancient measures of wine, seed, and grain would be, except that a 'bath' was an ordinary household measure, and a homer probably ten times an ephah. However, the exact amounts do not matter. All the prophet was saying was that as a result of the property-owners' greed, their lands would be laid waste and the yield reduced to almost nothing.

5.13: Therefore my people go into exile...dying of hunger...parched with thirst. Verses 13–17 seem to be a separate oracle inserted between the two sets of 'woes'. The punishment it describes is fitting enough for all those to whom the 'woes' were addressed. It may be that Isaiah gave this warning message during the last days of the Northern Kingdom, because he foresaw that a similar danger of destruction was looming for Judah also. The leaders' 'want of knowledge' (3.13) was not a matter of school-learning: what they lacked was understanding and wisdom. Compare Hosea's message to the Northern Kingdom some years earlier: 'My people are destroyed for lack of knowledge' (Hos. 4.6). 'Lack of knowledge' is the equivalent of the leaders' failure to 'regard the deeds of the LORD...' in Isaiah 5.12.

5.14: Sheol has enlarged its appetite: In the destruction which the invading Assyrians would cause, Sheol, the lifeless and Godless underworld, or 'place of the dead', would be like a man-eating beast, ravening for its prey. Leaders and people alike would fall into the open jaws of death.

5.15,16: 'Men are brought low, and the eyes of the haughty are humbled. But the LORD of hosts is exalted': Some scholars have suggested that the whole section, vv. 13–17, is part of a further 'woe', the beginning of which has been lost. However, since vv. 15,16 so closely echo the refrain in 2.9,11,17, others consider that it may originally have formed part of that message of judgement.

5.17: Then shall the lambs graze...fatlings and kids feed among the ruins: The Hebrew of v. 17 is unclear and translations vary. The Septuagint has 'aliens' instead of 'kids', and some interpreters see this verse as a picture of the once-fat landlords and the invading armies searching for food among the ruins the latter had created.

5.18,19: Those who draw iniquity with cords of falsehood…sin as with cart ropes, who say: 'Let him speed his work that we might see it': This is clearly a reference to sceptics or 'practical atheists', as they have been called, who deliberately tie themselves to their sin and flaunt their independence from God. They are not merely careless or forgetful of God, but actually mock His power and question His ability to hurt them. Translators vary in their treatment of v. 18. The AV has 'cords of vanity' and some versions merely 'sheep's tether' or 'chariot traces'. 'Falsehood' however, provides a link with the two following 'woes', addressed to 'those who call evil good and good evil' (v. 20), and 'those who are wise in their own eyes' (v. 21). All three groups were guilty of much the same sort of active and deliberate sin, i.e. a reversal of the truth about God and His work in the world, and what their own relationship with Him ought to be.

5.22: Those who are heroes at drinking…valiant men…who acquit the guilty…and deprive the innocent: A similar 'woe' to that in vv. 11,12, and again the prophet's words are sarcastic. This time the accusation includes corruption and moral cowardice as well as self-indulgence (compare 1.23 and 3.13–15).

Notice that throughout 5.8–23 the people whom Isaiah was addressing were not the ordinary citizens and work-people of Judah, but the rich and powerful, the appointed rulers and judges who were the leaders of society, just as such people are today. They were the 'honoured men…the nobility…living in large and beautiful houses' (vv. 13,14,9). They had responsibility for administering the law which God had given, for defending the country, and for looking after the people, and *ought* to have been truly 'wise…heroes…valiant men' (vv. 21,22) in all their doings.

THE OPPRESSIVE LEADERS

In some other messages Isaiah seems to have been making more general accusations against the leaders and the masses of the people together. But many of his hearers, including the leaders and the king to whom he was special adviser, refused to heed his warning. They said it was not for them, they knew better (see 6.9,10; 7.10–12). They deceived themselves into thinking that God would never punish them (5.18; 9.21; and see 30.8–11). So in these 'woe words' the prophet singled out one group after another, and described very clearly the ways in which each group were knowingly disobeying God's law, and failing to 'regard the deeds of the Lord or see the work of his hands' in what was happening around them (see 8.5–8).

In the first 'woe' he was addressing the wealthy landowners. As in many countries today, a few rich people were getting possession of all the land and houses, and even using criminal means, as shown by the story of King Ahab's seizing of Naboth's vineyard in 1 Kings 21. So God's punishment upon them would be a fitting one. If seclusion from poorer neighbours was what these high and mighty people wanted, that is what they would get. With more houses and land than they could live in or keep up, they would be left 'desolate' (v. 9), their land would become increasingly unproductive (v. 10), and with the coming of invaders the 'beautiful houses' would be torn down and the cultivated land would return to wild. And many of the poorer people, who had already been suffering at the hands of such grasping landlords, would share in the suffering that would fall on the nation as a whole because its leaders were so self-seeking and irresponsible.

Isaiah's description of the desolation that would result from the landlords' greed may remind us of what is happening in many parts of the world today. Besides all the havoc caused by war, careless use of chemical fertilizers and pesticides in farming and uncontrolled clearing of forests for profit have led to changes in the weather, and to erosion and poisoning which destroys the soil's fertility so that it will no longer yield any crops. Then there is drought and famine, and people starve (see v. 13).

In one way or another the same would be true of the other groups of leaders to whom Isaiah's message was 'woe', and whose modern counterparts we can also recognize in our own society today.

There are the 'idle rich' who use their money and position for selfish purposes only. They may sometimes make a show of working for others, but are quite unwilling to take any responsibility.

There are today's materialists and humanists, who see religion as merely a prop for the weak, and themselves claim to have no need of it. Perhaps Isaiah was also addressing some self-righteous religious and other leaders, who deceived themselves by assuming that their outward show of 'vain offerings...many prayers' were all that God demanded. We can recognize these also: so long as they keep up an appearance of virtue such people believe that God can hold no punishment in store for *them* (vv. 18,19).

Then there are the people who deliberately exploit the weakness of others for their own profit: professional thieves and thugs; armament manufacturers who sell guns to terrorists; sellers and advertisers of hard drugs and tobacco and patent medicines that will harm rather than help those who buy them; builders and factory-owners who fail to observe safety regulations. These too end by convincing themselves that what they do is right rather than wrong (v. 20, and see 29.15,16).

And the same is true of some politicians, military leaders, officials, and even teachers who base their policies and decisions on prejudice or expediency, rather than on God's law – or on reason or humane principles. They refuse to listen to anyone else, or to God Himself.

Isaiah was referring here to the king's military advisers who insisted on alliances with Egypt. But he may have thought to include the religious leaders as well, who encouraged the people to follow the strict letter of the law with regard to outward religious observances, and even to take part in worship of idols, instead of urging them to care for others and worship the Lord alone (see 30.1–3; also 1.11; 2.6).

Finally there are the people who make a great parade of their power and their qualities of leadership so long as they are not called on to show such qualities in action – moral cowards who are quite ready to pervert the course of justice, rather than risk unpleasantness or unpopularity or loss to themselves (vv. 22,23, and see 1.22,23).

Of course not all people in these categories are 'oppressors' of others. No doubt *some* of the leaders in Judah were honest and just, and there are plenty of generous landlords, fair and honest traders, conscientious lawyers, and high-principled and courageous politicians today. But the temptation to take the 'easy way out' is always there.

In v. 22 as in vv. 11 and 12, Isaiah may have condemned his hearers for drinking too much because of the effect alcohol can have on people's sense of responsibility and powers of judgement, and because the more people drink the harder they find it to stop. But this was not his chief accusation against them. It was not the 'stupor' caused by alcohol he was chiefly condemning, but the mental stupor and blindness of self-seeking and self-satisfied people who forget God, and 'stagger' because they can no longer 'perceive' God's will nor find the strength to obey it (see 6.9).

THE NATURE OF SIN

Isaiah was preaching about particular evils which he saw in people's lives and in the life of the nation. He was not trying to provide a comprehensive answer to the question 'what is sin'. Nevertheless, there are certain facts about sin that we can learn from his words, which are as true in our time as they were for his.

1. Sin is *social*. The sins Isaiah lamented are not merely the private mistakes of individuals. They are like the symptoms of a disease which affects the whole community. Individual greed, drunkenness, corruption, conflict, are all signs of much larger problems affecting society as a whole. They cannot be overcome by individuals alone. Society as a whole must change, though it is individuals who must work to achieve reform.

2. Sin is *serious*. The sins Isaiah spoke of were not only spoiling the lives of those who committed them and those who suffered the

'Human beings are to some extent capable of cleansing themselves...We can fight against the power of sin' (p. 47).

A little Indonesian girl can cleanse her baby brother with water from the stream, fighting against dirt and disease.

How does cleansing from dirt and disease differ from cleansing ourselves of sin?

'I will make it a waste...men are dying of hunger' (5.6, 13).

'The landlords' greed may remind us of what is happening today...uncontrolled clearing of forests' – as here in Brazil – 'destroys the soil's fertility so that people starve' (p. 55).

How can such selfish and sinful waste of God's gifts to us be prevented?

57

immediate consequences. Multitudes of 'innocent ones' too were being dragged headlong towards disaster, and the whole 'throng' of the people would 'go down' along with the leaders. The sins of the leaders were actually endangering Judah's chances of survival as a nation, and the people's own chances of salvation.

3. Sin is *costly*. The sins Isaiah spoke of were more than outward actions which could be reversed at a moment's notice. They were the expression of a wholly mistaken way of thinking, an attitude to life which left God out of account. The only solution was a complete renewal of people's ideas and inner life, and a whole new direction in the structure of society and the life of the nation, and this would be costly. Sin always demands some sort of cross and death before there can be resurrection. For Christians, Christ has paid the price and shown the way. But there is no less expensive answer.

STUDY SUGGESTIONS

WORD STUDY

1. Which *four* of the following words are nearest in meaning to the word 'woe' as used in 5.8–23?
   wariness   warning   pain   doom   anger
   weeping   shame   curse   remorse   disaster

REVIEW OF CONTENT

2. Isaiah gave the messages in 5.8–23 in the traditional form of a particular sort of song. What sort of song was it, and why did he use that form for his messages?
3. 'We should note that throughout this passage Isaiah was not addressing the ordinary citizens and work-people of Judah' (p. 54). Who was he addressing?
4. For what two chief reasons did Isaiah condemn those who were joining 'house to house' and adding 'field to field'?
5. 'Isaiah may have condemned his hearers for drinking too much... but this was not his chief accusation...it was not the stupor caused by alcohol he was chiefly concerned about.' What *was* Isaiah chiefly concerned about?
6. 'The leaders' want of knowledge was not a lack of school-learning' (p. 53). What was it?
7. What did Isaiah mean when he said that 'Sheol has enlarged its appetite' (v. 14)?

BIBLE STUDY

8. Read Hosea 4.1–13. Which verses contain accusations similar to the 'woe words' in Isaiah 5.8–23, and to which verses in the Isaiah passage do they correspond?

9. 1 Kings 21.1–25 describes the sort of sinful behaviour that Isaiah was condemning.
   (a) In this passage, what sort of person was guilty of that sinful behaviour, and what made it specially sinful, according to Leviticus 25?
   (b) Which verse in Isa. 5.8–23 refers to this sort of behaviour?

10. (a) Read Matt. 12.22–37. Which group of leaders in Judah could we compare to the Pharisees whom Jesus is said to have called a 'brood of vipers'?
    (b) Read Luke 18.9–14. Which group of leaders could we compare to the Pharisee in the parable?
    What do you think Jesus would have said to the Judean leaders in each case?

APPLICATION, OPINION, AND RESEARCH

11. Isaiah used the word 'woe' as a combined accusation, rebuke, threat, and lament. Do you think a modern preacher could effectively use the word in making similar accusations and threats against today's leaders? If not, what other word or words do you think would be more effective?

12. Which of the six sorts of sin described in 5.8–23 are most likely to bring 'disaster' to your own country today? What sort of disaster would it be, and which groups of people would be the guilty ones?

13. 'Woe to those who run after strong drink...tarry late till wine inflames them' (v. 11). If excessive drinking is a problem in your country, collect newspaper articles, radio reports, etc. about drunkenness among both important and ordinary people, and its effect on the community, on family life, and the lives of individuals. What other habits can cause similar problems, and how can they be overcome?

14. In vv. 22,23 Isaiah was condemning the leaders and judges for what we today would call 'moral cowardice' – something which many people feel they have been guilty of at one time or another. What do you think is the best way to overcome one's moral cowardice?

NOTE: At this point, instead of going straight on to study the remainder of chapter 5, we jump ahead to chapter 6, because most scholars agree that the section 5.24–30 belongs with 9.8—10.4. Perhaps it was shifted to its present position to provide a follow-up to the second group of 'woe' words, in the same way that 5.13–17 provides a follow-up to the first two 'woes'. Or it may have been to add emphasis to the 'woes' by describing more fully the punishment to come. Or it may simply have been misplaced in error by a later scribe. In any case its links with 9.8—10.4 are so clear that we shall study it later, along with that passage.

Special Note 1
The Historical Context of
the Book as a Whole

In the Introduction to this guide we described the historical situation during Isaiah's lifetime in general terms. We pointed to the various events which prompted him to speak out against the policies of successive kings in Judah, and against the injustice and corruption of the national leaders and the leaders of the surrounding countries. We also noted the relative lack of evidence in Isaiah 1—39 as to when the events described took place, and the general uncertainty about the dates of the Judean kings of that period.

However, evidence from non-Biblical sources shows that the so-called 'Syro-Ephraimitic' war, during which Israel joined Syria in attacking Judah, took place in 734/733 BC. So King Ahaz must have been ruling at that time (see 7.1–17). In the same way we know that Hezekiah was king in 701 BC, during the siege of Jerusalem by the Assyrians under King Sennacherib (chapters 36,37).

We know, too, that in 721 Sargon II of Assyria completed Shalmaneser V's conquest of Samaria, the chief city of Israel, and took its inhabitants away into captivity (see 2 Kings 17). This final defeat of the Northern Kingdom must have been a terrible shock for the Israelite people as a whole. But there is no direct reference to it in the Book of Isaiah. Perhaps the people of Judah did not feel much sympathy for the people of Israel at that time because the Northern Kingdom had sided with Syria in the war of 734/733.

Dates for events *after* the time of Isaiah can be fixed more closely.

We know that King Josiah died in 610 or 609 BC, when Judah was at war with Pharaoh Neco of Egypt, and that he reigned 31 years (2 Kings 22.1; 23.29,30). So he must have become king about 640 BC. About 625 BC, when the so-called neo-Babylonian Empire was founded by Nabopolassar, Assyrian power began to decline. This gave King Josiah the chance to regain the Northern territory of Israel, and the 'reform' of the Israelite religion which he began in the 18th year of his reign must have started about 622 BC (see 2 Kings 22.3–6).

In 605, less than five years after Josiah's death, Pharaoh Neco himself was defeated at Carchemish by the Babylonian Prince Nebuchadnezzar, and Judah became a vassal of Babylon instead of Egypt. Soon, however, the new Judean King Jehoiakim rose in rebellion, and some years of unrest followed, during which Babylon incited other vassal peoples to make raids into Judah (2 Kings 24.1–7). Then in 597 came the first Babylonian attack on Jerusalem itself. And when Jehoiakim's son Jehoiachin surrendered, Nebuchadnezzar took most of Judah's fighting men and craftsmen away into captivity, and set Jehoiachin's uncle, renamed Zedekiah, on the throne instead (2 Kings 24.8–17).

Before long, Judah rebelled again, and in 587 Nebuchadnezzar's army of Chaldeans attacked Jerusalem again. This time the siege went on for 18 months, and in the end, not only was the city taken and Zedekiah captured, but the Temple was burnt down and its treasures carried off. The whole city was destroyed, and most of the people were taken away as prisoners to Babylon, leaving only a few of the poorer farmers to cultivate the land (2 Kings 25.1–21). The year 586 is therefore usually taken as the beginning of the Exile, though many people had already been exiled in 597.

While Nebuchadnezzar lived, the Babylonian Empire remained strong, but a period of instability followed his death in 562, and the Median and Persian kingdoms to the east became more powerful. In 550 the Persian King Cyrus II fought and defeated the Medes, and went on conquering other kingdoms until he controlled an empire stretching from the Persian Gulf to the Aegean. In 539 Babylon too fell into Cyrus's hands, and a year later he proclaimed his famous Edict, allowing all subjugated and captive peoples to follow their own customs and religions.

Soon after this the Jewish exiles were allowed to return home from Babylon, and to take with them some of the Temple vessels which Nebuchadnezzar had seized. In 535 Sheshbazzar, the Judean Prince whom Cyrus had made governor of Jerusalem, was able to lay the foundations of a new Temple there. And in 515, under the Persian King Darius, it was completed by Zerubbabel, whom the prophets Haggai and Zechariah had been urging to finish the work on it since 520 (see Ezra 5.1—6.15).

The work of rebuilding the city went on over the next 100 years, as we learn from the books of Nehemiah, whom the Persian king made governor of Judah about 445, and of the priestly Scribe Ezra, who seems to have returned with other exiles around 438, and who played an important part in rebuilding the religious life of the people (see especially Nehemiah 2.7–9; 5.6–16; 12.27–44; Ezra 7.1–10).

Throughout this time all Palestine was under Persian domination. This continued until the latter part of the 4th century, when the Persian Empire fell to Alexander the Great, who conquered all the Eastern Mediterranean lands for Greece. After Alexander's death, his former generals Ptolemy (from Egypt) and Seleucus (from Mesopotamia) competed for authority over Palestine, and thus over Judah. By 198 the Seleucids had gained control, and under their rule Greek religious practices were introduced. In 167 Antiochus IV (who had also made himself King of Egypt) passed a decree prohibiting Jewish custom and religion, and demanding that idols should be worshipped in the Temple (1 Macc. 1.41–61).

The Jews responded to this by rising in revolt, led first by the priest Mattathias and then by his son Judas Maccabeus (1 Macc. 2.1—3.12). The struggle continued until in 133 Judas's brother Jonathan Maccabeus requested the help of the Romans against the Seleucids, and in 63 BC Judah became a Roman province.

Although, as we saw in the Introduction, it is chapters 40—55 of the Book of Isaiah which belong to the period of the Exile, and chapters 56—66 which clearly relate to the time of the return of Jerusalem, we should nevertheless bear all this later history of the Near Eastern lands in mind as we study chapters 1—39. There are many passages in these chapters which show very clear links with ideas and beliefs which people only began to hold as a result of experiencing defeat and deportation. And many of the oracles of promise are so unlike Isaiah's stern attitude towards the sins of injustice, oppression, and above all disobedience to the known will of God, that it seems almost certain that they belong to a later date.

STUDY SUGGESTIONS

1. Which 'super-power' or 'powers' ruled most of the Near East during Isaiah's lifetime?
2. Who was king of that superpower:
   (a) at the time of Isaiah's call to be a prophet?
   (b) at the time when he is described as advising King Ahaz of Judah?
   (c) at the time when he was advising King Hezekiah?
3. When was the Northern Kingdom of Israel finally defeated, and by whom? What happened to the people as a result of that defeat? What is the probable reason for the lack of reference to Israel's defeat in the Book of Isaiah?
4. What happened to Jerusalem in 701 BC?
5. Which superpower finally defeated Judah, and when? What happened to the people of Judah at the time of its defeat?
6. Who was Cyrus, and for what was he chiefly famous?

7. For approximately how long were the people of Judah in Exile, and what effect did their experiences have on them?

8. What was the importance of Alexander the Great in the history of the Jews?

9. Who was or were chiefly responsible for the rebuilding of the Temple in Jerusalem after the return of the exiles from Babylon, and when was it completed?

10. Who was Antiochus IV, and what was his importance in the history of the Jewish people?

11. Can you think of any part of the modern world in which the political and/or military situation in recent years has resembled that of Judah in the time of Isaiah? If so, give details of the similarities and of any differences you can see.

12. Can you think of any peoples or races in the modern world, or in history, whose experiences can be compared to those of the Jewish people in the time of Isaiah and after? If so give details.

6.1–13
Isaiah's Vision and his Call

INTRODUCTION AND OUTLINE

In chapter 6 the collection of 'prophetic' messages is interrupted by Isaiah's own account of the visionary experience in which he received God's call to him to become a prophet, and his own response to that call. We may wonder why this passage does not come at the beginning of the Book of Isaiah, since all his prophetic messages naturally follow from his call. But, as we have seen, the messages are not arranged in chronological order. Chapter 6 may originally have been the first part of a collection describing Isaiah's experiences from the time of his call to the end of the Syro-Ephraimitic war (6.1—8.18).

The words of chapter 6 are very familiar to most Christians, and for good reasons. They are among the most beautiful, the most important, and the most influential words in the entire Bible.

V. 1: Isaiah records the occasion of his call and his vision of God.

V. 2–3: In the vision he sees seraphim surrounding and praising God.

V. 4–5: The effect of God's presence and voice on the place and on the prophet himself.

V. 6–7: Isaiah is cleansed of his guilt.

V. 8: God calls Isaiah and he responds.

V. 9–10: Isaiah is warned that people will refuse to accept his preaching.
V. 11–13: Isaiah is commanded to go on preaching even through times of disaster and exile.

NOTES AND INTERPRETATION

6.1: In the year that King Uzziah died: The actual date of Uzziah's death is disputed (see general Introduction). Also, we do not know exactly when Isaiah wrote this account of his call. Traditionally there are two viewpoints about it:

1. That Isaiah recorded his vision when it happened or very soon afterwards, and the reference to Uzziah's death and other events described in chapters 6—8, are predictions.

2. That Isaiah recorded it later – perhaps many years later, remembering and interpreting events in the light of his long and sad experience as a prophet, when he could see a significance in the circumstances of his call that would not have been clear at the time.

This second view assumes that chapter 6 was part of Isaiah's own records (see the Introduction to the Outline above and Special Note 2). It does not cast any doubt on the date of the call, or on its significance for later historical developments, but rather emphasizes these.

The time when Uzziah died turned out to be the beginning of a period of drastic change for both Israel and Judah. After a long period of relative peace and prosperity, with little trouble from neighbouring countries, Assyria regained power with disastrous effects for the two kingdoms. Israel was destroyed and Judah became a vassal of the Assyrian empire. It was just when everything was beginning to change that God called Isaiah to be His spokesman to His people.

6.1, 5: I saw the Lord…and I said '…I am lost…for my eyes have seen the LORD of Hosts': See note on 1.1. Obviously this was not the same sort of 'seeing' as when we say 'I saw a man', or 'I saw the president'. Our physical eyes can see only physical things. But God is Spirit. No human being can actually and physically see God Himself. Clearly Isaiah meant another sort of seeing: the seeing we experience in our imagination and in our understanding, or in dreams, when we are aware of the appearance of things even though we do not see them with our physical eyes.

Just as God's name 'YAHWEH' was considered too holy to be spoken, so it was generally felt in Old Testament times that God was too holy to be seen directly by sinful human beings. In most instances in the Old Testament, where people are described as experiencing God's presence the emphasis is on *hearing* rather than seeing. It was the 'word' or 'voice' of the Lord which came to the prophets and told them what they were to do and say (see e.g. 1 Kings 19.9–18; Amos 1.1,2; 3.7,8).

Moses is said to have seen 'the form of the LORD' (Num. 12.8), and to have spoken with God 'face to face'. But even so, he was told that he could not 'see' God, 'for man shall not see me and live' (Exod. 33.11, 17–20). Even Ezekiel, who claimed to have seen 'visions of God...in *the likeness as it were* of a human form', gives no further detail, but describes what he saw as being '*as it were* the appearance of fire, and the appearance of *the likeness* of the glory of the LORD', rather than the actual shape and appearance of God Himself (see Ezek. 1.1–6, 26–28). Matthew 5.8 must of course be understood as referring to the reward of the pure in heaven, and not to physical seeing during life on earth.

However, the fact that we cannot know just what Isaiah 'saw', does not make his visionary seeing any less 'real' than the sort of seeing we do with our physical eyes.

6.1: His train filled the temple: 'His train', that is, 'his attendants'. We cannot be sure where Isaiah was when he had this vision. The references to 'throne...smoke...burning...altar' suggest that the Temple in Jerusalem was the scene in the vision itself, and this in turn suggests that Isaiah may have experienced it during a worship service. Perhaps it was prompted by one of the great festivals when the kingship of God was celebrated with great pomp and splendour of processional choirs, incense, and burning sacrifices. Many of the visions recorded in the Old Testament were related to things seen in the physical world, e.g. when Jeremiah saw a rod of almond and a boiling pot (Jer. 1.11–14), and Amos saw a builder's plumbline and a basket of fruit (Amos 7.7–9; 8.1–3). Isaiah's experience of his call has all the features of such a vision. However, there is no firm evidence to prove that it was so.

6.2: Above him stood the seraphim: As Isaiah describes them, these seraphim (plural of seraph) were heavenly beings, partly human in shape ('faces', 'hand'), partly bird ('wings'), perhaps partly snake (the Hebrew word is also used to mean flying or fiery serpents – Num. 21.4–9; Deut. 8.14, 15; Isa. 14.29). In Revelation 4.8, which describes a similar vision of six-winged beings serving God and praising Him in almost identical words, they are called 'living creatures', and some interpreters think that Isaiah simply meant angels.

6.3: 'Holy, holy, holy': See note on 1.4 and p. 67 below. To say that God is 'holy' is to say that He is completely different from human beings – *different*, not distant. It also emphasizes His mystery.

'His glory': See note on 2.19. The word 'glory' is used to describe the creative, judging, and saving acts through which God reveals Himself, making human beings aware of His presence. When used of God it implies much more than the respect, wealth, or power which it means when used of men and women. By means of His glory, which many Bible writers describe as manifesting itself as light and splendour, God shows in the world what can only be partly shown. The full extent of His being and of His holiness remains hidden in mystery.

In Isaiah's time every nation was believed to have a god or gods of its own to protect and fight for it (see 36.18–20). But, as Isaiah continually reminded his hearers, the living God who had made the Israelites His people was greater by far than any of these. 'The whole earth' was filled with His glory.

'LORD of Hosts': God is 'Lord' of many different sorts of armies. (See notes on 1.9 and especially 24.21).

6.4: The foundations...shook...the voice called...the house was filled with smoke: Isaiah gives a vivid description of his own physical sensations during his vision, both in order to gain his hearers' interest, and to remind them how other prophets had described their experience of God's presence (see note on 4.6).

6.5: 'Woe is me...I am lost': See note on 5.8–10. All the three meanings of the word 'woe' suggested there seem to be combined in Isaiah's exclamation as he realized the full significance of his vision. But here the 'woe' is addressed to himself, not to others. (See note on v. 1 above.)

A man of unclean lips...a people of unclean lips: See note on 1.4. Isaiah's 'unclean lips' (the part of a person which most often and most clearly reveals his wrongfulness) symbolize his whole 'unclean', i.e. un-holy, person and personality. Confronted with God's otherness and His perfect holiness, Isaiah was jolted into awareness not only of his own sinfulness as an individual, but the sinfulness of the society to which he belonged.

6.7: 'This has touched your lips, your guilt is taken away, you are forgiven': Once again 'lips' stands for the whole person. See note on 1.19 and the interpretation of 4.2–6, p. 47, para. numbered 2. Isaiah could repent, but only God could fully cleanse him, and 'take away' his sin. The description of his vision shows the divine power at work in him through the action of the seraph and the burning coal.

6.8: 'Whom shall I send, who will go for us?' '...send me': At this point in the vision Isaiah heard what he could not hear before: God's voice calling for someone to announce His judgement to Israel. It seems that the call was not addressed to Isaiah personally. But the vision of God made so great an impression on him that he immediately volunteered his service, and he continued to serve God faithfully in spite of the difficulties and frustrations he suffered in doing so.

6.8: 'I...us': We need not be puzzled by the fact that both the singular 'I' and the plural 'we' are used in recording what God said. In many languages, very important people are expected to speak of themselves in the plural. Compare Genesis 1.26, and the English 'royal we' used by the sovereign when speaking officially.

6.9: 'This people': That is, God's people, Isaiah's people.

Hear and hear...see and see: In Hebrew, repetition of this sort implies continuity. The meaning is: 'go on hearing...seeing!'

6.10: Make the heart of this people fat: In Isaiah's time the heart was thought to be the centre of a person's thought and will and power of decision. To be fat was regarded as healthy and desirable, but in this context it seems to imply being *too* well fed, too rich and self-satisfied, and therefore insensitive to God's command.

The whole of vv. 9 and 10 is difficult to understand, unless we recognize that v. 10, especially, describes what is to be the immediate result of Isaiah's preaching, rather than its ultimate purpose.

6.13: Though a tenth remain...it will be burned again like a terebinth or an oak whose stump remains: The Hebrew text of this verse is unclear and there is no general agreement as to its meaning. Translations vary widely. The last line: 'The holy seed is its stump' is omitted from the Septuagint. All we can safely say is that it seems to complete the picture of total destruction described in vv. 11 and 12, though some interpreters take the 'tenth' and the 'stump' as referring to the faithful 'remnant' who will survive to carry on the life of God's people (see notes on 4.2,3; 10.20,21; 11.11).

We know almost nothing about Isaiah's situation in life, or what his ideas and beliefs were before the time of his call. But clearly what he believed and preached about the nature of God was very largely shaped by his experience in this vision. And although he does not seem to have intended his account of it as a 'message', there is much that we can learn from it.

ISAIAH'S IDEAS ABOUT GOD

The vision gave Isaiah a very strong awareness of three important truths about God which he stressed again and again in his messages: God's *holiness*, His *glory*, and His *sovereignty*.

1. *God is holy.* We have already discussed some aspects of God's holiness (see notes on 1.4 and on v. 3 above). The holiness of God was strongly emphasized in Isaiah's vision, and so it became one of the chief emphases in his preaching. When theologians speak of the relationship between God and the world, they say that God is both immanent (in the world) and transcendent (beyond the world), and 'holiness' is the measure of His transcendence. It describes the feeling people have when they experience the numinous, that is 'divinity' in any form.

In many religions the idea of 'taboo' is very strong. Taboo is the belief that certain beings and certain things are so sacred, so holy, that they cannot be approached or touched, or even seen, without great danger (see Lev. 27.9,10,26–29). To say that God is holy is to say that He is not limited by place and time as we are. He 'lives' outside the world of nature and of time, and is the creator of all things, the first cause of all events. Human beings can experience God's presence, but can never fully know His nature or His will. His transcendence sets Him beyond our understanding. Sinful human beings can become holy only through repentance, and by being redeemed by God Himself.

2. *God's presence is glory:* But God is not only transcendent, outside and above nature, He is also immanent. We experience Him in and through the material world around us. Sometimes God makes Himself known in a special way and for a special purpose, as in the case of Isaiah's vision. Many of the Bible writers describe the glory which people then experience as some sort of brightness, a great light or fire which is more than human eyes can bear (see Exod. 34.29–35; Luke 2.9; Acts 22.6–11; Rev. 15.7,8). But God's glory can also be experienced as the expression of His presence in all that He has created, and for many people the awareness of God's immanence in the world around them is a vital part of their daily lives.

Those who experienced God's perfect presence among them in Jesus Christ often spoke of Him as 'God's Glory' (see John 1.14; 2.11; 17.4,5).

3. *God is 'Sovereign Lord of all':* God's first commandment to His people was that they should honour no Lord but Himself. He rules over the world He has created, and His power alone sustains and keeps the world in being. The kings whom He had given to Israel were His representatives. But although their descendants failed to rule as He had commanded, so that His people looked forward to a time when a more perfect king would come to rule them, Isaiah made it very clear that God's rule is not something in the distant future. He shows His presence and His power as well as His mystery in the great and small events of nature and of history.

VISIONS OF GOD

Some people, when they note that Isaiah may have experienced his vision during worship in the Temple, expect to experience God's presence in a similar way when they worship Him in church. Some are disappointed if they do not experience such visions, and feel that their worship is useless or unacceptable to God. Some even think that in vv. 9–13 Isaiah was implying that if his hearers would only forsake the wrong ways of worship described in 1.10–15, they would 'hear' and 'see' God (6.10) as he had done.

But in 6.1–10 Isaiah was simply describing his own experience as a prophet. If we find these verses difficult to understand, it may be because Isaiah did not intend them as a message. We need to recognize the difference between such 'narrative' and historical passages, and those in which the prophet was acting as God's spokesman, and clearly intending to arouse people and call them to repentance.

However, Isaiah's description of his vision does tell us something of

'Isaiah volunteered his service...speaking out in God's name...in spite of difficulties and frustrations' (see pp. 66 and 71).

The Korean poet and playwright Kim Chi Ha suffered many years' imprisonment for speaking out, as a Christian, against oppressive Government policies.

How far would *you* be willing to speak out, and suffer, for what you believe to be right?

the way in which God 'speaks' to human beings. People who have such experiences often find them difficult to explain to others, and, as we have seen, such inward visions are often related to some particular object or event through which God chooses to speak to people who are ready to hear – or even to those who (like Paul) are *not* ready, nor expecting such a direct spiritual experience.

Some Christians think that such visions or experiences can come only when people are asleep, i.e. in dreams, or in a trance, and others believe that *all* of our dreams bring us messages from God. Certainly God can speak to us in any way He chooses; but what psychologists have discovered about the causes and meaning of our dreams seems to show that they are usually messages from our subconscious or unconscious mind, rather than from any direct intervention from God in our lives.

For most Christians, of course, the most direct 'seeing' of God which they experience is through their knowledge of Jesus who is 'the image of the invisible God' (Col. 1.15), and through their experience of His presence and power in their lives (John 14.8–11,15–17,21).

EXPERIENCES OF WORSHIP

As we have said, some people consider that Isaiah's vision of God was an example of what should ideally happen to all Christians when they worship. Clearly it was not a typical experience of worship; in many ways it was unique. But our understanding of each step in Isaiah's experience can help us, as we ourselves try to worship God, both privately and with others in church.

1. Isaiah *recognized God*: 'I saw the LORD' (v. 1). Worship should be a meeting with God and recognizing His presence with us.

2. The seraphim *adored* and *praised* God: 'one called to another …"holy holy holy is the LORD"' (v. 3). Our adoration and praise of God can take many forms: speaking, singing, dancing – or silence.

3. Isaiah *recognized himself*: 'Woe is me' (v. 5). In God's presence we become painfully aware of our own sin.

4. Isaiah *confessed his sin*: 'I am a man of unclean lips' (v. 5). Too often we tend to hide from our sin, or make excuses. In God's presence such pretences are impossible.

5. Isaiah *received forgiveness*: 'Your guilt is taken away' (v. 7). We cannot ourselves overcome our sin. But God 'is faithful and just, and will…cleanse us' (1 John 1.9). Some people find it difficult to accept this, unless they hear God's forgiveness spoken by someone else (e.g. a pastor or priest), as Isaiah heard it from the seraph. Others believe that God speaks directly to each individual person.

6. Isaiah *heard God's word*: 'I heard the voice of the Lord' (v. 8). God speaks in many ways to those who worship Him: through a preacher, a Scripture reading, through music or art or nature or other

people's words and actions – or secretly in our hearts. Preachers need to be very careful that their words are 'from God', not merely their own.

7. Isaiah *offered himself*: 'Here am I! Send me' (v. 8). We can offer ourselves to God in many ways: by helping others, giving money, trying to overcome habits of selfishness or carelessness, speaking out in His name, as Isaiah did, for what we believe to be the right.

Of course these are not the only steps we can follow in worship, and we should not force ourselves to follow them. But they do provide a helpful framework for people who find it difficult to prevent their minds from wandering during times of worship. They can also be useful for pastors and other leaders who have the task of planning worship services for a congregation.

STUDY SUGGESTIONS

WORD STUDY

1. Which *four* of the following phrases are nearest in meaning to the words 'I saw' or 'I have seen' in 6.1 and 6.5?
   I dreamed of   I beheld   I imagined   I foresaw   I perceived
   I pictured   I understood   I had a vision of   I conceived
   I recognized
2. In what ways does Isaiah's use of the word 'woe' in 6.5 differ from his use of it in 5.8,11,18,20,21 and 22?
3. Match each of the following words with one of the definitions below:
   imminent   immanent   eminent   emanent
   (a) indwelling, universally present   (b) flowing out
   (c) outstanding or distinguished   (d) coming very soon.

REVIEW OF CONTENT

4. What was the political situation in Judah and Israel at the time when King Uzziah died?
5. What evidence can be found in the passage to suggest that Isaiah experienced his vision of God during or after a service of worship in the Temple?
6. 'I am lost; for I am a man of unclean lips'. Why did Isaiah use the phrase 'unclean lips' to describe his own sinfulness?
7. Explain the apparent contradiction in verses 9 and 10, where God commands Isaiah to go and speak for Him, but also seems to command him to tell the people not to hear or understand.
8. What three important truths about God are expressed in this passage, which are stressed in many other parts of the Book of Isaiah?

BIBLE STUDY

9. In each of the following passages the words of God to Isaiah as recorded in 6.9,10 are quoted. Say in each case (i) who was speaking these words on what occasion and (ii) what teaching were the words used to help explain?
(a) Matt. 13.10–23   (b) Mark 4.10–25   (c) Luke 8.4–18
(d) John 12.20–41   (e) Acts 28.16–28

10. Each of the following passages describes a 'call' by God. Say in each case who was called, and for what special purpose, if any.
(a) Rom. 8.18–20, 28–30   (b) 1 Cor. 1.26–31
(c) Eph. 4.4–16   (d) 2 Thess. 1.11,12
What general truths do we learn from these passages about the way in which God calls people to serve Him?

11. Isaiah's visionary experience changed his life. What were the experiences which changed the lives of each of the following, and in what ways were they changed? (A Concordance may help you to discover the answers.)
Jacob   David   Matthew   Paul

APPLICATION, OPINION, AND RESEARCH

12. God called Isaiah to be His spokesman. What sorts of people do you think God calls to be His spokesmen today? How can we tell whether those who claim to be God's spokesmen have really been called by Him?

13. 'Some Christians feel that their failure to experience visions of God means that their worship is unacceptable to Him' (p. 68). What is your opinion?

14. If possible, discuss with a group of friends or fellow students the different ways in which people experience God's presence. In what ways do you yourself chiefly experience God's presence? In what chief ways are you conscious of God's *transcendence*? In what ways are you conscious of His *immanence* in the world?

15. If you know anyone who claims to have had a vision of God, what is your opinion of their claim? What effect, if any, did the experience have on their life?

16. Do any of the religious leaders in your country claim to be 'prophets' of God? If so, in what ways does the story of how each was 'called' compare with Isaiah's description of his call?

17. How would you answer someone who said: 'Most people who claim that God has called them to serve Him are simply following their own inclination, and doing what *they* want to do'? How can we tell the difference between what God calls us to do and our own inclinations?

7.1–9
Isaiah's Warning to Ahaz

OUTLINE

A further narrative passage, mainly in prose, describing Isaiah's warning to King Ahaz at the time when the Northern Kingdom joined Syria in trying to conquer Judah, so as to strengthen themselves against Assyria (see Special Note 1, p. 60). Unlike chapter 6 (and chapter 8) it was written in the third person, presumably by Isaiah's disciples.

Vv. 1,2: Syria and Israel attack Jerusalem without success, but panic spreads as the king and people hear of the alliance against them.
Vv. 3–8a,9: Isaiah meets the king and tells him there is nothing to fear, if only he will trust in God's protection.
V. 8b: A specific reference to the break-up of the Northern Kingdom: probably a comment added at a later date.

NOTES AND INTERPRETATION

7.1: Syria and...Israel came up to Jerusalem: Little is known about this invasion, but it seems that the aim of Israel's alliance with her old enemy Syria was to unite all the small nations of Palestine against the growing power of Assyria (see 2 Kings 15.29; 16.1,5,6 and pp. 1, 2, 60).
7.2: The house of David: That is, the king, Ahaz, who was a descendant of David, and his court.
Ephraim: The strongest of the northern tribes of Israel. Its name was sometimes used to mean the Northern Kingdom as a whole.
7.3,4: 'Go...to meet Ahaz, you and your son Shearjashub...and say to him': The name Shearjashub means 'a remnant shall return'. It was common in the ancient Near East, as in many places today, to name children after events or places which were significant at the time of their birth, or which carried a message from God (e.g. Samuel, Elijah, Jesus). No doubt Isaiah was to take the boy with him because his name would convey to the king either a warning ('only a few will return') or a promise ('at least some will be saved'), according to whether or not he heeded the prophet's message. Prophets often used the words 'Say (or Speak) to him (or them)' to introduce their messages. Scholars sometimes refer to these words as 'the messenger formula'.
At the conduit of the upper pool: Clearly Isaiah was to give the king God's warning at a moment when it would have most effect, that is, when Ahaz was preparing for the expected invasion and probable siege by inspecting

the city's water supply. This was especially important for a city which was built, as Jerusalem was, on a rocky outcrop.

Fuller's Field: The place where a cleansing process in cloth-making was carried out, usually an open field near to a source of clean water – hence, perhaps, a camping ground for troops defending the city.

7.4: 'Take heed, be quiet, do not fear...these two smouldering stumps': Isaiah began his counsel to the king with a simple warning and word of comfort: 'Keep alert' (GNB), 'do not be frightened' (NEB). The king was fearing the wrong danger. Syria and Israel were not the real threat to Judah. Kings Rezin and Pekah had once been dangerous enemies, but now had lost their strength like fires that are nearly out. In spite of their plans to conquer Judah, Ahaz need only keep calm and quiet and the danger would pass.

The son of Tabeel: Probably a Syrian prince whom Rezin and Pekah planned to set up as puppet king in Jerusalem.

7.8b: Within 65 years Ephraim will be broken: The reference to '65 years' is puzzling, and although this sentence (in the RSV) seems to have been added at a later date, it does not match known historical facts. But its general meaning in the context of vv. 7–9(a) seems clear: neither the overall aims of Syria and Israel nor their plan to force Judah to join them would succeed.

7.9b: If you will not believe...you shall not be established: Isaiah ended his poetic warning with a play on words which would make it stand in the king's memory. In Hebrew the last word in each of the two phrases has almost the same sound: *taaminu* 'believe', and *teamenu* 'be established'. We can compare this with the word-play which gave such a forceful end to the poem in 5.1–7.

PROPHECY AND HISTORY

We have already seen that the prophets of the Old Testament spoke to God's people about God's will for them in particular situations (pp. 2–6). This becomes clear as we read Isaiah chapters 7 and 8, which show that a true prophet impressed people, not by an ability to forecast events in the far future, but by the ability to interpret correctly the events of his own time.

Isaiah was speaking to the leaders of the nation at the time of the Syro-Ephraimitic war (about 735 BC). Everyone in Judah was in a panic, including King Ahaz and other leaders, and seemingly with good reason, as the country was being invaded by its neighbours on three sides (see 2 Kings 15.29–38; 16.5,6; 2 Chron. 28.17,18). But seeing this immediate danger, they were blinded to the much greater danger from Assyria.

Isaiah, however, saw beyond the immediate situation. Syria and Ephraim were no stronger than their capital cities, Damascus, and

Samaria, which already paid tribute to Assyria, or their weak kings whose plans would come to nothing. Isaiah saw too that Assyria's strong leader Tiglath-pileser III was not likely to stand idly looking on while these vassal states tried to persuade their neighbours to form an anti-Assyrian alliance.

Ahaz, in his terror at the thought of invasion, declared that he would turn to Assyria for help against Syria and Israel. But Isaiah saw that far from making Judah safe, this policy would only turn the nation into a vassal of Assyria like the others. In return for Tiglath-pileser's 'protection' the people would be made to pay heavy tribute, and to introduce Assyrian religious symbols and ways of worship into the Temple (see 2 Kings 16.7-18).

The whole purpose of the message in 7.3-9, therefore, was to prevent Ahaz from carrying out his decision to go to Assyria for help rather than trusting in God's power to save His people. The Hebrew words translated 'believe' and 'be established' in the word-play both contain the sense of 'firmness' or 'safety' for the dynasty as well as the nation (NEB translates v. 9: 'Have firm faith or you will not stand firm'). Ahaz's lack of any firm commitment to, or trust in, the God of Israel could only lead to disaster, as described in the remainder of chapter 7.

RELIGION AND POLITICS

Many people today, including some Christians, think that religion and politics ought to be kept separate. They say that religion should be concerned only with people's souls, and that the Churches (and other religious authorities) have no right to try to influence government policy, nor even to comment on the political opinions and activities of their own members.

In ancient times, however, religion and government went together. In Israel God was regarded as ruler of the nation, and the king as His representative. It was the religious leaders, elders and judges, who interpreted the law, settled disputes, and acted as advisers to the kings on foreign policy and military strategy, as well as on home affairs. Any separation of religion from politics would have been unthinkable.

When the prophets spoke out against oppression and injustice their words may have been unacceptable to the politicians, as Isaiah's were (see 5.24b), but no-one thought to accuse them of 'meddling in politics'. Government was a prophet's business, as well as spiritual matters. All prophets were expected to receive and proclaim God's word about how the country was ruled, and to remind the leaders and people of their covenant relationship with God. Some were regarded almost as official advisers to the kings (though, like Isaiah, they were not always listened to). They emphasized that the only true and firm basis for the nation's safety was firm faith and quiet obedience to God's law, not military alliances with bigger nations. And they continually denounced the sacrificial pagan worship with which both priests and kings hoped to placate the Lord, even while continuing to rule unjustly.

The task of Christian 'prophets' today is in some ways more difficult. Although in a few countries the head of state is also head of the Church, most modern nations are intentionally secular. This does not mean that they are necessarily anti-Christian (though some are), merely that they will not favour one religion more than another. Church leaders also face the fact that true prosperity and security are no longer benefits that one nation can expect to enjoy at the expense of other nations. Oppression and injustice in one nation affects that nation's relationships with others. Only world-wide international efforts to promote peace can prevent further wars of aggression. Christian leaders not only have to overcome the opposition of many secular leaders to the Church's involvement in discussion or decision-making on political issues. They may need to re-think quite radically the biblical ideas about the relationship between Church and state, and about their own responsibility for proclaiming God's word not only to His own people, the Church, but also to His world at large (see 2 Cor. 5.16–20; Rom. 9.30—11.36).

STUDY SUGGESTIONS

WORD STUDY

1. What is meant by: (a) 'The house of David', and (b) 'Ephraim' in v. 2?
2. What is the literal meaning of the name 'Shearjashub'?

REVIEW OF CONTENT

3. Why did Syria and Israel want to conquer Judah, and what did they plan to do after they had conquered it?
4. (a) Where was Isaiah told to meet King Ahaz, and for what particular reason was he told to meet him there?
   (b) Why was Isaiah to take his young son with him to meet the king?
5. What did Isaiah mean when he called Rezin and Pekah 'smouldering stumps of firebrands' (v. 4)?
6. (a) What was Isaiah's advice to Ahaz, and why?
   (b) What, if anything, did Ahaz actually *do* as a result of Isaiah's message as recorded in Isaiah 7.4–9?

BIBLE STUDY

7. Read (i) 2 Kings 15.29–38 and 16.1–20 and (ii) 2 Chron. 28.
   For each of these passages write a short summary in your own

words of the historical events which it reports. Then make an analytical table to show which of these events are contained in: (a) both passages, (b) the Kings passage only, (c) the Chronicles passage only. Which of these three lists do the events recorded in Isaiah 7 most nearly match? Are there any contradictions between them?

8. Make a sketch map of the Near East, showing the boundaries of Judah and of the neighbouring countries which were allied against her at the time of the Syro-Ephraimitic war. Show also, by means of arrows, the advances into Palestine which Assyria made at that time. Show as far as you can the various places listed in the passages studied under question 7 above. (The general Introduction and Special Note 1 will help you in making this map, but you may also need to use a Bible Atlas and Bible Dictionary.)

APPLICATION, OPINION, AND RESEARCH

9. Isaiah had given his son a name which carried a message that would stand in the king's memory (see p. 73). In many countries today people give names with a religious message (or a prayer) not only to people, but to their houses, vehicles, etc. What do you think is their purpose in doing this? If you can, give examples of such names, with an explanation of their purpose.

10. If your country was threatened with invasion today, who would have the responsibility of deciding whether to fight back, surrender, or seek military help from an ally? Whose responsibility would it be to give advice on such questions?

11. 'Many people today, including some Christians, think that religion and politics should be kept separate' (p. 75). What is your opinion?

12. What is the relationship between Church and state in your country? Do you think it is a satisfactory relationship? If not, in what ways do you think it should be changed? Give your reasons in each case.

7.10–25
The Sign of Immanuel

OUTLINE

The remainder of chapter 7 falls into two main sections. Verses 10–17 contain a further narrative passage, and verses 18–25 a series of oracles.
Vv. 10,11: Isaiah offers Ahaz a sign from God as proof that the message in vv. 4–9 was true.

V. 12: Ahaz refuses to 'test' God in that way.

Vv. 13–15: God will send the sign in any case, in the birth of a boy to be named *Immanuel*, 'God with us'.

Vv. 16,17: The meaning of the sign: Ahaz's lack of faith in seeking help from Assyria against Syria and Israel, instead of trusting God, will cause Judah to suffer greatly.

Vv. 18,19: An oracle threatening that Egypt and Assyria, like devouring insects, will devastate the land.

V. 20: The weapon (Assyria) which Ahaz hoped to use against Israel and Syria will turn in his hand and destroy Judah instead.

Vv. 21,22 and 23–25: The survivors will return to the hardship of a nomadic life, and the cultivated farms and vineyards will revert to wild.

NOTES AND INTERPRETATION

7.10: Again the LORD spoke to Ahaz: 'Again' – that is, as before, God 'spoke' to Ahaz through the prophet Isaiah.

7.11: Ask a sign of the LORD your God...as deep as Sheol or high as heaven: The Hebrew word translated 'sign' was used by many of the Old Testament writers to mean something which gave evidence of God's presence and activity in the world. A sign could be anything: an object, an event, particular words, a particular person. Many of the Old Testament prophets were given signs to show that God was truly calling them. Many of them pointed to signs to show that the message they proclaimed truly came from God. Often the sign would be something remarkable, perhaps even what we might call 'miraculous', like the holding up of the sea (Exod. 14; Num. 14.22,23). Thus a sign was both a call for faith in God and also a guarantee that such faith would be justified (see e.g. Psalm 145).

Sometimes signs were mysterious, like a riddle. But they were not necessarily miraculous, though they might appear to be. Sometimes God gave signs of His presence through quite ordinary happenings like a plague of insects, a rainbow, or, as in this passage, the birth of a child. **Deep as Sheol or high as heaven:** Ahaz had apparently taken no notice of the sign given in the coincidence of Shearjashub's name with the message about Rezin and Pekah (see note on 7.3). Now Isaiah offered him any sign he chose to ask for, from Sheol (see note on 5.14) upwards.

7.13: Hear then, O house of David...you weary my God also. Therefore the Lord himself will give you a sign: Coming after the words '*your* God' in v. 11, this seems to be both a reminder that, as king, Ahaz had special reason to put his trust in God's promise that King David and his descendants would be 'made sure' forever (2 Sam. 7.12–17). It was also a warning that, because Ahaz still shilly-shallied, God would not wait any longer to be asked. He would provide the sign Himself: a child soon to be born, within whose early years Ahaz's lack of faith would bring its own punishment.

7.14: A young woman shall conceive and bear a son, and shall call his name Immanuel: The exact meaning of this verse has been the subject of much discussion among biblical scholars over the centuries. As the RSV footnote indicates, the AV and some other English translations have the word 'virgin' instead of 'young woman', chiefly because the Greek word used in the Septuagint translation normally means a virgin. This has naturally led to speculation as to whether the sign Isaiah spoke of was the coming of the promised Messiah, and hence the coming of Jesus Himself. But the original Hebrew word, *almah*, simply means a young woman of marriageable age, who may or may not be a virgin. And Isaiah's own words seem to show that the message which this sign carried was not really about the child himself, or the nature of his birth. It was about what was to happen (Syria and Israel would be laid waste and Judah itself overrun by the Assyrians), and how soon it would happen (within the space of time between the child's birth and his becoming old enough to know right from wrong). And the child's name was part of the sign, showing that these happenings could be avoided, if only Ahaz would remember God's promise to be 'with' His people always, and would trust in that promise rather than in help from Assyria.

7.15,22: Curds and honey: Some interpreters link these words with Exodus 3.8 and other passages where milk and honey symbolize the richness of the promised land to which God's people would come after the Exodus from Egypt. They therefore take v. 15 to mean that the child of the sign would belong to a rich family, perhaps even the royal family itself, and some even suggest that Isaiah was pointing to Ahaz's son Hezekiah. Isaiah's words of promise in chapter 9 about a child who would succeed to the throne of David in divine power and light seem to support this interpretation, though it does not tie up with the probable date of Hezekiah's birth.

Others, however, point to the context of the words in v. 22, which suggest just the opposite: the food of nomadic tribesmen dependent on the milk and other produce of the few cattle left to them, and such wild food as they could find.

It seems in fact that Isaiah may have had both ideas in mind, and many scholars now support the idea that the 'young woman' was Isaiah's own wife ('the prophetess', 8.3), thus adding a third child to the 'signs and portents' (8.18) of darkness followed by light (8.22; 9.2). Like many of the prophetic signs in the Old Testament, this one may carry a double meaning: that is, (1) the threat of disaster brought about by Ahaz's lack of faith, and (2) the reminder that God *is* with His people always, and that after the time of darkness He will bring them into the light (see 9.2).

7.17: The day that Ephraim departed from Judah: That is, the time some two hundred years earlier when Solomon's kingdom split up and a period of conflict between small nations followed (see also note on 7.2).

7.18: The fly...the bee: Another reminder of the plagues of Egypt, but this time the plagues which God would send would be upon His own people, not their oppressors.

7.20: The Lord will shave with a razor which is hired beyond the River: This does not only mean that Judah would be stripped bare of power and prosperity. The Jews customarily wore their hair and beard long and cut them only as a sign of mourning, so that to be 'shaved' meant that the nation would experience shame and sorrow.

The River: That is, the Euphrates. Here as in v. 17 the words 'the king of Assyria' were probably added by a later scribe to make sure that readers would understand the allusion. The land of Assyria lay beyond the Euphrates, and it was from there that the instrument of God's wrath would come.

After the time of Isaiah, some Jews came to see the sign of Immanuel as a prophetic allusion to the hoped-for Messiah. And it was natural that the early Christians, whose personal knowledge of Jesus made them feel that in Him God had indeed been 'with' them, regarded Isaiah's description of a baby boy to be named 'God with us' as a prediction of Jesus's birth (see Matt. 1.22,23). Certainly there are many passages in the Old Testament which have been seen as pointing to Jesus's coming, and this is one of them.

But we must not forget that Isaiah's chief concern was the immediately dangerous situation in Judah, and the King's refusal to accept his warnings about it. He may well have been trying to boost Ahaz's morale by suggesting that the traditional belief in a future ideal king might soon be fulfilled. And v. 13 seems like a cry of frustration: 'God help Judah indeed,' Isaiah seems to be saying, '(and Syria and Israel too), if you will persist in bringing back the bad old days of dependence on Assyrian power!'

The description of devastation in vv. 18–25, too, has the strength of a much-repeated warning, containing many echoes of oracles we have already studied, especially those in chapter 5.

STUDY SUGGESTIONS

WORD STUDY

1. What connection, if any, can you see between the word 'sign' as used in vv. 11–14, and the custom which requires people to 'sign' such documents as cheques, contracts, letters, etc.?

REVIEW OF CONTENT

2. Why did Isaiah accuse Ahaz of 'wearying' God?
3. (a) What was the 'sign' which God would give Ahaz?
   (b) Briefly summarize three possible ways of interpreting that sign.
4. Which other verse in chapter 7 refers to the 'land' mentioned in v. 16?
5. In v. 17, what is meant by:
   (a) 'Your father's house'?
   (b) 'The day that Ephraim departed from Judah'?
6. For what chief reasons have Christians assumed that in vv. 14 and 15 Isaiah was fortelling the birth of Jesus?
7. Which verses in chapter 5 describe the sort of disaster pictured in 7.18–25? Make a list of verse references of the matching descriptions from the two chapters.

BIBLE STUDY

8. What was the purpose of the signs described in each of the following passages and in what way, if any, was the sign fulfilled?
   (a) Gen. 1.14   (b) Gen. 9.8–14   (c) Exod. 4.1–9
   (d) 1 Sam. 10.1–9   (e) 1 Kings 13.1–10   (f) Isa. 19.19,20
9. What was the attitude of the people towards the signs described in each of the following passages?
   (a) Matt. 4.1–6   (b) Matt. 12.22–32
   (c) Mark 8.11,12   (d) Luke 2.8–12
10. Study the ways in which the Hebrew word *almah*, translated 'young woman', is used in the following verses, and say in each case whether or not the passage seems to suggest that the girl is a virgin.
    (a) Gen. 24.43   (b) Exod. 2.8   (c) Prov. 30.18,19
    (d) Song 1.3   (e) Song 6.8
11. Use a Concordance to find other passages where the phrase 'curds and honey' is used. Notice in each case whether the context suggests that the phrase was used to mean 'poverty', or 'plenty'. Compare the passages where the words 'curds and honey' are used with some of those where the words 'milk and honey' are used instead.

APPLICATION, OPINION, AND RESEARCH

12. Some Christians believe that whenever they are faced with a difficult problem, or have to make a difficult choice, they should ask God to give them a sign to help them to know what His will is. Others disagree, saying that Christians should have sufficient faith to trust in God's power without demanding any outward sign of it. What is your opinion?

13. From what sources, other than God, do people chiefly seek 'signs' to show them what they should do at difficult times in their lives? What is your own opinion about the usefulness of such signs?

14. In 7.18–25, we find descriptions of the effect that invasions and oppression by the Assyrians would have in Israel and Judah. In what chief ways, if any, would the effects of invasion and oppression by an occupying power be similar, or different, today?

15. According to v. 12, when Ahaz refused to ask God for a sign, he gave as excuse that it would be unlawful to 'test' God in that way. That is, he hid behind the 'letter of the law' (see Deut. 6.16). What are some of the ways in which Christians today may be tempted to hide behind religious rules?

8.1–22(23)
'Bind Up the Testimony!'

OUTLINE

A continuation of the prose narrative, together with further messages which were probably grouped together here because they relate to the Syro-Ephraimitic crisis.

Vv. 1–4: Once again God commands Isaiah to deliver a message in the form of a name to be given to a newborn child. This time Isaiah is to record the message and have it attested by reliable witnesses.

Vv. 5–8a: A message of warning that Judah as well as Syria and Israel will be submerged by the rising tide of Assyrian power.

Vv. 8b–10: A message of hope if only Judah will be faithful.

Vv. 11–15: A message of support for Isaiah in his stand against the mistaken opinion and faithless behaviour of the rulers and people of both the Israelite kingdoms.

Vv. 16–20: Since no-one heeds his words, Isaiah declares he will say no more. If people look to wizards and mediums for guidance instead of turning to God, they will have to suffer the consequences.

Vv. 21,22 (or –23): Those consequences will be a dark time of great distress and hunger.

NOTE: In the RSV chapter 8 is shown as ending at v. 22. But in some of the Hebrew manuscripts the verse numbered as 9.1 (and in other manuscripts the first sentence of it), is included with chapter 8 as verse 23, and chapter 9 has only 20 verses (see RSV footnote). Other English versions vary in their numbering of these verses, according to which manuscript they are based on.

NOTES AND INTERPRETATION

8.1: A large tablet...common characters: The Hebrew words do not give an exact description of how the message was to be recorded, and English translations vary: e.g. GNB: 'in large letters', JB: 'in ordinary writing'. But obviously it was to be set down as plainly as possible, for all to understand, so that when the threatened disorder occurred everyone would recognize that Isaiah had spoken truly.

8.2: Reliable witnesses to attest for me: In the same way, it is customary in many countries today for anyone signing an important legal document to get witnesses to attest to its validity.

8.1–4: Maher-shalal-hash-baz: As we saw, the prophetic name Shear-jashub could be understood either as promise or as threat (see note on 7.3). The same is true of the name Maher-shalal-hash-baz, meaning 'the spoil speeds, the prey hastens' (GNB has 'quick loot: fast plunder'). Assyria would despoil the nations which Judah feared, but would afterwards prey on Judah also.

8.3: The prophetess: Isaiah's wife.

8.4: Before the child knows how to say 'father': Compare 7.15,16. This message too shows how soon the expected events will happen.

8.6,7: The waters of Shiloah: Probably a conduit bringing water into Jerusalem from the Gihon spring, which seems to have been associated with the anointing of Judah's kings (see 1 Kings 1.38–45 and Isa. 7.3). **The River:** See notes on 7.20. Isaiah gave this message in the form of a parable, contrasting the gentle but strong support which God promised to Judah's kings with the dangerous support of the King of Assyria, which would come flooding over the land like a spring torrent.

8.8: Outspread wings: It is not clear what 'wings' are meant. If (a) this verse belongs with the preceding message, this may be a reference to the winged God 'Asshur' who was believed to help the Assyrians in battle (see note on 9.9,10). Or (b) the verse could be an introduction to the hymn which follows, and the wings would then refer to the protecting power of God (see e.g. Ps. 57.1).

O Immanuel: If interpretation (a) of 'outspread wings' is correct, 'Immanuel' seems here to be a call for the help that Judah will need:

'God be with us, help us!' If interpretation (b) is correct, then it is a reminder of God's promise, and a call to the rulers and people to 'walk in his paths' (2.3).

8.9,10: Be broken, you peoples...gird yourselves and be dismayed: Some interpreters consider these verses to be a later addition, but they can be compared with 7.3–9, and seem to be part of a hymn which declared the futility of opposing God's purpose for His people, and which perhaps carried the refrain: 'God is with us'.

8.11,12: The LORD warned me not to walk in the way of this people...Do not call conspiracy...what they fear: Another reference to the Syro-Ephraimitic plan to dethrone Ahaz and put a puppet king in his place (see 7.5–7). Isaiah was right in taking a stand against those people who feared this so-called conspiracy. Their refusal to believe and 'fear' the words of God, that is, to trust and obey Him, was a far greater danger and stumbling-stone to them, as they would discover (see note on 11.2 and 1 Peter 2.7,8).

8.16,17: Bind up the testimony...among my disciples...I will wait for the LORD who is hiding his face...and I will hope in him: As no-one but Isaiah's close followers heeded his preaching, he put the written record of God's warnings into the hands of those disciples, who could witness to the truth of his words. Now he would stop speaking for a time, as God seemed to have set His face against His disobedient people, and had no more to say to them. Even so, Isaiah himself would not despair, but continue to wait in hope, trusting that in the end God's will must prevail.

8.18: I and the children whom the LORD has given me are signs and portents: Isaiah did not use the word 'sign' in telling about either Shearjashub or Maher-shalal-hash-baz, as he did in the message about the child to be named Immanuel. But their names carried a significance which should have been just as clear to the king and other leaders as the actual message of warning or promise which the prophet spoke on God's behalf (see notes on 7.3; 7.14; and 8.2,3 above).

8.19: Consult the mediums and wizards: Seeking guidance from the spirits of the dead was forbidden under the covenant law (see Lev. 19.31; Deut. 18.9–14). But people continued the practice, especially in times of trouble and confusion. No doubt when the prophet's words displeased them, or he had no immediate message to give, people looked to the mediums and magicians for counsel instead (see note on 2.6). But that could only lead them into darker distress.

As we saw in chapter 6, God warned Isaiah at the time of his call that people would shut their ears and their eyes to his teaching, and we saw in chapter 7 how this warning was fulfilled. Not only did the people turn a deaf ear to Isaiah's preaching, but the king refused to listen to his words either of encouragement (7.4–8) or of doom (7.13–20).

Here in the narrative section of chapter 8 we see the prophet at the end of his patience. He had warned King Ahaz again and again that the policies he was pursuing could only end in ruin for the nation, for Ahaz himself, and for the people. One last time Isaiah offered to give the king any proof he chose to ask for, to show that national safety lay in obedience to God rather than in foreign help. But again Ahaz refused. So Isaiah would say no more. He would disassociate himself entirely from the action taken by the king and other leaders of the nation. But he also took care to make a written 'testimony' of the warnings he had given, and had it sealed by those who could vouch for the truth of his words when the time came (as it surely would: 'I will wait for the LORD' (v. 17)) to say 'I told you so!' In the meantime Isaiah himself and his sons with their ominous names would remain as living 'signs' of what was to come.

The king might get approval for his policies from other advisers, and through the mediums and sorcerers who claimed to receive messages from spirits of the dead. But that advice and approval would be worthless, and would lead only to distress and hunger. Then the people would curse the king's folly, and would even curse God for turning against them (vv. 16 and 21).

We can feel Isaiah's exasperation, and the vehemence of his words, throughout this chapter. What hope could there possibly be for people who chose to ignore the clear warnings they had been given? 'Surely for this word they speak there is no dawn' (v. 20).

THE DANGERS OF NATIONALISM

Throughout history there have been small countries who chose to place themselves under the protection of a more powerful nation when threatened by an enemy, rather than rely on their own resources. Sometimes this saves them, but there is always a risk that the smaller nation will be swallowed up by its powerful allies, or lose much of its cultural heritage and national identity under the influence of foreign tastes, values, habits, and beliefs. There may be enrichment, but there may also be great loss. Much depends on what sort of values and beliefs the stronger nation has.

In the case of Judah, dependence on Assyria brought a flood of destruction, oppression, and exploitation, in which the little nation nearly drowned. And it brought the imposition of moral codes and religious practices which included the worship of false gods in the holy places of Jerusalem.

Clearly the chief aim of Ahaz and the other leaders was to *save* Judah, even though their policies were mistaken. And it seems that Isaiah's criticism of these policies made him so unpopular that he decided to withdraw from public preaching and keep silent for a time.

'Ask a sign of the Lord' (7.11). 'In times of crisis people find it difficult to go on trusting God....They are tempted to ask for "signs" from astrologers and mediums instead' (p. 87).

On the wall of her apartment in Washington, USA, the well-known clairvoyante and visionary Jeane Dixon has photographs of the many grateful – and influential – people whose 'futures' she has foretold.

In what circumstances, if at all, should we as Christians seek guidance about the future in this way?

Today too we are accustomed to thinking of 'patriotism' as being a virtue in all circumstances. 'Nationalism' and the struggle to achieve a 'national consciousness', is a very strong force today, especially in countries which have recently become independent after years of colonial rule. To oppose official military policies on moral grounds is to be treated as unpatriotic, or even as a traitor to the state. For example, Americans who opposed the war in Vietnam were called 'un-American'; Russians who work for human rights in their country are imprisoned or forcibly sent to hospital as 'insane'; Africans who oppose violence in the struggles for liberation are labelled 'colonialists'.

CONFLICTING LOYALTIES

Christians in many countries are faced with the choice which God told Isaiah he must make: they have to decide what they will 'regard as holy', and what they will 'dread' (v. 13). Which comes first, loyalty to what seem to be the best interests of the nation, or what they believe to be their duty to God? For the Israelites, because of God's promises, these two things were the same. But we have to recognize that the survival of any particular nation as such – including our own – may *not* be part of God's purpose.

In times of national crisis and distress, as of personal trouble, many people, including some Christians, find it difficult to go on trusting God. They feel helpless and confused, and unless their faith is very strong they are tempted to look for guidance from political leaders, or to ask for 'signs' from astrologers and mediums instead, as the Israelites did. And when this leads to disaster, they blame these 'guides' and the 'signs' they give, or even God – rather than themselves.

But if we truly seek God's guidance He will show us the right path. 'Should not a people consult their God?...To the teaching and to the testimony!' (vv. 19b, 20a). Jesus never promised His followers that they would be protected from all danger, nor that they would always be able to understand why things happen as they do (John 14.27; 16.33—17.2: 17.13). But 'in everything God works for good with those who love him, who are called according to his purpose' (Rom. 8.28).

STUDY SUGGESTIONS

WORD STUDY

1. Why did Isaiah call the record he made of his prophetic words 'the testimony'?

REVIEW OF CONTENT

2. (a) Why was Isaiah told to write down the message about the name Maher-shalal-hash-baz, and what does the name mean?

(b) For what reasons do people usually have documents which they have written 'attested' as Isaiah did?

3. Explain in your own words the meaning of the message contained in verse 4.

4. (a) What were the two 'waters' which Isaiah contrasted in vv. 5–8? What were the chief differences between them, and what did they symbolize?

(b) What 'land' was Isaiah referring to in v. 8, and why did he refer to it as belonging to 'Immanuel'?

5. To what 'conspiracy' was Isaiah referring in v. 12?

6. What did Isaiah mean when he said that God would be a 'stone of offence and rock of stumbling' to Israel and Judah?

7. Why did Isaiah say that the king and people should not consult 'mediums and spirits'?

BIBLE STUDY

8. Compare Isaiah's use of each of the following terms in this passage with the ways in which they are used in the passages given. (Using a Concordance you could extend this study by comparing their use in other passages also.)

(a) 'wings': Exod. 25.20; Ruth 2.12; 2 Sam. 22.7,10,11;
Ps. 91.1–4; Jer. 48.40–44; Mal. 4.2; Matt. 23.37.

(b) 'the way': Gen. 3.24; 24.25; 2 Chron. 23.19; Judges 8.7,8;
Ps. 1.6; 18.30; Prov. 7.4,5, 25–27; John 1.23; 14.6; Acts 27.15;
1 Cor. 10.13.

(c) 'rock (or 'block' etc.) of stumbling': Lev. 19.13,14;
Jer. 6.19–21; Ezek. 7.19,20; Rom. 9.30–33;
1 Cor. 1.23,24; 8.8,9.

(d) 'signs and portents': Gen. 1.14; Exod. 4.1–17;
1 Sam. 10.1–9; Joel 2.28–31; Matt. 16.1–4; Luke 21.10,11;
John 2.1–11; 1 Cor. 12.12.

(e) 'darkness': Deut. 28.28,29; Job 19.5–9; Ps. 18.28;
Isa. 5.20; Matt. 8.10–12; Acts 13.9–11; 1 John 1.5–8.

APPLICATION, OPINION, AND RESEARCH

9. (a) Isaiah wrote down his prophetic message as testimony of what would result if Ahaz continued to ignore his warnings. What 'prophets' can you think of, religious or otherwise, of the past or the present time, who have given written warnings against policies of military leaders which seemed likely to lead to disaster? Were the warnings heeded, and what in fact were the results of the policies?

(b) What other steps might a present-day 'prophet' take (besides writing them down) to ensure that his words are not forgotten?

10. What do most people in your country today believe about 'mediums and wizards' (or similar 'guides')? What do they believe about communicating with spirits of the dead? What are your own beliefs in these matters, and why?
11. How easy or difficult is it for people in your country to oppose the official policies of the government? What are the likely consequences of such opposition? What if anything can ordinary people (as distinct from 'prophets') do to change such policies if they disagree with them?
12. 'I and the children whom the LORD has given me are signs and portents' (v. 18). In what ways if any do you think that children of religious leaders (or ordinary clergy) are or can be 'signs and portents' today?
13. Give some examples from the past or present of small countries who have relied on the military support of stronger nations. What were the results in each case, and what effect did it have on the traditions and culture of the smaller nation?

9.1–7
The Hoped-for King

OUTLINE

V. 9.1: As already noted, in the Hebrew Scriptures the verse numbered 9.1 in the RSV and other English versions was made the final verse of chapter 8, i.e. 8.23. Perhaps written later than either 8.15–22 or 9.2–7, it seems to have been inserted as a connecting link between the gloom of the former passage and the promise of bright hope in the latter, rather than belonging to either.

The rest of the passage follows the usual pattern of a hymn or psalm celebrating the accession of a king, and reaffirming God's promises to David (we may compare such 'royal' psalms as Pss. 21, 72, 89.1–37).
Vv. 2,3: God's people rejoice as He brings them out of the darkness into the light of His deliverance.
Vv. 4,5: God has put an end to warfare and oppression.
Vv. 6,7: A new king comes to occupy David's throne, the hoped-for ideal king (Messiah) who, God has promised, will bring permanent peace, justice, and righteousness to His people.

NOTES AND INTERPRETATION

9.1: The land of Zebulun and...Naphtali...the land beyond the Jordan, Galilee: The northern tribes of Zebulun and Naphtali, and trans-Jordan, were the areas of Israel most exposed to foreign influence and invasion, which Tiglath-pileser despoiled in 735–33 (see 2 Kings 15.29). It seems that the reference to Galilee gave support to the early Christian interpretation of the passage which follows as a direct prediction of the coming of Jesus (see Matt. 4.12–17).

In the latter time: See note on 2.2. Here the phrase links the time of hope for those taken captive from these areas with the traditional hope for the coming of God's chosen King, which was further developed after the Exile (see note on vv. 6,7 below).

9.2–4: The people who walked in darkness have seen a great light...Thou hast multiplied the nation: Darkness can here be understood to have a double meaning. These were the people whose minds and hearts were darkened with the lack of understanding and lack of faith, which in turn led to the darkness of eventual defeat and oppression. Use of the past perfect tense in these verses, as though the events had already happened, reflects the customary style of the praise poems used at a king's enthronement. It expresses certainty that the hoped-for events *will* one day have happened.

9.4: The yoke...staff...rod of his oppressor, thou hast broken as on the day of Midian: The 'yoke', 'staff', and 'rod' are symbols (as is 'boot' in the next verse) of the alien power to which God's people have been subject, and over whom God's victory will be like the victory of Gideon, whom He called to deliver His people from the Midianites and other enemy tribes (see Judges chapters 6—8).

9.6,7: To us a child is born...a son is given; and the government will be upon his shoulder: See notes on 4.2; 8.13,14. The tradition that one day a perfect king would come to rule was common to many peoples in the ancient Near East. Isaiah's poem is probably the most important and most beautiful expression of the hope and expectation felt at the ceremonial enthronement of every new king: that he will be a great, just, and righteous ruler who will have God's full support and backing. But many other Bible writers too give glimpses of this idea of a chosen 'Messiah' (Hebrew: 'anointed one') who would be a descendant of David (see e.g. Ps. 2.6: 'I have set my king on Zion'; and also Deut. 17.14–20; Ezek. 37.24–28).

The government...upon his shoulder: Perhaps a reference to some symbol of royal honour and responsibility placed or worn on the king's shoulder. (We may compare the way in which the honour of knighthood is conferred by the touch of a sword on the shoulder, or the responsibility of being sheriff is symbolized by wearing a badge in the shape of a star.)

His name will be called 'Wonderful Counsellor, Mighty God, Everlasting Father, Prince of Peace': The people proclaim four 'throne-names' for God's new king. Giving such names was customary, as it still is in some present-day monarchies.

Some interpreters suggest that the name 'Mighty God' means that this king would be God Himself, and this has been taken as prophetic evidence for the divinity of Jesus. But the Hebrew words could be translated 'God of a hero' (NEB has 'in battle godlike'), and the prophet does not otherwise seem to suggest that the coming king would be more than divinely inspired.

9.7: The zeal of the LORD of hosts will do this: The Hebrew word translated 'zeal' really means 'jealousy', in the sense of being wholly devoted to someone or something. JB translates it here as 'jealous love'. (Compare e.g. 2 Sam. 21.2; Zech. 8.2; 2 Cor. 11.2,3.)

In this poem Isaiah was concerned to comfort and encourage the people, and to give them hope which he expressed in two ways which are closely related:

1. God will not allow the disaster which the king and people bring upon themselves to last for ever. He will set them free from those who humiliate and oppress them.

2. God will give them a new king, specially chosen to rule for ever in accordance with His will.

THE MESSIANIC HOPE

During Isaiah's lifetime, many people thought that Ahaz's son Hezekiah would be this ideal king or Messiah. A century later others thought that King Josiah was the Messiah. After the Exile some proclaimed Zerubbabel to be 'the anointed' (Hag. 2.23; Zech. 4.6–14), and a hundred years before Christ, many welcomed Judas Maccabeus in the same way. Each of these leaders did seem to have been chosen by God to rescue His people; and each did partly fulfill the promise, but only partly.

But in describing the tragedy of the people of the Northern Kingdom, who experienced the full force of Assyrian cruelty after they had been conquered in 721 BC, the prophet was describing the suffering war brings to conquered and oppressed people in every age. In describing the people's joy when they were being liberated, he was describing feelings familiar to many today. And in expressing the hope that the promised time of peace and justice would go on 'for ever more' (v. 7), he was expressing what all such people feel, and feel the more strongly the longer the time of oppression lasts.

In Israel the hope of a deliverer and just ruler became more and more widespread as the people became more and more disappointed because the kings who followed David failed either to rule justly or to protect the nation against outside enemies (see Exod. 20.1–7; Deut. 17.14–20; and 1 Sam. 8.11–18!).

By the time of Jesus's birth, when Palestine was under Roman rule, many of the Jews were hoping for a Messiah who would 'restore the kingdom'. Some believed he would be a purely spiritual leader. Some (like Judas Iscariot and the Zealots) hoped he would be a leader of political rebellion like the Maccabees. Some believed that he would come from God in some mysterious way, and would live for ever.

Jesus seems to have seen Himself as a leader whose suffering would heal the nation's wrong. He began His ministry by announcing that He had been specially anointed to do something about oppression. His work was to be: 'To bring good news to the poor,... to proclaim liberty to the captives, recovery of sight to the blind, to set free the oppressed' (Luke 14.18, GNB, quoting Isa. 61.1,2 and 58.6).

In this way Jesus seems deliberately to have encouraged people to accept Him as their liberator. By becoming human, God in Christ revealed His solidarity with poor and oppressed people (see Matt. 8.20; 2 Cor. 8.9; Phil. 2.5,6). Like the prophets, He spoke harshly against injustice and exploitation (see e.g. Matt. 23.1–11, 23–26; Mark 11.15–17; 12.38–40). The purpose of His life, and especially of His death, was to set men free, whether from bondage to others or to their own weakness and sin (John 8.36; 10.11,12; Gal. 3.23–28). In fact, most modern liberation movements directly or indirectly owe their inspiration to Him.

Certainly the disciples believed that the prophecies in the Book of Isaiah were fulfilled by the coming of Jesus (see e.g. Isa. 53; Matt. 8.14–17; John 12.37–50). And it was because of this that Paul and others referred to Him as the 'Christ' (from the Greek for 'anointed').

We may note that Jewish people today still await the coming of a Messiah whom they believe God will send to rule over them all for ever in power and peace.

STUDY SUGGESTIONS

WORD STUDY

1. What is the meaning of the following words and phrases as used in Isaiah 9.1–7?

   (a) darkness   (b) the latter time   (c) government   (d) zeal.

2. What is the connection between the two words 'Messiah' and 'Christ'?

REVIEW OF CONTENT

3. Why did Isaiah refer especially to Zebulun, Naphtali, the Jordan, and Galilee (v. 1)?
4. (a) What symbols of oppression did Isaiah mention in describing the Assyrian occupation of the Northern Kingdom?
   (b) What happened on 'the day of Midian'?
5. (a) What is meant by the phrase 'Messianic hope'?
   (b) For what chief reasons was this hope particularly strong among the Israelites at the time of Isaiah, after their return from Exile in Babylon and at the time of the birth of Jesus?
6. For what chief reasons did the early Christians regard this passage as a prediction of the birth and life of Jesus?

BIBLE STUDY

7. In this passage Isaiah used the word 'darkness' to mean suffering under defeat and oppression, and 'light' to mean the joy of liberation and life under a just and peaceable ruler. What is the meaning of each of these two words as used in each of the following passages?
   (a) Isa. 2.5   (b) 5.20   (c) 5.30   (d) 8.22
   (e) 10.12   (f) John 1.5–8   (g) Eph. 5.8   (h) 1 John 1.5–7
8. Make a brief summary of the ideas about the ideal king and the qualities he would possess, as expressed in the following passages: 2 Sam. 7.16–26; 23.1–5; 1 Kings 11.30–35; Ps. 132.
9. In which of the following passages does the term 'anointed' or 'anointed one' seem to mean the hope for a Messiah or ideal king, and in which does it seem to have some other meaning? Give reasons for your choice in each case.
   (a) 1 Sam. 15.17–21   (b) 1 Chron. 16.19–22   (c) Ps. 132.8–18
   (d) Lam. 4.16–20   (e) Dan. 9.24–27   (f) Hab. 3.9b–13

APPLICATION, OPINION, AND RESEARCH

10. What sort of picture-language did Isaiah use in describing how the Israelites would rejoice when freed from Assyrian oppression (v. 3)? Would such language be meaningful to people in your country today? If not, what alternatives can you suggest?
11. The four 'throne-names' in v. 6(b), and the words of v. 7, show what qualities and behaviour people looked for in the hoped-for king. Are these the qualities and behaviour people would look for in an ideal national leader today? If not, what other qualities and behaviour would they look for, and why?
12. Read the so-called 'royal Psalms', 21, 72, 110, and 132, which scholars believe were used at enthronement ceremonies in Israel.

What promises and demands does each make to the new king, and what other 'praise names' for him do they contain? Compare these with any ceremonial songs, prayers, or praises used at the coronation, enthronement, or installation, of heads of state in your own country and elsewhere today. How seriously do you think such leaders take these ceremonies?

13. Christians believe that Jesus is the Messiah whom God promised to His people. What difference, if any, does this make to the expectation of eventual 'peace on earth' among people in so-called Christian countries?

14. In most countries today government is carried out by elected politicians, rather than by hereditary monarchs. Even where the head of state is a king or a queen, the power is in the hands of political leaders who were elected, or who gained power by force or cunning. Is it possible for such leaders to be 'chosen' by God to rule according to His will? If not, what should be the attitude of Christians toward such leaders?

9.8—10.4 and 5.24–30
God's Anger against His People

INTRODUCTION AND OUTLINE

See NOTE on p. 59. Like many poems intended for speaking or singing aloud, this group of poetic oracles about God's punishment of His people have a common refrain or chorus which is repeated at the end of each section. Most scholars agree that the passage 5.24–30 (RSV) provides a conclusion to them, though it may originally have followed 9.8–21. The form of 10.1–4 is like that of the 'woe' words in 5.8–23, and seems to be addressed to Judah, but it has the same refrain as in 5.25, and in 9.12, 17, and 21, which relate to Israel.

9.8–12: God has sent a 'word' to the Northern Kingdom, but the people are too proud to take the warning seriously, so He stirs up 'adversaries' against them.

9.13–17: 'Therefore' *everyone* in the land will suffer: leaders and people, the strong youngsters and the helpless aged.

9.18–21: Chaos spreads throughout Israel like wildfire, one tribe attacking another, and then turning against Judah also.

10.1–4: As the oppressors have no mercy on anyone, so they have no hope of escaping God's punishment.

94

5.24–25: A reminder of the disasters which have overtaken Israel, and which should have been taken as warnings.

5.26–30: A clear prediction of the final blow to come, when God will 'whistle for' (that is, call up) the Assyrian army. Efficient and powerful, it will come 'like the whirlwind', and 'none can rescue'.

NOTES AND INTERPRETATION

9.8: The Lord has sent a word against Jacob: For 'word' see notes on 1.1 and 2.1. Here it clearly means an event or events of some sort which the active power of God's 'word' actually caused to happen. For 'Jacob' see note on 2.3,5. Here the mention of Israel, Ephraim, and Samaria clearly shows that Isaiah was referring to what had happened in the Northern Kingdom.

9.9,10: Bricks...dressed stones...sycamores...cedars: Bricks and sycamore wood were ordinary building materials; dressed stones and cedar wood were more expensive. In spite of the devastation which foreign invaders caused, the people of the Northern Kingdom were so proud and self-satisfied that, far from taking their losses as a warning from God, they boasted that they would not only rebuild their cities, but build them better than before.

9.11,12: The LORD raises adversaries against them...Syrians...Philistines: The original Hebrew actually says 'adversaries of Rezin', but as Rezin was king of Syria, this must be an error, and the RSV translators are correct in omitting the name. (Perhaps the Hebrew should have read: 'adversaries, that is Rezin'.)

9.12: His hand is stretched out still: See notes on 1.25 and 11.11. The second line of the refrain is a twin or 'parallel' for the first, and God's hand is outstretched to punish, not protect. God's hand (or arm) had originally created and saved the Israelite people (see Exod. 6.6; Deut. 4.34; Ps. 136,12; Isa. 30.30). But not so now!

9.14: Head and tail, palm branch and reed: Picture-language (perhaps from a familiar saying or proverb – see also 19.15) simply meaning *everyone* in the land. From the highest to the lowest *all* suffered, not only the oppressors but the oppressed also. Compare v. 16: 'Those who...lead them astray, and those who are led.'

9.15: The elder and honoured man...the prophet: Many interpreters think that this explanatory verse and v. 16 are a later insertion.

9.17: The Lord does not rejoice over their young men: For a clearer translation see GNB; 'the Lord will not let any of the young men escape'.

9.18–20: Wickedness burns like a fire...no man spares his brother. They snatch...they devour: The description of anarchy, destruction, famine, and conflict in these verses relates to the period of upheaval, conquest,

'The Lord stirs up their enemies.... Against a godless nation I send him ... to take spoil and seize plunder' (9.11; 10.6).

Under the eye of an enemy soldier, frightened villagers in Vietnam wait to learn what their fate will be. As food and supplies run short in war-torn Central America, people start looting and destroying the shops of their fellow-citizens.

Who are the 'godless' in today's wars? Who are the innocent?

and civil wars under a series of ambitious and violent kings which led up to the fall of Samaria to the Assyrians (see Special Note 1).

9.20: Each devours his neighbour's flesh: See RSV footnote. The original Hebrew, 'flesh of his arm', or 'of his offspring', clearly describes a situation of very great want. At such times people were tempted to steal food from their neighbours, and unwanted babies and very old people might even be left to starve. But it is unlikely to mean actual cannibalism.

9.21: Manasseh, Ephraim...together they are against Judah: See notes on 7.2 and 7.4. Manasseh was another of the tribes in the Northern Kingdom.

10.1: Those who decree iniquitous decrees: That is, the Judges and other officials whose job it was to administer the law, issue regulations (decrees), and pass sentence in the courts. Instead of doing all this in accordance with God's covenant law, they were using their powers unjustly to cheat and rob (see e.g. Exod. 23.2,3,6–8; Deut. 24.17,18; and compare Isa. 1.21–23; 3.14,15; 5.21–23).

Writers who keep writing oppression: 'Writers' does not mean authors or journalists, but the clerks and Scribes who recorded the decisions of the unjust Judges accused in the first half of the verse.

10.3: The storm which will come from afar: A clear reference to foreign invaders, presumably Assyria (compare 8.7,8).

5.25: The anger of the LORD was kindled against his people, and he...smote them, and the mountains quaked; and their corpses were as refuse in the streets: This seems to refer to an earthquake – perhaps a reminder of the one which occurred in Uzziah's reign (see Amos 1.1).

5.26: He will raise a signal for a nation afar off...from the ends of the earth: See notes on 10.3 above and 11.10,12. The vivid description in the verses which follow, of a great army mobilized and advancing in perfect battle array, makes it quite clear that the nation Isaiah meant was Assyria.

5.30: Behold, darkness and distress. This verse was probably inserted here because the allusion to 'growling' and 'roaring' seems to link it to the comparison of the Assyrians to 'young lions' in 5.29. But it is really closer in style and content to the description of stricken Judah in the final verses of chapter 8.

THE PURPOSE OF GOD'S WRATH

Isaiah often referred directly to God's 'wrath', that is, His anger, and many of his messages show God acting in anger towards His sinful people (e.g. 1.24,25; 2.12–19; 3.9,11; 5.5,6,24). In fact, we cannot fully understand Isaiah's ideas about God until we recognize Him as One who acts in anger. At the same time, it is important that we should clearly understand what the Bible writers mean by God's 'anger' or 'wrath'.

We have already seen (notes on 4.4,5) that God's final purpose is to restore and save His people. His anger is not like the anger of human beings, which is very often the result of our selfishness and lack of love, our malice, spite, envy, greed, or wounded pride. Human anger is often unreasonable and uncontrolled. God's anger is not like that.

1. We could say that God's anger is the anger of a *Holy* God. His anger and His love do not conflict. Indeed, His anger shows that He truly loves us and therefore cannot accept our disobedience and our refusal of His love.

2. His anger is also the anger of a *saving* God. His ultimate purpose is always to rescue people and bring them back into a loving relationship with Him. Even when He allows them to suffer the consequences of their own lack of love, it is so that they may learn the importance of living in accordance with His will (see notes on 1.25, and pp. 14–27).

3. God's anger is also that of an *eternal* God. He does not change, and His anger is not capricious like that of human beings. It can always be foreseen, as the inescapable result of sin.

THE CHRISTIAN UNDERSTANDING OF GOD'S WRATH

The truth about God's anger lies behind the messages of Isaiah and the other Old Testament prophets, but it was not until the coming of Jesus that the full meaning and importance of God's anger became clear. The death of Jesus on the cross perfectly reveals the way in which God's anger works. It is important, therefore, that Christians should not misrepresent the words of Old Testament writers, who sometimes seem to suggest that God's wrath is the most important thing we know about Him. Through Jesus we know that the most important thing about God is the *love* from which His anger springs.

This does not mean, however, that we should take a passive or fatalistic attitude, and regard all the disasters and distress which occur in the world as coming from God. In some religions people are taught to accept as 'the will of God' everything that happens in the world, whether good or bad. And there are some people in every culture who take this attitude because they are too lazy or too selfish to care. But even when it seems clear that such suffering and disaster as we experience are the direct consequence of our own bad actions, our response should be active repentance, not passive acceptance, and this may involve the costly process of clearing up the results of our sin.

The Church has always accepted that it must take responsibility for helping the needy' and 'the poor' (10.2), especially those among its own members (see e.g. Matt. 10.42; Luke 10.25–37; James 2.14–17; 1 John 3.17,18). But too often it does so in ways which increase people's helplessness, rather than enabling them to help themselves. Giving money or food to meet people's immediate need is easier than working to change other people's attitudes towards them, to change laws and conditions which made them helpless in the first place, or to oppose the rich and powerful who abuse and exploit them.

STUDY SUGGESTIONS

WORD STUDY

1. In 9.8 what is meant by (a) 'word', and (b) 'light'?
2. (a) Which of the following words would you use to describe God's anger? (b) Which would you only use to describe human anger?
   burning   resentful   petulant   fierce
   uncontrolled   slow   spiteful   arrogant
3. For each of the following words write a short sentence in which it has the same meaning as in 9.8—10.4.
   arrogance (9.9)   adversaries (9.11)   devour (9.12,20)
   spare (9.19)   spoil (10.2)   decree (10.1)

REVIEW OF CONTENT

4. What is the link between the oracles in Isaiah 9.8—10.4 and those in 5.24–30?
5. What was the significance of Isaiah's reference to different sorts of building materials in 9.10?
6. In what ways were the leaders in Judah leading the people astray (v. 16)?
7. What did Isaiah mean when he said that the Lord would cut off 'head and tail, palm branch and reed'?
8. What did Isaiah mean by the phrase 'his hand is stretched out still'?
9. Who were (a) 'those who decree' and (b) 'the writers', referred to in 10.1?

BIBLE STUDY

10. Isaiah described the Lord's anger as being 'kindled against' His people (5.25). How was God's anger described in each of the following passages, and in what ways, if any, does the description differ from that of Isaiah?
    (a) Num. 11.10   (b) Neh. 9.16–31   (c) Psalm 35   (d) Psalm 69.24   (e) Psalm 86.15   (f) Jer. 4.8   (g) Zeph. 3.8.

APPLICATION, OPINION, AND RESEARCH

11. Isaiah spoke of people who 'devour' their neighbours. Give examples if you can of any who 'devour their neighbours' among your own people. What sort of people are those who devour, and

what sort are those who are devoured? What, if anything, can be done to prevent it?

12. Isaiah described particular sorts of disasters which God would cause to fall upon His people. What explanations do people commonly give today for such disasters as
    (a) civil war?
    (b) foreign invasion?
    (c) political upheaval or 'anarchy'?
    (d) famine and starvation?
13. Do you think that God still uses the activities of the super-powers in the world to correct and punish people today? Give reasons for your answer, with examples if possible.
14. Are any of the laws of your own country used to benefit certain people at the expense of others? If so, how is this done? How can a country's legal system be made to protect everyone equally?
15. Who do you think is chiefly responsible when there is injustice in a country, those who make the laws or those who administer them?

10.5–34
God Controls History

INTRODUCTION AND OUTLINE

This passage contains sayings and poems about Assyria's invasion of Palestine, and Judah's later deliverance. The varying style suggests that they may come from different periods. The prose passage, vv. 20–27b, is similar to chapters 24—27 which were probably written after the Exile. Some scholars suggest that it may have been intended as an interpretation, to comfort people when the more threatening passages were being read at worship services.

Vv. 5–14: A poem or poems, in which vv. 5–11 and 13,14 are joined by the prose link-verse 12. They show that Assyria is simply a tool which God will use to punish His people, though the Assyrians do not realize it but boast of their great strength and of the many small kingdoms who are their vassals.

Vv. 15–19: When Assyria has done what God requires, she too will be destroyed (see also v. 12).

Vv. 20–23: These verses and vv. 24–27b point to the future, promising that some at least of God's people will survive the Assyrian conquest, and return to true worship of their own God.

Vv. 24–27b: Another message of comfort and assurance of eventual deliverance.

Vv. 27c–34: A description of the advancing armies moving through village after village as they approach Jerusalem.

NOTES AND INTERPRETATION

10.5,6: Assyria, the rod of my anger, the staff of my fury: See also vv. 15,24,26, and also 9.4. A rod and a staff were (and still are) used by shepherds to control and defend their sheep. Kings (8.1) and other leaders were regarded as shepherds of the people, and a staff and rod were symbols of their authority to rule (see notes on v. 15 below and on 3.1).

10.6: I command him to take spoil and seize plunder: These words echo the name of Isaiah's son Maher-shalal-hash-baz (see note on 8.1–4).

10.9,10: Calno...Carchemish...Hamath...Arpad...kingdoms of the idols: These were powerful cities to the north which Assyria had already defeated by about 715 BC (see general Introduction and Special Note 1). The Assyrians regarded Jerusalem's God as just another idol or 'graven image', like the gods of these pagan cities which had failed to protect them (see note on 8.8 and p. 102 below).

10.11: As I have done to Samaria: Again, a reference to Assyria's conquest of the Northern Kingdom.

10.15: Shall the axe vaunt itself...or the saw magnify itself...?: These two questions may in fact be a proverb or proverbs which Isaiah's hearers would recognize. The prophet was contrasting the Assyrian king's arrogant idea of his own greatness with his true role as a tool in the hand of God.

Not wood: Israel's God is the *living* God, not mere wood or clay like the man-made idols of other nations. Assyria's king might wield his own 'rod and staff', but he and his armies were symbols of *God's* greatness, and would be punished for their arrogance when God had no more use for them.

10.16: A wasting sickness...under his glory a burning: Isaiah combined two word-pictures to describe the punishment of the Assyrians: (a) an epidemic sickness among the soldiers (for 'under his glory' other translations have e.g. 'within his flesh' – NEB; 'in their bodies' – GNB and see 37.36), and (b) a forest fire.

10.17: The light of Israel: i.e. God Himself, who is a danger to Israel's enemies.

10.20–23: A remnant will return...to the mighty God: See notes on 2.11; 4.2,3; and 7.3. As when Isaiah named his son Shearjashub, these words can contain both a promise and a threat.

In 7.3 Isaiah seems to have been chiefly concerned to persuade Ahaz against relying on Assyrian help, by promising him that at least some of the people would survive the military disaster that was threatening, if only he would rely on God instead, while at the same time warning that these survivors would be very few.

In 10.20–23 much of the Hebrew is unclear, but it does show the characteristic style of later additions to the words of Isaiah, written after the Assyrians had not only destroyed the land but carried many of the people into captivity and separated them from their traditional ways of worship (see e.g. 11.11.16; 37.31). Here Isaiah seems to mean by 'return' what he means at 30.15; that is, not so much physical survival but repentance and a return to wholehearted trust and obedience to God by a 'remnant' who would remain faithful through all the disasters.

10.26: When he smote Midian at the rock of Oreb: See note on 9.4.

As it did in Egypt: a reference to the Exodus.

10.27c: He has gone up from Rimmon: The meaning of the Hebrew is uncertain here and translations vary: e.g. GNB and NIV omit any reference to Rimmon (a place south of Jerusalem).

10.28–31: Aiath...Migron...Michmash...etc., etc.: The string of place-names, no doubt well-known to Isaiah's hearers, would give greater urgency to his message, describing the rapid advance of the Assyrian armies as they come nearer and nearer to Jerusalem from the north and finally reach Nob, a hill about 2 km north-east of the city.

10.33,34: The Lord...will cut down the thickets...Lebanon will fall: Lebanon was famous for its forests of tall cedar trees – Isaiah's word-picture for the haughty leaders of the Palestinian nations.

Throughout the Near East at the time when Isaiah was preaching there were many small kingdoms such as Judah and Israel, each with its own god or gods who were believed to control the affairs of that nation. People thought that if a nation was powerful, that was because its god was powerful. Or if a kingdom was conquered, they thought its god had been defeated by the god of the conqueror (see notes on 8.8 and 9.10 above).

So when Isaiah declared that Assyria's success in battle was not due to the power of its gods, nor to its military skill, but to the power of *Israel's* God, who was using Assyria to punish and cleanse His own people, this must have seemed nonsense to his hearers.

GOD ABOVE ALL GODS

Isaiah's interpretation of the events of his time was based on two important ideas which people found difficult to accept, though other prophets before him had spoken out of the same conviction that:

1. The Lord God of Israel was and is the most powerful God of all. Other gods might exist (though Isaiah does not discuss this), but only

the LORD has complete authority: 'The whole earth is full of his glory' (6.3), there is no other God like him.

2. The Lord God of Israel controls the events of human history according to His purpose and plan, not only for His own people Israel, but for the whole of the world He has created.

This view of history differs, not only from the ideas generally held in Isaiah's time, but from the various secular ideas of history which suggest that events are part of an endless cycle, repeating itself over the centuries, or like a lottery in which everything happens by chance, or like a machine which can be controlled and directed by whichever nation happens to be the most powerful at the time.

THE IDEA OF THE 'REMNANT'

In Isaiah's view, however, although God guides and shapes the history of nations, He nevertheless still allows people choices and responsibilities. Some, like Ahaz, refuse to follow God's guidance; they will necessarily suffer the consequences of their wrong actions, but God can use their actions to further His purpose. Isaiah seems to have had no real hope that either Israel or Judah as a political state would be saved. But he did believe that there would always be some of the people – a 'remnant' – who would have faith enough to 'return' in penitence and trust to the way God had shown to be His will.

This tradition of a faithful few, who turn aside in endurance and obedience from the road to disaster, occurs again and again in Israel's history. Believing and obeying God's command, Noah saved himself and others from the flood while the rest of the people drowned (see Gen. 6). Similarly, when sin had broken the relationship between God and man, Abraham's obedience and trust in God led him to make the long journey to a new land and become the founder of a new nation (Gen. 12.1–5a; 22.1–28). At the time when King Ahab was introducing the worship of idols, Elijah was able to persuade 7,000 people to remain faithful to the Lord (1 Kings 19.17,18).

Other prophets of the 8th century also proclaimed the idea of the 'remnant', and it became more and more important among the Jews, especially after the Exile in the 6th century. Those who were 'left', and eventually able to return to Jerusalem, saw themselves as the 'remnant' of Judah and Israel (see Ezra 9.8,13–15; Neh. 1.1–3). This gave them a sense of identity and of purpose, both as a nation and as the people of God.

STUDY SUGGESTIONS

WORD STUDY

1. List the names by which God is named in 10.5–34, and say in each case why the name is suitable for the particular message or context in which it is used.
2. What is meant by each of the following words or phrases as used in 10.5–34?
   (a) rod of my anger (b) spoil (c) kingdoms of the idols
   (d) Lebanon will fall

REVIEW OF CONTENT

3. What is it that Assyria 'does not so intend, does not so think', as stated in 10.7?
4. Why did the prophet compare Calno and Carchemish, Hamath and Arpad, with Samaria and Damascus (10.9)?
5. What was the Lord's 'work' in Mount Zion and Jerusalem that He was to 'finish', according to 10.12?
6. In what way did the Lord say that He would 'punish' the King of Assyria, and for what reason was he to be punished?
7. What sorts of picture-language are used in the passage to describe the Lord (i.e. to what is He compared), as He acts against Judah or Assyria?
8. Who were the 'remnant of Israel' and to what would they 'return' (vv. 20,21)?

BIBLE STUDY

9. Use a Concordance to find all the verses in Isaiah 1—39 in which the word 'remnant' is used. Look for any differences in the meaning of the word as between one verse and another, and make a list of the various ways in which it is used.
10. The prophets Amos and Micah also preached about the 'remnant'. Compare what they said in the following passages with what Isaiah said. What, if anything, does either of them *add* to what Isaiah said? Amos 3.12; 4.11; 5.3; Micah 2.12,13; 5.7,8
11. In the following passages other prophets speak of other empires, later than the Assyrian. In what ways are their messages similar to Isaiah's message about Assyria, and in what ways are they different?
    (a) Jer. 25.8–14 (Babylon) (b) Isa. 44.24—45,6 (Persia)
    (c) Dan. 7.1–14 (?Greece) (d) Rev. 17.1—18.3 (Rome)

APPLICATION, OPINION, AND RESEARCH

12. 'Rod' and 'staff' are described as symbols of kingship and authority (p. 101). What are some of the symbols of this sort used in different countries today?
13. Give examples of occasions in the past, or in recent times, when Christians have been a 'remnant' in one country or another.
14. In what ways, if any, do you think that God uses nations or other 'organizations of people' as a tool to punish others in the world today?

11.1—12.6
The Perfect King and the Second Exodus

INTRODUCTION AND OUTLINE

These messages of hope for Israel's future seem to belong to different periods. Most interpreters consider that the oracles in 11.10–16 about the wide dispersion of the Jewish people and their subsequent restoration must have been written after the Exile. Some have suggested that the same is true of 11.1–9, but there is little evidence of this. These verses so closely echo and develop Isaiah's description in 9.2–7 of the hoped-for Messiah and the return to ideal conditions, that they may well be by Isaiah himself. The two short psalms in chapter 12 cannot be dated; they seem to have been inserted here by an editor to round off the whole important collection of prophetic messages in chapters 1—11.

11.1: Announces the coming to power of a new king of David's line.

11.2–3a: God's Spirit will give this king the qualities of an ideal ruler.

11.3b–5: He will rule in righteousness, equity, and faithfulness.

11.6–9: His rule will bring peace to the whole world.

11.10: He will provide a standard and a rallying-point for all nations.

11.11–16: In a new 'Exodus' God will lead the scattered remnant of His people back to Palestine.

12.1,2: There will come a time of thanksgiving to God for salvation – and

12.3–6: – a time when all of God's people will praise Him for His greatness.

NOTES AND INTERPRETATION

11.1: 'A shoot from the stump of Jesse...a branch out of his roots: That is, a descendant of King David, son of Jesse (see notes on 7.2 and also 7.13). Some interpreters suggest that the use of the word 'stump' means that the Davidic dynasty had been cut off, and so the passage must be dated later than 507 BC, long after Isaiah's time. But 'shoot' and 'branch' can simply mean a new or different line of descendants within the royal family. Compare this passage with 9.6,7 and Micah 5.2–4. None of these passages contain the title 'Messiah' or 'anointed', but it is clear that all three refer to the hoped-for ideal king (see notes and interpretation on 9.6,7).

11.2: The Spirit of the LORD shall rest upon him, the spirit of wisdom and understanding and the fear of the LORD: Notice the difference between the 'Spirit of the LORD' (spelt with a capital S in the RSV), i.e. the power of God Himself, and the spiritual gifts (with a small s) which God bestows. (Not all Bibles show the distinction in this way.) 'Wisdom' is often shown as leading to 'fear' of God, which means having faith in Him, and responding to His care with trust and obedience (see note on 8.12, and Ps. 111.10).

11.3–5: He shall not judge by what his eyes see...his ears hear...but with righteousness...equity...faithfulness: Not, that is, by outward appearances, nor by hearsay, but faithfully and impartially according to the Law which God has given.

11.4: He shall smite the earth with the rod of his mouth: 'Earth' may be an error in the Hebrew. NEB and JB have 'smite the ruthless'. For 'rod' see notes at 9.4 and 10.5,6. Here, clearly, the *word* of royal authority is meant, and the emphasis is on the use of this authority as a tool or weapon to punish the wicked.

11.5: The girdle of his waist...the girdle of his loins: The 'girdle' was a loincloth worn under all other clothing. This word-picture means that the king's judgements and actions would be bound as closely by the qualities of faithfulness and righteousness, as his body was bound by the girdle he wore.

11.9: All my holy mountain: I.e. Mount Zion, that is, Jerusalem/Judah (see note on 2.2).

11.10,11: In that day: See note on 2.11 and its detailed interpretation.

11.10,12: An ensign: That is, a flag or signal, like the 'standard' which provides both a rallying-point in battle and a symbol of identity for the particular nation or group to which it belongs.

11.11: The Lord will extend his hand yet a second time to recover the remnant...of his people: See notes on 1.25 and 9.12. 'A second time' is in relation to the 'first time' when God had stretched out His arm to save His people (see Exod. 6.6). The 'nations' listed in v. 11, as well as those named in 11.14, were all at one time or another enemies of the Israelites, and in battle would have carried away any of God's people whom they could take prisoner.

Coastlands of the sea: An expression already used in ancient Egypt to mean the most remote parts of the known world, i.e. distant countries around the Mediterranean or the Red Sea.

Remnant: See notes on 10.20–22 and p. 103.

11.15: Tongue of the Sea of Egypt: A reference to the long stretch of water reaching up into Egypt from the Red Sea, today called the Gulf of Suez.

The River: See note on 8.7.

11.16: There will be a highway from Assyria: As in v. 15, the writer was saying that God would remove all hindrances to the return of His people to their own land.

12.1–4: In that day: See notes on 11.10,11.

12.3: The wells of salvation: I.e. God Himself, the source of salvation (see Jer. 2.13).

We have already, in our study of chapters 9 and 10, discussed two of the three very important ideas which are also the subject of the oracles in chapter 11:

1. The hoped-for ideal king or Messiah, whose rule will be a time of perfect justice and peace, when all conflict and violence is ended.

2. The 'remnant' of God's people, who were to remain faithful to the Torah though scattered all over the world.

3. God's eventual deliverance of His people from all their enemies, and their 'return' to the holy places and religious practices which He had ordained for them.

Here, as in 9.7, the ideal king is identified as being descended from David, whose dynasty had ruled the Israelites for over 200 years by the time of Isaiah. But the important thing about this Messiah is not so much the family he belongs to, as the fact that he is to be chosen and inspired in all he does by the 'Spirit of the Lord'.

THE IDEA OF PARADISE RESTORED

Just as the prophet describes a ruler who perfectly obeys God, so he also describes a world in which God perfectly rules. In that world all creatures, including human beings, have returned to the relationship with the Creator and with one another which, according to Israelite tradition, existed 'in the beginning', before sin brought in conflict, violence, and fear (see Gen. 1.29,30; 9.2–6; 3.13–19).

This idea of a 'paradise', a perfect world in which all men and animals live in harmony, is common in many cultures. Among the peoples of Africa and Asia, for example, a majority of the traditional stories or 'myths' about the creation of the world describe the original state of mankind as one of happiness, plenty, and immortality. As in the Biblical account, these myths also describe the separation of men from God as being the result of disobedience. And many of the great religions of the world teach that order, peace, and immortality depend on a proper relationship with God, and, especially in their more popular forms, offer the hope of a future 'paradise' for the faithful.

This hope for a restored world was common among the prophets of Israel (see Isa. 32.17–18; Ezek. 47.1–12; Joel 3.18; Amos 9.13–15; Zech. 14.4–11). Isaiah and others believed it would be brought about by the ideal ruler whom God would send.

In Isaiah chapters 11 and 12, prophetic messages about Israel's restoration (11.10–16) are set alongside the hope for the ideal king and a world restored to tranquillity. The Israelites who were scattered among the nations of the Near East would return to Palestine, rallying around the signal-flag of the Messiah, and even the age-old jealousy and fighting between the Northern and the Southern tribes would stop.

We have seen that although Isaiah prophesied doom, he promised that some at least of the people would survive the coming disasters. He was also saying something which at the time people wholly failed to understand: that mere physical survival was not enough. God offers salvation freely, as a gift of His grace. It cannot be earned or bought. But neither can it be received or enjoyed except by those who accept the responsibility, and are willing to give God their whole trust and obedience in return.

THE 'SECOND EXODUS'

Isaiah spoke some comforting words about the survivors whom God would 'recover' from the Assyrian and other enemies (e.g. 1.9; 4.3; and here in 11.11). But he also said that the *true* 'remnant' would be the few who remained faithful: 'the remnant of Israel will lean upon the Lord' (10.20); 'in returning and rest you shall be saved; in quietness and in trust' (30.15). Like the few plants left alive after a fierce bush-fire, this scattered remnant experienced the withering judgement of God, and would become the 'seed' for a new, purified kingdom which would regenerate in place of the old. (See 6.11–13.)

This promise of a 'second Exodus' for the faithful few became one of the great themes of prophetic preaching during the Exile (see Isa. 35.1–10; 40.3–5; 48.20–21; Jer. 30.1–10; 31.31–34). And it was after the return of the exiles and the rebuilding of the Temple in the 6th century, that Israel's hope for a Messiah grew and developed more strongly. As we have seen, many Jews still entertain this hope, and regard the establishment of the present-day state of Israel as the beginning of God's fulfillment of all these promises.

Christians, of course, believe that God has already fulfilled them in

'The hoped-for ideal King or Messiah whose rule will be a time of perfect justice and peace'...is chosen and inspired by 'the Spirit of the Lord' (p. 107).

'Ethiopian' Christians in Africa, and Rastafarians like this Jamaican, believe that the Emperor Haile Selassie (in the portrait) was an incarnation of God, and await the birth of a successor who will rule a free and united Africa.

How does this belief differ from that of Isaiah, and from the belief in Jesus as King and Messiah?

the person of Jesus, and see in Him both the hoped-for Messiah and the faithful remnant whom God rescued from death and raised to life in order that He might rescue others from sin. By His suffering, death, and resurrection Jesus conquered all the forces of evil, not merely enemy nations, and has opened the 'wells of salvation' to all the peoples of the earth, not only the actual 'inhabitants of Zion' (12.3–6).

STUDY SUGGESTIONS

WORD STUDY

1. (a) Which *three* of the words listed below are nearest in meaning to 'righteousness', as used in 11.4,5 to describe a quality of the ideal king?

(b) Which *three* words are nearest in meaning to 'equity' as used there?

(c) Which *three* are nearest in meaning to 'faithfulness' there?

fairness trustworthiness piety fidelity
goodness morality integrity changelessness
impartiality godliness love correctness

2. The word 'knowledge' is used with a special meaning in 11.2 and 11.9. In which of the following sentences is its meaning closest to that special meaning?

(a) Paperback books have brought an explosion of knowledge in our country.

(b) The old man sadly told us that knowledge of lake fishing is rare in these hills.

(c) Sarah and Matthew's knowledge of each other became a model for their children.

REVIEW OF CONTENT

3. Rewrite 11.11 in your own words: (a) using a different sort of picture-language, and (b) in plain terms, using no picture-language at all.

4. What difference in meaning is shown by the use of a capital 'S' for the word 'Spirit' in the first line of 11.11 in the RSV, and the use of a small 's' for it in the remaining three lines of the verse?

5. What were the three most important qualities of the hoped-for king as described in 11.4,5?

6. For what particular reason did the prophet choose to name the places listed in 11.11, and the tribes and people mentioned in 11.13 and 14?

7. What does the prophet mean by each of the following phrases?
(a) 'A highway from Assyria' (11.16).

(b) 'Thou wast angry with me' (12.1).

(c) To 'draw water from the wells of salvation' (12.3).

8. In chapter 11 verses 10 and 11 are both introduced by the phrase 'in that day', and the same phrase occurs in 12.1 and 12.3. Does the prophet mean the same day in each case, and if so what day does he mean? Is it the same day as in 7.18,20,21 and 23? If not, what is the difference?

BIBLE STUDY

9. What is meant by the word 'salvation' in each of the following passages? (Note particularly the twin-words for 'salvation', which may help to give the answer for the Isaiah passages.)
   (a) Micah 7.4–7   (b) Hab. 3.12–13   (c) Hab. 3.17–18
   (d) Jer. 3.23b   (e) Isa. 45.8   (f) 46.13   (g) 51.5,6   (h) 60.18

10. In 11.3 it is said of the hoped-for king that 'his delight shall be in the fear of the LORD'. Read Deut. 6.13–15; 10.12; Pss. 34.11; 111.10; and Jer. 32.39–40, and then write a sentence to say what is meant by 'the fear of the LORD'. Then read Acts 10.2,22; 13.26; and 1 John 4.18. What difference, if any, do you see between the meaning of the phrase 'the fear of the LORD' as used in the Old Testament, and its meaning as used in the New Testament? What light do all the other passages throw on the meaning of 1 John 4.18?

11. Compare the psalms or songs of thanksgiving which follow the 'second Exodus' (12.1,2 and 12.3–6) with some of the songs which were sung during the 'first Exodus', e.g. Exod. 15.20,21 and Exod. 15.1–18. In what ways are the two sets of songs alike, and in what ways are they different? Do they have a common theme, and if so, what is it?

APPLICATION, OPINION, AND RESEARCH

12. Read again 11.6–9. What sort of picture-language would you use to describe the peace and joy of 'paradise restored', if you were speaking today to:
    (a) a group of factory workers in an industrial area of South-East Asia?
    (b) a conference of diplomats and national leaders in Africa with responsibility for deciding on the foreign policy of their nations?
    (c) villagers in a remote island group in the Pacific?

13. What is the chief difference between the way in which rulers and other leaders were appointed in Isaiah's time, and the way in which they are appointed in most countries today?

14. It has been said that the description of the ideal king in 11.2–5 is 'just too good to be true – no human being could ever be as perfect as that!' What is your opinion?

15. In most countries there are certain 'national' or popular songs which were originally composed to celebrate a military victory. Compare any such songs you may know with the two songs in chapter 12. On what occasions are such songs usually sung today?

Special Note 2
How and Why Isaiah 1—39
was Put Together

In the general Introduction we pointed out that the Book of Isaiah includes messages, some in poetic form and some in prose, which seem to have been spoken or written not only by the prophet Isaiah himself, but by a number of different people at different times. The chief purpose of all these authors was to make known to the leaders and people of Judah God's will for them in their immediate situation; and to warn, exhort, or encourage them, according to how they were behaving or what was happening to them at particular times. But the chief concern of those who compiled the Book as we have it today was to put together a collection of prophetic words to be read to the people in worship services, which would help them to understand the Torah through the teaching of important religious leaders of earlier days.

As we study the literary questions raised by the text itself, we have to consider these points very carefully. We can see at once that the various passages which make up the present Book of Isaiah do not belong together in their present order. When we try to understand the reasons for this order, and those for a probable earlier order, we may be able to recognize some of the religious and theological intentions of those who wrote, collected, compiled, and edited the book in its present form.

THE ORDER OF THE CONTENTS

The two 'introductions' or beginnings in 1.1 and 2.1 are no doubt the result of putting together two collections of the prophet's oracles, without omitting the second introduction (2.1) although it was no longer really needed.

As we read chapters 6—8 we noticed that while 6 and 8 are written as personal reports by the prophet himself, chapter 7 is a report *about* Isaiah written by someone else. Some scholars believe that chapter 7 too was originally written by Isaiah. In fact the change from first person to third person can be explained in several ways, but most likely it was due to the mistake of a copyist, who took the 'to me' in 7.3 as an abbreviation for 'to Isaiah', as in Hebrew both words begin with the same letter. In any case scholars believe that the section 6.9—9.6 (9.7 in English translations) was a collection put together either by Isaiah himself or by an editor, because all were written as personal reports by the prophet. This explanation can be supported by the present order of passages. The section 6.1—9.6 (or 9.7) interrupts the series of oracles in 5.1–30 and 9.7 (or 9.8)—10.1. This indicates that the 'little autobiography' – as 6.1—9.6 (7) is sometimes called – was put in as it stands, so causing an interruption in style.

On the other hand, the oracles in 5.1–30 and 9.7 (8)—10.1 are *not* preserved in their original order. Some of these oracles have the same *introductory* formula ('Woe to those...' in 5.8; 5.11; 5.18; 5.20; 5.22; 10.1). Others have the same *concluding* formula ('and his hand...' in 5.25; 9.11, etc.; 10.4), almost like a 'refrain' or chorus. But the oracle in 5.26–30 has no such formula, and is a separate oracle unconnected with the others.

So it seems that the latest editor must have arranged chapters 1—11 as they now stand, and added a psalm or two at the end (chapter 12), thus completing the first section of this part of the Book, consisting very largely of Isaiah's messages to the leaders and people of Judah.

The oracles in the second section, chapters 13—23, are also similar in form and content. They too come from various sources. Chapters 20 and 22 at least are Isaiah's own oracles, and the editor put them together with all the others to form a section which consists mainly of oracles against other nations.

The third section, chapters 24–35, also has a common theme: the future punishment of the enemies of God's people, and the salvation of God's people themselves. This section too contains one group of oracles (in chapters 24—27) which probably stood as a separate collection before it was included in this part of the Book of Isaiah. Chapters 28—33 contain many oracles which were obviously spoken by Isaiah himself, but apparently some of them did not quite agree with the expectations of the later editor, who seems to have made some changes, especially in 29.5–8 and 31.4–5.

The fourth and last section, chapters 36—39, is almost identical with 2 Kings 18.13,17—20.19, though the version in Isaiah has been slightly revised in some places and Hezekiah's psalm (Isa. 38.9–20) has been added. The editor clearly placed these chapters here as a kind of 'historical appendix', because they were about the prophet and the king with whom he had to deal (see the detailed Introductions to the study of these chapters, below).

113

THE AIM OF THE COMPILERS

Leaving this last section aside, we can see that the editor had a definite aim when he arranged the material of Isaiah 1—39 in the three main sections: chapters 1—12, chapters 13—23, and chapters 24—35. The main themes of these three sections: (1) Judah, (2) foreign nations, and (3) expectations for the future (i.e. eschatology), are the same as the themes of the three parts of the Book of Ezekiel. The contents of the Book of Jeremiah, too, were originally in this same order, and still are so in the Greek translation, though for some unknown reason a later Hebrew editor rearranged the Book of Jeremiah in its present form. So we see that the contents of each of these three important prophetic books conforms to a similar pattern.

The editor or editors who arranged these prophetic books in this way did so for theological reasons connected with the historical experience of the Jewish community. They believed that they, like their forefathers, were the 'chosen people' of the God of Israel. But in spite of this, they suffered. And although their suffering had originally been God's punishment for their misdeeds, by the time these books were written that was no longer the case. The suffering was being inflicted upon them by godless enemies. So although the people were willing to accept the prophets' reprimand, they also looked to them for words of comfort, and for reassurance that God would fulfil the promises He had made to Moses and to David. So they looked forward to a time when God would punish the evil powers, and to their own salvation. This same viewpoint and expectation is found in all the later books of the Old Testament, and those of the Apocrypha, and in various other religious writings of the time.

STUDY SUGGESTIONS

1. What were the chief aims of the prophets and writers whose spoken and written words are contained in the Book of Isaiah?
2. What was the chief concern of the editor or editors who compiled the Book of Isaiah in its present form?
3. Isaiah 1—39 falls into three main parts or sections, plus a so-called 'historical appendix'. What are the main themes or subjects of each of these four sections?
4. What relationship is, there, if any, between Isaiah 1—39 and the Books of Jeremiah and Ezekiel?
5. 'The editor(s) who arranged these books in this way did so for theological reasons.' What sort of arrangement was it, and what were their reasons?

13.1—17.14
The Fate of the Nations – Part 1

INTRODUCTION

Apart from chapter 22 and some verses in chapters 14 and 17, which in RSV are prose, chapters 13—23 consist of a sequence of poetic oracles describing what was to happen to various nations. Most of these nations were, or at one time or another had been, either enemies of the Israelites or a threat to the purity of Israel's religion. Other prophetic books contain similar collections (e.g. Jer. 46—51 and Ezek. 25—32).

Oracles of this kind were spoken by many of the prophets of Israel, so they are difficult to date. Some are certainly the words of Isaiah. In some, historical references show that they must have been spoken or written much later. Some seem to be based on traditional sayings and beliefs that were handed down from one generation of prophets to another.

Much of what is in these chapters repeats or overlaps with the contents of other chapters in the Book of Isaiah, so we shall study in detail only those oracles which are not paralleled elsewhere. And although it makes sense to think of these chapters as forming a single unit, because of its length we divide our study of it into three parts. The Outline, Notes and Interpretation, and Study Suggestions for chapters 13—17 will be Part 1, those for 18—21 will be Part 2, and those for 22 and 23 will be Part 3.

OUTLINE

13.1–22: 'The oracle concerning Babylon' describes the 'destruction from the Almighty' which came upon that city some 200 years after the time of Isaiah.

14.1–4a: A short prose link-passage declaring that the fall of Babylon will be a sign of God's compassion on His people, who will return from exile and take their former oppressors as slaves, and will taunt them with the poem which follows.

14.4b–21: A 'taunt-song', mocking the oppressors who 'ruled the nations in anger' and thought to make themselves 'like the Most High', and who are now 'brought down to Sheol, to the depths of the Pit'.

14.22,23: Like v. 4a, these prose verses seem to have been inserted to show that the taunt-song is here addressed to Babylon, though it may have been composed much earlier.

115

14.24–27: An oracle by Isaiah announcing the Lord's plan to 'break the Assyrian'.

14.28–32: An oracle in which Isaiah warns the Philistines of the danger which will come 'out of the north', i.e. from Assyria, of which Philistia was a vassal.

15.1—16.14: A collection of laments and threats about the doom of Moab, parts of which seem to be by Isaiah, parts to date from different times.

17.1–11: Short oracles threatening the destruction of Damascus (vv. 1–3) and of the Northern Kingdom (vv. 4–6), and warning of the 'grief and pain' to come upon the children of Israel who have forgotten the 'God of their salvation' (vv. 7–11).

17.12–14: An oracle against 'those who despoil us' whom God will 'chase like chaff before the wind'.

NOTES AND INTERPRETATION

13.2: Raise a signal: See notes on 5.26 and 11.10,12. There the army being raised was that of Assyria, which would punish Judah; here it is an army to punish Babylon, the ruthless enemy of God's people.

13.6,9: The day of the LORD comes: See Note on 2.11 and its following interpretation. Although as described here the 'day' will make the earth a 'desolation' (v. 9), it will be followed by the return of God's people to their own land (14.1).

13.9–12,20: To make the earth a desolation…the sun will be dark and the moon will not shed its light. I will punish the wicked…lay low the ruthless…the earth will be shaken…Babylon, the glory of kingdoms…will never be inhabited: See Introduction to chapters 24—27 and notes on 24.1,6,19,23; 26.21; 27.10,13.

13.17,19: I am stirring up the Medes against them…and Babylon, the splendour and glory of the Chaldeans, will be like Sodom and Gomorrah when God overthrew them: These verses show that chapter 13 must have been put together at the earliest around 518 BC, when Babylon was captured by the Persians who were united with the Medes (see also Dan. 5.31). It reflects the mood of the Jews in exile, longing for liberation from Babylonian oppression – a mood which is expressed in some of the Psalms (see Pss 44; 68.20–23, 28,31).

14.1,2: The LORD…will again choose Israel, and will set them in their own land…the peoples will bring them to their place and the house of Israel will rule over those who oppress them: 'Again' – that is as He did in Egypt. Compare 10.26. These two verses by a later writer, express the firm hope, first, that the exiled Israelites will be freed, and secondly that Israel will regain the power to fulfil God's purposes for His people. Compare chapter 49 and especially 49.5–7, 13, 22–26, which describe what was to happen when the Persian armies (including Medes) overthrew the power of Babylon, and their leader Cyrus allowed all exiles in Babylon to go back to their own lands. The Jews were among the first to leave, and returned to build a new Jerusalem.

14.4a: This taunt against the King of Babylon...the oppressor: Only this introductory verse and the brief 'epilogue' or conclusion in vv. 22,23 relate the taunt to Babylon. The poem itself, vv. 4b–21, does not refer to any particular 'oppressor'. Its language and the mythical allusions it contains (e.g. in vv. 9 and 12–14) suggest that it may have been a traditional song composed very much earlier, and perhaps was used by Isaiah against the Assyrians.

14.4b–6: The oppressor has ceased...the LORD has broken the staff of the wicked...that smote the people...that ruled the nations with unrelenting persecution: Compare 10.5–7 and see notes on 10.5,6.

14.12–14: O Day Star, son of Dawn!...you said 'I will ascend to heaven...sit on the mount of assembly'...but you are brought down to Sheol: These are all references to traditional myths belonging to the Caananite religion, which Isaiah accused the religious leaders of introducing into the Temple worship in Judah. He was using them to describe the arrogance of the Assyrian kings, who boasted of their conquests and set themselves up as higher than the gods. It was these religious practices imported by the Assyrians which Isaiah encouraged King Hezekiah to rebel against and 'do away with' (2 Kings chapters 17—19 – compare especially 2 Kings 19.21–24, and see note on 5.14).

14.18–20a: The kings of the nations lie...each in his tomb; but you are cast out...clothed with the slain...who go down to the stones of the Pit: Compare vv. 9–11. 'The stones of the Pit' may be a reference to the common grave of those slain in battle. 'Pit' was also an alternative term for 'Sheol', but the sense here seems to be that the cruel and arrogant tyrant is so loathed that he will be cast out unburied, or at best in an unmarked grave.

14.20b–23: Prepare slaughter for his sons because of the guilt of their fathers...I will...cut off from Babylon name and remnant, offspring and posterity: Verse 21 may be an addition to the poem; its theme being more like that of vv. 22,23. As we have seen, the whole poem is in many ways similar to 10.5–11, 13–19, and for this reason many scholars think it was composed by Isaiah himself.

14.24–27: The LORD of Hosts has sworn: 'I will break the Assyrian...and upon my mountains trample him...his yoke shall depart...and his burden from their shoulder'...his hand is stretched out and who will turn it back?: Threats against Assyria, which echo many of Isaiah's accusations against Israel and Judah, and also his promises that eventually the Assyrian oppressor would be punished and God's people freed. The passage also reflects the popular feeling that Jerusalem, as God's special dwelling place, could never be captured. See notes on 1.9; 2.12; 5.25; 9.12,17,21; and 10.4.

14.28: In the year that King Ahaz died: Although the oracle in vv. 28–31 is dated in this way, scholars are not agreed as to how, if at all, it may relate to Ahaz's death. It seems that Isaiah was referring to the time when Ahaz had averted the danger from the alliance between Syria and Israel, at the cost of inviting the far greater danger of 'aid' from Assyria (see 2 Kings 16.5–9, and compare 7.17—8.8).

14.29,31: From the serpent's root will come forth an adder...For smoke comes out of the north: That danger to Judah from the Assyrians endangered Philistia too. Isaiah probably spoke both oracles during the same period. The threats in these verses are not an expression of hatred against Philistia – they simply warn that the Philistines cannot escape the general destruction that is to come. The threat to one Palestinian nation was a threat to all, and they often tried to unite against the danger from the north.

14.32: What will one answer the messengers of the nation? 'The LORD has founded Zion and in her...his people find refuge': Some interpreters have suggested that vv. 28–31 refer to an attempt by the Philistines, after Ahaz's death, to draw Judah into a plot against Assyria; and that Isaiah was warning against this, proclaiming that the only refuge for the people of God was in the city the Lord had founded for them.

But this verse, with its promise of special status for Zion, closely resembles Zephaniah 3.12, and is probably by a later writer. See notes on 1.26–28, and section on 'the City of righteousness', p. 29. This verse and vv. 24–27 reflect a very ancient tradition, that of the 'Holy City', which has had far-ranging influence over the centuries. Very many ideas and ideals, political as well as religious, have been linked with hope for a 'new Jerusalem' and for 'a new heavens and a new earth' (Isa. 66). St Augustine of Hippo's great book *The City of God* has had an immense influence on the development of theology since that time. And most of us are familiar with the way in which the word 'Zion' has been used, both by pious Christian individuals, and also by many of the Independent Churches around the world, as a sort of 'standard' as well as a symbol of their intentions and ideals.

15.1,2: Moab is undone...Moab wails: Moab was Judah's nearest neighbour state to the east, across the Jordan and on the farther side of the Dead Sea. The list of places 'laid waste in a night' (see vv. 1–5) suggests that the disaster described in these verses must have struck with great suddenness.

15.5: My heart cries out for Moab: The two countries had much in common in the way of history and language, and the tone in most of chapters 15 and 16 is one of sympathy, perhaps in the face of a common threat as in Isaiah's time when the Assyrians took control of southern

Palestine (compare the Book of Ruth with e.g. 16.9 and 16.11). Moabite refugees seem to have come streaming into Judah: 'Let the outcasts sojourn among you' (16.4). But for most of the Old Testament period there was emnity between them.

16.1: They have sent lambs to the ruler: From the time of David, Moab was a vassal paying tribute to Israel (see 2 Sam. 8.11,12), but after Ahab's death the Moabites achieved independence (2 Kings 3.4–27).

16.6,13: We have heard of his arrogance...pride...insolence – his boasts are false...upon the high place, when he comes...to pray, he will not prevail: The prophets of Israel condemned the religious and social practices of Moab (see 15.9; etc.).

16.14: In three years, like the years of a hireling: An unusually exact prediction. A 'hireling' was contracted to work for a stated period.

A rather longer collection of oracles prophesying doom for Moab appears in the Book of Jeremiah. There too, some sections are sympathetic: e.g. 'My heart moans for Moab like a flute' (Jer. 48.36), while others are strong warnings of punishment impending: 'His boasts are false, his deeds are false...Moab shall be destroyed...because he magnified himself against the LORD' (Jer. 48.30,42). The reason for Jeremiah's enmity may have been either jealousy (Jer. 48.11,12), or anger because Moab rejoiced in the destruction of Israel and Judah – though we do not find these feelings expressed by Isaiah.

17.1,3,4: An oracle concerning Damascus...Ephraim...Syria...and Jacob: The heading in v. 1 actually applies only to vv. 1–3, and the combined threat against Damascus/Syria and Ephraim/Jacob suggests that Isaiah spoke these words around 733 BC, during the Syro-Ephraimitic war (see 2 Kings 16.5–9; Isa. 7.1–3; and compare with Isa. 7.8,9).

17.2: Her cities: RSV translates from the Greek Septuagint (see RSV footnote). Some versions (e.g. AV, NIV) have 'cities of Aroer' from the Hebrew, but there is no Aroer in Syria, and the verse may have been inserted here in error.

17.3: The remnant of Syria: Here the word 'remnant' as used about the Syrians simply means 'survivors' – comparable to the few remainders of grain and fruit left after the harvest, which farmers were obliged by law to leave for the poor to 'glean', i.e. to gather up for their own use (17.5,6).

17.3,4: The glory of the children of Israel...the fat of his flesh: The Northern Kingdom was in fact stronger and richer than Judah.

17.7–9,11: The altars, the work of their hands...the Asherim...slips of an alien god that you plant: Both the two brief words beginning 'In that day' (vv. 7–9), in prose, and also the oracle which follows in vv. 10,11, are accusations and threats against God's people for apostasy, that is, for abandoning their faith in God and putting their trust in man-made idols, and participating in the worship of foreign gods who have no power to save. The 'Asherim' were wooden symbols of the fertility goddess Asherah, and 'slips' refers to plant cuttings grown in honour of a Canaanite god (see note on 1.29 and compare NEB: 'gardens of Adonis').

17.9: Hivites and Amorites: These were peoples who had lived in forest and mountain areas of Palestine before the coming of the Israelites, and had eventually been driven out or conquered by them.

17.10: You have forgotten the God of your salvation...the Rock of your refuge: These ways of describing God show clearly that the oracle is addressed to the Israelites, and suggest that it comes from a later writer, though vv. 7–9 may be compared to the words of Isaiah in 10.20–23.

17.12,13: Ah, the thunder of many peoples...the roar of nations...like mighty waters!...but he will rebuke them and they will flee far away: The oracles in vv. 12–14 clearly refer to Assyria, though no nation is named (compare these phrases with e.g. 5.29,30; 8.7; 13.4). It may refer to Sennacherib's attack in 701 BC on Jerusalem's 'mountain of God', which ended in the Assyrians' withdrawal (see chapters 36, 37). But the statement in v. 14 that 'those who despoil' God's people 'are no more' suggests that it is probably by a later writer.

Some interpreters think that the whole of chapter 17 is of later date than Isaiah, and that the accusation of idolatry refers, not to leaders and people in Judah (like 1.28,29 and 2.6–8), but to the time after the Exile when the proper interpretation of God's commandments in Deuteronomy 13 was an important issue for the Jews.

The oracle in 17.12–14 (like 14.24–27) presents the question raised by all oracles which contain threats against Assyria. We know from 1.4–9, and also 22.1–14, that Isaiah understood that the Assyrian attack on Jerusalem and Judah would be God's punishment of His faithless people. But, as we have seen, many oracles in the Book of Isaiah not only show that the Assyrians themselves will eventually be punished for their cruel exploitation of the peoples they conquered, but seem to promise that God will *always* save Jerusalem from its enemies: 'They will flee far away' (14.27b; 17–13). Does this mean that Isaiah changed his mind? Or that *all* oracles threatening the eventual downfall of Assyria are by later writers? We cannot be sure, because later editors sometimes misunderstood Isaiah's words and changed them (see Introduction to chapter 29 and notes on 29.1–8 and 31.1–5). They did so because of the 'Mountain of God' tradition that Zion could not be captured (see notes on 2.2 and also Pss. 15.1; 48.1–3; 68.15,16).

We know of course that in 587/586 BC Jerusalem did fall to the Babylonians, and that later still it came under the control of the Seleucids, and then of the Romans. And in AD 70 it was again destroyed, and the Temple pillaged, by Titus. But there is certainly a sense in which

Jerusalem as the 'City of God' is indestructible. Throughout these chapters, alongside the warning that for those who have 'forgotten' God the inescapable consequence is 'grief and incurable pain' (17.11), there is the repeated promise that for the faithful remnant there will be rest and refuge after the conflict, and God's good purpose for His people *will* be fulfilled.

STUDY SUGGESTIONS

WORD STUDY

1. For each of the following words write a short definition to explain its meaning:
   apocalyptic apostasy idolatry apostleship

REVIEW OF CONTENT

2. By which of the powers (j)–(o) below was each of the peoples (a)–(i) defeated?

   (a) Philistia
   (b) Damascus
   (c) Ephraim
   (d) Babylon
   (e) Assyria
   (f) Hivites
   (g) Moab
   (h) 'Many nations'
   (i) Chaldeans

   (j) Yahweh/The Lord
   (k) Medes
   (l) Israel
   (m) 'the rod'
   (n) Persia
   (o) Assyria

3. Look up the following words and phrases in Isaiah 13—17, and explain in each case who the prophet was condemning, and for what particular attitudes and/or actions.
   (a) The day of the Lord comes...to make the earth a desolation
   (b) I will punish   (c) I will put an end
   (d) It will never be inhabited   (e) Sheol is stirred up to meet you
   (f) You are brought down...to the Pit
   (g) I will trample him under foot   (h) Let everyone wail
   (i) Her cities will be deserted   (j) The fortress will disappear
   (k) Wail, O gate   (l) The harvest will flee away
   (m) Before morning they are no more

4. Verses 1 and 2 of chapter 14 each describe the same event, but from different points of view. Read 49.13 and 60.9,10, and then say what was the event, what or whose were the viewpoints, and what was the reason for the difference between them.

5. What differences are there between the predictions of disaster in (a) Isa. 14.22,23; 15.1–9; 16.1–5, 8–11,13,14, and those in (b) 14.5–20;

16.6,7 (see also Isa. 5.8–10, 11–17). Why is it important to recognize the distinction between these two different sorts of disaster in order to understand the words of the prophets?

BIBLE STUDY

6. For what sin was the king of Babylon to be 'brought down to Sheol' (14.11–16)? What does this passage have in common with the passages listed below, and what is the link between all these passages and the 'First Commandment' (Exod. 20.2,3)? Ezek. 28.2–10; Dan. 11.21,31,36; Acts 12.21–23; 2 Thess. 2.3,4.

7. In 14.9–11,15,18–20 the underworld, or 'place of the dead', is referred to as 'Sheol' or 'the Pit'. Read Job 17.13–16; 26.5,6; Pss. 88.4–12; 95.3,4; Matt. 16.18; 1 Peter 3.19; 4.4–6,4.6. What do these passages show about the way in which people's ideas about life after death gradually developed, as compared with those expressed in Isa. 14?

8. The oracle in 17.10,11 is an accusation and threat against God's people for apostasy. Read Deut. 13.1–8; Hos. 2.2–6; 7.14–16; Jer. 2.14–19. Why did the writers of these passages consider apostasy to be the most serious sin? What is the link with Exodus 20.2–6?

APPLICATION, OPINION, AND RESEARCH

9. Read again 14.24–27 and 17.12–14, and also Zech. 9.9; Matt. 21.5; Heb. 12.18–24. In what ways do you find these ideas about 'Zion' helpful or unhelpful in thinking about such topics as 'salvation', 'heaven', 'the Kingdom of God'?

10. Compare and contrast 14.1–3 and 14.4–21 with any hymns and songs about liberation which you know, especially any of the American 'spirituals' which are popular today. What are the chief similarities and differences between them, and why? What do these songs tell us about the sufferings and hopes of people in Old Testament times, and of people today?

11. 'The tone in most of chapters 15 and 16 is one of sympathy for Moab.' Why was this, according to 16.6,7,12? For what reasons might one nation or its national leaders offer sympathy to another nation or withhold it today? If you can, give examples.

12. According to 14.24–27 and 17.12–17 the Lord 'planned' to 'break' the Assyrians because they had despoiled and plundered their weaker neighbours. In what ways do stronger nations exploit, plunder, and oppress weaker nations today, and for what chief reasons? Do you think God punishes such nations, and if so, how?

18.1—21.17
The Fate of the Nations – Part 2

OUTLINE

18.1–7: A poetic oracle by Isaiah, addressed to ambassadors from the 'Ethiopian' 25th dynasty in Egypt some time after 715 BC, predicting the downfall of that dynasty. Verses 3 and 7 are probably later additions.

19.1–25: A collection of oracles mainly about Egypt, of which vv. 1–15 is a poem threatening civil war, famine, and confusion. Verses 16–25 consist of five short eschatological predictions in prose, promising a time when the God of Israel will be worshipped in Egypt, and will bless Israel, Egypt, and Assyria alike.

20.1–6: A prose passage concerning Assyria's victory over the Ethiopians in Egypt as symbolically foretold by Isaiah, with a warning to the Philistines who risked the same fate.

21.1–10: A vivid poetic oracle, almost certainly by a later prophet, predicting the imminent fall of Babylon.

21.11–17: Three short oracles threatening Dumah (vv. 11,12), Dedan (13–15), and Kedar (16,17), all clans of Northern Arabia.

NOTES AND INTERPRETATION

18.1,2: Ah, land of whirring wings... beyond the rivers of Ethiopia; which sends ambassadors by the Nile... a nation, tall and smooth, mighty and conquering: We cannot be sure what 'whirring wings' means; perhaps swarming insects in the Nile valley or the flapping sails of the river boats (NEB), or kites and vultures hovering over the bodies of the slain (v. 6). But the reference is to the Ethiopians who overran Egypt and became the ruling family there from about 715 BC till about 665 BC. 'Ethiopia' at that time meant the land south of Egypt, or what is now Sudan, rather than the present-day country of Ethiopia. The 'ambassadors' had come to persuade Judah, perhaps under King Hezekiah, to join an alliance against the Assyrians. But Isaiah made very clear his view that there was no future for Judah in military power or political alliances, even with such a seemingly 'mighty' people as the Ethiopians (other English versions have 'Woe' instead of 'Ah' in v. 1, as the Hebrew is the same as in 5.8; 10.1; 28.1 etc.).

Isaiah sent the ambassadors back with a message to say that those who had sent them need only wait 'quietly'. The time would soon come, 'before the harvest' (v. 5), when the Lord's judgement would 'cut off' the Assyrians, their corpses would be left to the vultures, and the Ethiopians themselves would bring tribute to Him. In the meantime the Assyrians under Esarhaddon did indeed conquer a large part of Egypt in 672. We may compare Isaiah's words here to the advice he gave when King Ahaz wanted to seek military help from Assyria (7.49).

19.1: The LORD is riding on a swift cloud...and the idols of Egypt will tremble at his presence: The figure of a god 'riding' upon a cloud was common in Canaanite as well as Hebrew mythology, though the Old Testament writers more often used the idea of a cloud as symbolizing the mystery of God's presence (e.g. Exod. 14.24; 24.15,16; Ps. 99.6–8). In the religion of Egypt many gods were worshipped, but they would have no power to help against the judgement of the Lord.

19.2–4: They will fight, every man against his brother...city against city...I will confound their plans...and I will give over the Egyptians into the hands of a hard master...a fierce king: We cannot be sure whether Isaiah was here referring to the period of upheaval in Egypt just before the Ethiopians became masters there (see note on 18.1,2), or whether the oracle refers to the time of general disintegration fifty years later when the fierce Assyrian king Esarhaddon conquered much of the country. If the latter, then it is almost certainly by a later writer. In either case the true 'conqueror' was 'the Lord, the LORD of Hosts' (see note on 1.9).

19.5: The waters of the Nile will be dried up...all that is sown by the Nile will dry up...the fishermen will mourn and lament; those who are pillars of the land will be crushed: The whole country of Egypt depends exclusively upon the Nile for its water supply, and for the fertility of its crops. The drought referred to in 19.5–10 most probably occurred in a year or years when the annual rains failed in the mountains of 'Ethiopia', and in the equatorial regions to the south, which normally feed the great river. This may have coincided with a time of invasion and conflict, but is almost certain to have been a natural disaster rather than a man-made one, and would thus have been regarded at the time as the direct work of God.

19.10: Those who are pillars of the land: Cotton and flax were important crops in Egypt, and the Hebrew word translated 'pillars' here is a typical term meaning 'weavers', rather than the leaders of the people whom we might call 'pillars of the land' today.

Some interpreters point out that 19.1–10 can be read as a Jewish 'Midrash' or 'exposition' of Exodus 14 taken in reverse order. It refers first to the confusion and defeat of the Egyptians (19.1–3, and see Exod. 14.24b, 25) caused by the action of God in the 'pillar of fire and of cloud' (19.1 and Exod. 14.24a), and then to the drying up of the waters (19.5–10, and see Exod. 14.21). We should not press this comparison too far, but in both passages a 'theophany', or appearance of God, made the Egyptians confused and powerless to defend themselves. Isaiah was clearly reminding his hearers of God's past action against Egypt on their behalf, so as to give weight to his warning against relying on Egyptian help against the Assyrians. The Lord had caused Egypt's defeat before, and would do so again.

19.11,13: The princes of Zoan are utterly foolish; the wise counsellors of Pharaoh give stupid counsel...the princes of Memphis are deluded ...the cornerstones of her tribes have led Egypt astray: Zoan and Memphis were both great cities in the northern part of Egypt; each had at one time or another been the capital. By 'cornerstones' the prophet meant the various local chiefs or leaders in different districts.

Verses 11-15 continue the warning about Egypt's weakness, but in this passage Isaiah is using the style and language of traditional 'wisdom teaching' such as we find in the Book of Proverbs and parts of Job and Ecclesiastes. Here, however, the emphasis is on the *lack* of wisdom in Egypt's leaders, in whom 'the Lord' had 'mingled a spirit of confusion' (v. 14), so that those whose counsel should have been wise, were in fact 'foolish', 'stupid', 'deluded', 'astray'. Compare e.g. Prov. 10.8,13,14; 21.16; Job 12.24,25.

19.15: Head or tail, palm branch or reed: See note on 9.14. This verse may be an addition.

19.16,17: In that day the Egyptians will...tremble...And the land of Judah will become a terror to the Egyptians...because of the purpose which the LORD has purposed against them: This first of the five prose oracles in 19.16-25, all beginning 'in that day', threatens that the Lord will use Judah to punish and subdue Egypt. Compare 19.1.

19.18: There will be five cities...which speak the language of Canaan and swear allegiance to the LORD...one of these will be the City of the Sun: The 'language' means either Hebrew, or the Aramaic more generally spoken by the Jews after the Exile. 'City of the Sun' probably means Heliopolis, where the High Priest Onias IV founded a temple in the 2nd century BC. But the Hebrew text is uncertain; some scholars suggest it may have been altered because many later Jews believed that the Lord should be worshipped only in Jerusalem. English translations vary; e.g. NIV has 'City of Destruction'.

19.19,21: There will be an altar to the LORD in the land of Egypt, and a pillar to the LORD at its border...and the Egyptians will know the LORD: There was certainly a Jewish settlement in Egypt in Jeremiah's time (see Jer. 44.26). Archaeologists have also discovered letters and other documents showing that there was a garrison of Aramaic-speaking Jewish soldiers at Elephantine about 419 BC and later, who were hired by the Egyptians to protect their southern border.

19.22: The LORD will smite Egypt, smiting and healing, and they will

'We have heard of the pride of Moab...his arrogance...his insolence...let Moab wail...he will not prevail....There will be a highway from Egypt to Assyria...the Egyptians will worship with the Assyrians' (16.6, 7, 12; 19.23).

Because of racist 'pride' this footbridge over a railway in S. Africa is divided – Blacks one side, Whites the other. But elsewhere in Africa new roads and rail links being built will join nation to nation.

What sort of 'highway' or bridge can bring all races and classes and castes of people to worship together'?

return to the LORD and he will heed their supplications: That is, God will treat the Egyptians not as enemies, as in the time of the Exodus, but as He treats His own people, punishing them in order to heal and save.

19.23: There will be a highway from Egypt to Assyria...and the Egyptians will worship with the Assyrians: Compare 11.10,11,16. The hope expressed in the preceding oracles, that the Egyptians will come to believe in the God of Israel, is extended to include Assyria. Here, and in vv. 24,25, 'Assyria' probably means not the Assyrian Empire, but a later power in Mesopotamia, either the Persians or the Seleucids (see Special Note 1).

19.24: Israel will be the third with Egypt and Assyria, a blessing in the midst of the earth: The eschatological hope which appears throughout these oracles is of a special kind, because it is a hope not only for 'Israel/Judah' but for other peoples also. Egypt, 'Assyria', and Israel/Judah *together* become the one people of God. We may compare this with the underlying theme of the Book of Jonah, and with some of the 'Servant Songs' in Isaiah 40—66 (see 42.1–4; 52.15). According to some other Bible writers, in the period of early Judaism (during and towards the end of the Exile) the Jews were very careful to keep themselves separate from other peoples (see e.g. Ezra 4.3; Neh. 13.23–25). But it seems from Isaiah 19.16–25 that they were not everywhere so exclusive.

20.1: In the year that the commander...sent by Sargon...came to Ashdod and took it: This is one of the verses which help us to date Isaiah's life and work, because we know from other historical evidence that Sargon II of Assyria captured Ashdod in 711 BC.

20.3,4: The LORD had spoken by Isaiah...saying 'Go, and loose the sackcloth from your loins, and...your shoes from your feet', and he had done so...as a sign and a portent against Egypt and Ethiopia: We may compare this prose narrative with chapters 6—8, which describe some of the ways in which Isaiah received and delivered his prophetic messages (see notes on 7.3,11–14: 8.1–3,18; and interpretation pp. 80 and 87). 'Sackcloth' was a sign of mourning (see 15.3 and 37.1,2), perhaps also customarily worn by Isaiah. 'Ethiopia' again refers to the Ethiopian dynasty in Egypt.

20.4–6: So shall the king of Assyria lead away the Egyptians captives and the Ethiopians exiles...and the inhabitants of the coastland will say...'Behold, this is what has happened to those...to whom we fled for help': The 'signs' which Isaiah gave to warn King Ahaz against seeking help from Assyria were in the form of symbolic names carrying a reminder or a threat or a promise (chapters 7 and 8). Here in chapter 20 his symbolic action in going about stripped of his garments like a prisoner of war pointed even more directly to the folly of relying on Egyptian aid. He was also calling on Judah to take warning from the fate of neighbouring nations. 'Coastland' here means Philistia, and in fact when Sargon threatened Ashdod (20.1), an important city there, Egypt not only failed to send the help the Philistines hoped for, but betrayed their leader to the Assyrians.

21.1: The wilderness of the sea: Some scholars believe that this was a term which the Assyrians used for Babylonia. In any case, other references in 21.1–10 show that it was almost certainly by a later prophet than Isaiah, and that the 'stern vision' (21.2) of coming battle and destruction relates to an occasion when Babylon was overrun, almost certainly its fall to the Persians in 538 BC. (Some suggest that it could relate to an earlier time of rebellion and unrest, but there is no certain evidence for this.)

21.2: Go up, O Elam, lay siege, O Media: See note on 13.17.

21.2,3: All the sighing she has caused I bring to an end. Therefore...I am bowed down...dismayed...my mind reels: It is important in this rather difficult passage to distinguish between the prophet's message from God: 'I (the Lord) bring to an end', and his own reaction to the horror of knowing what was going to happen: 'I (the prophet) am dismayed'.

21.5: They spread the rugs...eat...drink: As in many countries today, it was customary to sit or recline on the ground at meals, rather than on chairs. This vivid description of an interrupted feast may emphasize either the city's unpreparedness or the suddenness of the attack.

21.6,8: The Lord said 'set a watchman, let him announce what he sees...' **'Upon a watchtower I stand, O Lord':** Compare this description of the prophet with Habakkuk 2.1–3.

This whole poem is full of uncertain meanings. But the picture of dismay and confusion, of anxious waiting and watching for the coming of riders bringing deliverance, the broken idols and the shout of triumph 'fallen is Babylon' (v. 9), and the final word of comfort from the Lord to end the suffering of 'my threshed and winnowed one', resembles the general mood of Isaiah 40—66. So this passage may very well come from the period of the Exile (e.g. compare 42.22–25).

21.11,12: The oracle concerning Dumah. One is calling...from Seir, 'Watchman, what of the night?': This Dumah was an important town in the Arabian desert east of Edom (not the village of that name in Hebron), for which Seir was another name. The name Dumah appears in Genesis as belonging to descendants of Abraham, as do other place-names in vv. 13–15, hence their importance for Judah (see Gen. 25.1–3,12–15). As in 21.6, the 'watchman' is the prophet himself. 'Night' was a symbolic term for danger, and 'morning' suggests a new beginning and new hope (see 8.20–22 and Pss. 91.5; 130.5,6). This oracle could refer to an Arab uprising in the middle of the 6th century, but its meaning is very uncertain.

21.13,14: The oracle concerning Arabia...O caravans of Dedanites...O

inhabitants of Tema: The Dedanites were a North Arabian tribe and Tema an oasis southwest of Dumah. Both are mentioned by Jeremiah as having been made 'a desolation and a waste' when the Babylonian kings extended their empire southwards and Judah was conquered (see Jer. 25.17,18,23,24; and note on 21.11,12 above). The prophet's call to one group of people to help refugees from another is striking (v. 14, compare 15.5 and 16.3–5). He cannot have meant that people in Judah should help, they were too far away, but might perhaps have been addressing Jews who lived at Tema.

21.16,17: Within a year, according to the years of a hireling ... all the glory of Kedar will come to an end: See notes on 16.14; 21.11,12. Kedar was a powerful North Arabian tribe, and the name 'Kedar' actually means 'Arab'. This short prose passage seems to be an insertion to sum up and explain the preceding oracles. Expressing hatred for the threatened people (like 15.9 and 16.5,6), it probably comes from a time after the Exile when there were tensions between the Jews and the surrounding Arabs.

STUDY SUGGESTIONS

WORD STUDY

1. What do the following words and phrases mean or symbolize as used in chapters 18—21 and elsewhere?
   (a) head and tail, palm branch and reed (19.15; 9.14)
   (b) a cloud (19.1; 4.5)
   (c) coastland(s) (20.6; 11.11)
   (d) the years of a hireling (21.16; 16.14)
2. What, if any, is the difference between the meaning of 'cornerstone' as used in 19.13 and as used in 28.16?

REVIEW OF CONTENT

3. (a) What were the 'River' and 'rivers' mentioned in 18.1,2,7, and also in 7.20; 8.7; 11.15?
   (b) Why did the prophet refer to 'Ethiopia' and 'Ethiopians' in connection with Egypt?
4. For what chief reasons did Isaiah oppose Hezekiah's policy of military alliance with Egypt? Give references to support your answer.
5. What made the prophet say that he was 'dismayed', and that his horror had 'appalled' him?
6. Describe in your own words the events which led the prophet to call on the people of Tema to provide food and drink for the 'thirsty' and the 'fugitive'.
7. In what ways did God's treatment of the Egyptians, according to

19.19–22, chiefly resemble the way He treats His own people, the Jews?

BIBLE STUDY

8. In what ways is the symbolic language used in 21.11,12 like or unlike the language used in each of the following passages?
   (a) Isa. 9.2–4   (b) Job 36.20   (c) Ps. 30.5
   (d) Ps. 90.5,6   (e) Prov. 4.18,19
9. Compare and contrast 21.1–10 with Jer. 1.11–16; Jer. 6.16–19; Ezek. 3.16–21.
   (a) In 21.1–10, what was the watchman so worried about?
   (b) In Jer. 1.12, who was watching what, and why?
   (c) In Ezek. 3.16, what was the watchman's duty, and why was it so important?
   (d) In Jer. 6.17, how successful was the work of the watchman, and why?

APPLICATION, OPINION, AND RESEARCH

10. In what ways is the description of the Lord's punishment of Egypt in 19.1–10 like or unlike the descriptions of strange or disastrous natural events in (a) Judges 5.4,5; (b) Ps. 29.3–9; (c) Ps. 97.2–9? What was the purpose of God's action in each case? Are there any legends or traditions in the history or folklore of your country relating to similar natural events, and if so what do people generally believe was the cause of them? What do *you* believe?
11. What were the chief differences between the 'sign and portent' which Isaiah gave according to 20.1–6, and the signs and portents he gave according to 7.3–9,13,14 and 8.1–4,18? What signs and symbols have been used by religious or political 'prophets' in your country, in the past or at the present time? How effective have they been? What sort of 'signs' do you think are most likely to influence people today, and why?
12. Chapters 18—20 (and 23) show that Isaiah and other prophets regarded Israel/Judah as one nation among many, because God is the God of *all* people. What can we learn from this, in the light of such New Testament passages as Acts 2.5–13 and Gal. 3.28?

22.1—23.18
The Fate of the Nations – Part 3

OUTLINE

22.1–14: Stern messages of reproach in which Isaiah condemns, and weeps over, the senseless and inexcusable sin of Jerusalem.

22.15–25: Another stern warning in which Isaiah threatens the downfall of a corrupt official, and his successor.

23.1–18: Two oracles about Tyre. The first, in poetry and perhaps by Isaiah, describes the destruction of the city and the ruin of its trade by an invader, presumably Assyria (vv. 1–14). The second, in prose, of a much later date, promises its restoration (15–18).

NOTES AND INTERPRETATION

22.1,5: The valley of vision: Some versions, e.g. JB, have 'valley of Hinnom' – a valley outside Jerusalem which was traditionally a place for idol-worship and child-sacrifice to the Canaanite god Molech. In calling it the valley of 'vision', Isaiah was being sarcastic, though as a sacred place it was one where people might expect to experience visions (see Gen. 28.10–17). The whole of 22.1–14 in fact concerns Jerusalem: 'Daughter of my people' (v. 4 – see note on 1.8), and is perhaps the bitterest of all Isaiah's accusations against his own people.

Scholars differ about the occasion of this prophecy, but almost certainly it was in 701 BC. Jerusalem then narrowly escaped capture by the Assyrian army under Sennacherib, who lifted his siege of the city and withdrew after King Hezekiah surrendered and paid tribute to him (see notes on 1.7; 14.24–27 and 2 Kings 18.13–16 and 19.32–36).

22.1,2: What do you mean...exultant town? Your slain are not dead in battle...your rulers have fled...were captured. Therefore let me weep: After Sennacherib's conquest and occupation of other cities the people of Jerusalem were naturally relieved to be spared a similar fate. Isaiah, however, could not share their 'tumultuous' rejoicing: Hezekiah's dishonourable surrender meant that many people had died for nothing, and it would not save the city from eventual destruction.

22.5–7: The LORD...has a day of tumult and trampling and confusion... battering...shouting...chariots and horses: These verses, with 8a, may be an addition not by Isaiah. However their description of the Assyrian forces getting ready to attack Jerusalem, like the description in 8b–11 of the Jews' preparation to withstand the siege, helps to explain vv. 12–14.

22.8a: He has taken away the covering of Judah: This underlines the continuing danger for Judah. Its most important stronghold, Jerusalem, had just barely escaped, but neither the people nor their leaders had learnt their lesson. 'He' refers back to v. 5, i.e. the Lord, whom the people were still refusing to 'look to' (see v. 11).

22.8b–11: You looked to the weapons of the House of the Forest...broke down the houses to fortify the wall...made a reservoir...but you did not look to him who did it: The so-called 'House of the Forest', built by King Solomon with pillars of cedarwood, was now used as an armoury (1 Kings 7.2). This prose passage, coming between two poetic sections, shows some of the prophet's compassion for both the people and their leaders in Jerusalem, but also expresses his impatience and frustration with the latter. True, they had busied themselves with fortifying the city and seeing to its water-supply. But they had done it all 'in their own strength', without regard to the Lord who had given them their city, planned their future, and sent His prophets to remind them of His care and protection. This is the plain message of the verses which follow.

22.12–14: 'In that day the Lord...called to weeping, and girding with sackcloth, and behold, joy...eating and drinking...'Surely this iniquity will not be forgiven': Again and again the Lord had called upon them to turn to Him and repent of the stubborn folly which endangered Jerusalem. But in spite of many warnings they would not. And now they celebrated as if they had truly won a victory, instead of listening to Isaiah's efforts to make them aware of their mistakes.

The background to 22.1–11 is that King Hezekiah had started his reign by rebelling against the Assyrian overlords, refusing to pay them tribute, and removing all the idols and other religious objects placed in the Temple by Ahaz as the price of Assyrian help (see 2 Kings 16). Later generations praised Hezekiah for this as a 'reformer', and he is shown to have prayed for God's help against the Assyrians' invasion of his country (see 37.14–20; 2 Kings 18 and 19).

But Hezekiah was also involved in military alliances with Egypt and other nations. Just as Isaiah had warned Ahaz against political and military alignment (see notes on 7.1–9), so he had now told Hezekiah to have nothing to do with such policies. In both cases Isaiah demanded that the kings, the military leaders, and the people should simply be 'quiet' and 'return' to God in complete faith and trust (see 7.4 and 30.15 which relate to the same 'league' with Egypt (30.1)).

22.13: 'Let us eat and drink, for tomorrow we die': This suggests that the leaders did recognize the futility of their military policy, but they still refused to recognize what had happened as the judgement of God, or to believe that God would protect them if only they would put their trust in Him. So the whole nation would eventually have to suffer the consequences of their sin.

22.15: Thus says the Lord...go to this steward, to Shebna, who is over the household: Shebna was evidently a high official. The Hebrew title translated 'steward' means controller of the king's establishment, and chief political adviser. Elsewhere he is described as 'secretary' (see 36.3; 37.2 and 2 Kings 18.18 etc.).

22.16–19: What have you to do here, and whom have you here, that you have hewn here a tomb for yourself on the height...O you strong man...you shame of your master's house: No exact reason is given for Isaiah's threat against Shebna. On the rare occasions when the prophets addressed their words of reprimand to individuals, it was usually because someone had opposed their activities or contradicted their words (e.g. Jer. 20.6). Shebna was clearly powerful (vv. 21, 22 suggest the responsibilities of his office). He was also rich: to prepare one's own tomb was a sign of wealth (compare Matt. 27.57–60). Isaiah also referred to Shebna's 'splendid chariots' (v. 18), though the Hebrew of this verse is uncertain and some suggest that it simply means 'your splendid tomb'.

Perhaps Shebna had encouraged Hezekiah's mistaken policies. Some scholars have interpreted v. 16a as suggesting that he was a foreigner, or had resorted to bribery in the matter of his tomb. Or perhaps he had used his high position to enrich himself. Whatever he had done, Isaiah regarded it as so shameful as to deserve not only demotion but banishment – certainly there should be no honoured tomb for him in Jerusalem.

22.19–23: I will thrust you from your office and...I will call my servant Eliakim...and will commit your authority to his hand...and he shall be a father to the inhabitants of Jerusalem. I will fasten him like a peg in a sure place: These verses show the full responsibility of the office which Shebna had held and Eliakim was now to take on. They may be a later addition, not by Isaiah. The final verses describing Eliakim's eventual fall from office (vv. 24, 25) – apparently because of excessive nepotism, that is, granting too many favours to his own family – seem to have been added later to round off the story.

It seems that in spite of Isaiah's threats, although Shebna was demoted he was not banished, or not immediately. Assuming that the Shebna mentioned in 36.3 and 37.2 was the same person, he was among the delegates whom Hezekiah sent to treat with Sennacherib's officers over the lifting of the siege (see chapters 36, 37).

23.1,2: The oracle concerning Tyre: Wail O ships of Tarshish...be still O inhabitants of the coast, O merchants of Sidon: The title given to this threatening oracle by a later editor mentions only the important seaport of Tyre. But as other place-names and references in the passage show, it relates to the whole of Phoenicia, the northern coastland of Palestine which had grown rich as a result of its sea trade.

23.1: From the land of Cyprus it is revealed to them...when the report comes to Egypt they will be in anguish over Tyre: News that their home port is destroyed will shock the Tyrean ships abroad in Cyprus, just as it will shock Tyre's trading partners in Egypt ('Shihor' in v. 3 also means the Nile).

23.4: Be ashamed O Sidon, for the sea has spoken...I have neither raised young men nor brought up virgins: Here, as elsewhere in the passage, the meaning of the Hebrew is unclear, and interpretations vary. Some suggest that the sea itself mourns Sidon's loss of seapower, others that it disowns the defeated seafarers.

23.8: Who has purposed this against Tyre, the bestower of crowns...the honoured of the earth? The LORD has purposed it, to defile the pride of all glory: As we have seen, Isaiah again and again emphasized that the events of history are not mere accidents, but part of God's good purpose for the world. If people oppose His purpose they suffer. 'Bestower of crowns' is probably a reference to the rulers whom the Phoenicians appointed to the overseas settlements and colonies they established. It was not only God's purpose for his own country of Judah that Isaiah was concerned about, but God's purpose for the rest of the world also. Just as God punished the Jews for their pride and greed, so He would 'stretch out his hand' to shake other proud and vainglorious kingdoms (v. 11, and see notes on 1.25 and 9.12).

23.10: Overflow your land...O daughter of Tarshish: Here again the meaning is uncertain, but 'daughter of Tarshish' may mean Tyre's colonies, who must now rely on their own produce rather on support and protection from Tyre (see NEB, GNB, and JB translations of this verse).

23.13,14: Behold the land of the Chaldeans! This is the people; it was not Assyria. They destined Tyre for wild beasts...they made her a ruin... Wail, O ships of Tarshish: Most scholars agree that 22.1–12, and possibly vv. 13,14 also, were spoken in Isaiah's time, perhaps by Isaiah himself, and at that time referred to an invasion by Assyria. But v. 13 seems more likely to have been added later, so as to apply the poem to the siege of Tyre by the Babylonian King Nebuchadnezzar's Chaldean troops. Verse 14, repeating v. 1, might have been inserted at the same time, as a sort of concluding refrain to round off the poem.

The exact meaning or location of 'Tarshish' is not known. The term 'ships of Tarshish' was normally used for larger vessels than mere coasters (see 2.16). Some interpreters think it derives from Tartessa in Spain (hence the GNB reference to Spain in v. 10, and to 'ocean' throughout this passage). Others suggest a link with Tarsus in Cilicia.

23.15,16: In that day, Tyre will be forgotten...at the end of seventy years

it will happen to Tyre as in the song of the harlot: 'Make sweet melody...that you may be remembered': An alternative suggestion about dating is that the whole poem relates to the destruction of Tyre by Alexander the Great in 332 BC, but the majority opinion is that only vv. 15–18 belong to this later date. 'Seventy years' would then be the period between 332 and 274 BC when the city gained a new lease of life under Ptolemy II (see Special Note 1).

23.17,18: At the end of seventy years the LORD will visit Tyre...and she will play the harlot with all the kingdoms of the world...her merchandise and her hire will be dedicated to the LORD: Clearly in borrowing the words of a popular song this later prophet was not doing so in a negative or critical sense. He was simply describing, symbolically and in the most striking way he could, the city's return to remembered prosperity, and to its many relationships with foreign nations. It is clear from v. 18 that he was not accusing Tyre in the way that Isaiah accused Jerusalem in 1.21, nor was he implying that the rich proceeds of the city's trade were to be regarded as 'the wages of a harlot', since they were to be brought to Jerusalem and dedicated to God (see Deut. 23.18, and e.g. Isa. 60.5,11).

STUDY SUGGESTIONS

WORD STUDY

1. What do the following words and phrases mean or symbolize as used in chapters 22 and 23?
   (a) exultant city (22.2; 23.7)   (b) daughter of my people (22.4)
   (c) he has stretched out his hand (23.11; 5.25; 17.21; 10.24; 14.26,27)
   (d) baldness (22.12; 15.2)
2. In both 1.21 and 23.17 the word 'harlot' is used symbolically to describe a city. What city was concerned in each case, and what was the meaning of the symbolism as relating to that city?

REVIEW OF CONTENT

3. What was the probable location of the 'valley of vision' mentioned in 22.1 and 22.5?
4. What had the rulers in Judah done, which was so bad that it made Isaiah 'weep bitter tears'?
5. What had the people of Jerusalem done, which was so bad that Isaiah said 'this iniquity will not be forgiven you till you die'?
6. Who was Shebna, and what had he done which caused him to be demoted?
7. (a) What was the most probable date of the destruction of Tyre described in chapter 23, and of its subsequent restoration?

(b) What is the probable reason why the prophet called Tyre a 'bestower of crowns'?

BIBLE STUDY

8. Study again 22.15–21, and read 2 Kings 18.16–18. What additional information about the demotion of Shebna does the 2 Kings passage give us?
9. 'Let us eat and drink, for tomorrow we die.' Why did Paul liken the Christians at Corinth to the people of Jerusalem who had said these words, according to 1 Cor. 15.12–14, 29–34?

APPLICATION, OPINION, AND RESEARCH

10. Compare and contrast Isaiah's prophecy against Judah and Jerusalem in 22.1–14 with that in 1.4–9, and then write a short description in your own words of what was happening to the people and the country according to each prophecy, and what Isaiah felt about it in each case.
11. The phrase 'Let us eat and drink, for tomorrow we die' has been used as a sort of slogan by people wanting to justify a materialist view of life. In what sort of circumstances might people be likely to use it today? In what circumstances, if any, do you think people would be *justified* in using it?
12. Draw a sketch-map of the Near East, and mark on it the names of peoples and places in the order in which they appear in chapters 13—17, joining each place to the next as you go. Then do the same in a different coloured pen or pencil for the names of peoples and places in chapters 18—23. What, if anything, do you notice about the two different coloured lines you now have on your map? (A Bible Atlas, if you have one, will help you to carry out this exercise.)

24.1—25.12
Chaos to Come and Songs of Praise

INTRODUCTION

Chapters 24—27 consist of a collection of prophecies, prayers, and psalms almost certainly put together by an unknown author long after the time of Isaiah. They have been called the 'Isaiah Apocalypse' because some parts of them are similar to such apocalyptic writings as the Book of Daniel and the Revelation (which is also known as the 'Apocalypse') of St John.

The term 'apocalyptic' comes from a Greek word meaning to 'uncover' or 'reveal'. It is used for writings which 'uncover' the meaning of events which are happening or have happened in the world, usually through visions or symbolic pictures of great disasters which will affect the whole natural world of earth, sea, and sky, and of eventual salvation and triumph for God's faithful people at the end of time.

Many people in the past have misunderstood the Books of Daniel and Revelation, thinking that they foretell in detail events which would actually happen in the future. But scholars have come to understand that the writers of these books were describing the events of their own time and the experience of their own people. They used symbols and picture language because the purpose of their writings was a theological one: to show that God is at work in the events of history even at times of great oppression and persecution. The writer of Daniel, for example, was trying to encourage and comfort the Jewish people in the 2nd century BC when they were suffering under the harsh rule of the Seleucid King Antiochus IV (see Special Note 1) who forbade the practice of the Jewish religion under pain of death.

We have already seen that some of the early chapters of Isaiah contain certain phrases which often occur in apocalyptic writing, e.g. 'in that day', 'in those days...'. Of course, such phrases do not of themselves make a passage apocalyptic, but they suggest that it may be so. And parts of chapters 24—27 are clearly apocalyptic in character. As in other chapters, those phrases mark additions to earlier writings. We find them at 24.21 and 27.1,6,12,13, and they are elsewhere combined with an earlier passage so as to change its meaning, e.g. 26.1a with 26.1b–6; 27.2a with 27.2b–5,7,11. And 27.1: 'In that day the LORD... will punish Leviathan the fleeing serpent', further strengthens the apocalyptic interpretation.

All this shows that whoever put chapters 24—27 together wanted them to be understood as apocalyptic. In actual form and content, too, these chapters are very different from chapters 13—23 and from chapter 28 onwards. Whereas 13—23 refer to other nations as 'enemies' and are in the form of oracles, this is not the case in 24—27, which introduce the apocalyptic viewpoint of the *universal* disaster to come. Some interpreters have suggested that 24—27 were even meant to give an apocalyptic meaning to preceding passages, which would imply that they were among the latest to be added to the Book of Isaiah.

Throughout our study of these chapters we should remember that they were written by and for Jews during periods of great suffering and anxiety.

OUTLINE

24.1–23: Five descriptions of the universal disaster to come. All the people, high and low, will suffer (vv. 1–3); the land is polluted and all enjoyment is ended (vv. 4–13); songs of praise will soon die away (vv. 14–16); inescapable disaster will strike the whole earth (vv. 17–20); the disaster will be universal, sun and moon will be dimmed, only Zion will be safe as God comes to reign there (vv. 21–23).
25.1–5: A song about the downfall of alien rulers, and God's help for the poor and the needy.
25.6–8: God fulfills the longing of those who wait for his help; He provides a feast to celebrate His victory over death.
25.10–12: The fate of Moab.

NOTES AND INTERPRETATION

24.1: Behold, the LORD will lay waste the earth...and scatter its inhabitants: This clear statement, that it is the *Lord* who will cause the coming disaster, shows that the writer was describing the sort of suffering and destruction described in other prophetic books. That is, it was not seen merely as a natural event connected with the end of the world, but as a punishment due to human guilt. If we compare 24.4, 21–23a with similar passages in the Gospels, (e.g. Matt. 24.29–31; Mark 13.24–27; Luke 21.25–28), we find that the latter do seem to suggest that such wholesale destruction will be part of the 'end of the world' drama, and the same is true of the events prophesied in Revelation 8.

This shows that Isaiah 24—27 is still closer to the idea of the earlier prophets, and not really 'apocalyptic' in the full sense of the word. This passage emphasizes two points which will always remain valid:

1. History is not a series of accidental events, it is under God's control;

2. The activity of human beings – both as individuals and in community – plays a major part in what happens to this world and to human kind. Faith recognizes God's acts of grace and punishment in the events of history.

The Hebrew word translated 'earth' also means 'land' or 'country', i.e. here the lands of Israel and Judah. We should keep this double meaning in mind as we study these chapters. It helps to explain the phrase 'scatter its inhabitants' which is often used in writings about the exile of the Israelites and Judeans. (See also 'the land mourns...' in vv. 4–6 and compare Deut. 4.26,27; Jer. 4.28; Ezek. 28.25; 34.6; Hosea 4.3).
24.2: As with the people, so with the priest...the slave...his master...the maid...her mistress; etc.: This list of 'opposites' is simply a poetic way of saying that *all* the people, without distinction, will suffer the same

fate, resulting from the 'pollution' caused by the breaking of their relationship with God.

24.4: The heavens languished: English versions of the Hebrew word translated 'heavens' in RSV (and JB) vary. NEB has 'the earth's high places', GNB has 'sky'. In fact the Hebrew text itself seems confused; it actually reads 'the high (ones) of the people of the land'. This may be because people's understanding of the prophet's words changed. The original writer may have meant 'the exalted people of the earth', i.e. referring to the social position of the leaders (compare 26.5; Job 5.11). But later on people seem to have understood the passage in a more general way, as referring to the 'world' and 'heaven' suffering together. Because of the general apocalyptic character of chapters 24—27, this second meaning became dominant in chapter 24 also (compare vv. 18b,21).

24.5: The earth lies polluted under its inhabitants; for they have transgressed the laws, violated the statutes, broken the everlasting covenant therefore a curse devours the earth: See note on 24.2 above. The word 'polluted' is used in this same way in Jer. 3.1,2,9 and Ps. 106.38, to mean the worship of false gods. In following this pagan practice the people were disobeying God's law clearly laid down in the covenant God made with Moses (see Deut. 13, especially vv. 5b,12–16). The combined reference to 'laws, statutes, covenant' is unusual. But it shows that the 'laws' which the people had broken were not merely those made by the rulers, but those of God's covenant with His people.

The word 'pollution' has a rather different meaning today, but it is not far from our own experience. This passage may remind us that the biblical view of the close relationship between human activity and the world in which we live needs to be taken very seriously. The 'pollution' of idol-worship can be directly related to the selfish, greedy, and reckless exploitation of natural resources which is widespread in the world today. The results of this attitude are indeed a 'curse' (v. 6), bringing terrible suffering to great masses of the poor and weak. Today we face 'pollution' of water, air, soil, and of human relationships as part of this 'curse' which results from man's attitude to himself and to the world around him. Sincere scientists point out that unless this sort of development is halted, it means the almost inevitable self-destruction of the human race.

At the very time when this section of the Guide is being written, the news media are reporting that hundreds of thousands of people all across Africa are dying of starvation because felling of trees for profit has turned fertile forest into desert. Thousands more are dying in India from poisonous chemicals because careless industrialists failed to provide and supervise the necessary safety precautions. And in many areas of Europe and America there is poverty and social unrest because the leaders of the nations and the heads of commercial enterprises have been making money the measure of all things, rather than the welfare of the people. We have to face the possibility that unless the nations learn to live with one another in peace, nuclear war could destroy not only the human race, but the planet earth itself. Because of our disobedience to God's will, the apocalyptic threat of self-destruction is as real now as it was in the time of Isaiah and the Exile.

24.7–9: The wine mourns, the vine languishes...no more do they drink wine with singing: See note on 5.2. Many writers in the ancient world used 'wine' as a symbol of peace, blessing, and well-being. So these verses emphasize the misery to come.

24.10–12: The city of chaos is broken down: This phrase is a puzzle. We cannot be sure what city is meant. JB has 'city of emptiness'. The Hebrew word translated 'city' is elsewhere combined with 'evil-doers' (Hos. 6.8) or with 'the great king' (e.g. Ps. 48). Some scholars take it to mean Babylon, but it may simply emphasize that the people's sin had turned Jerusalem into a city of chaos instead of the city of God.

24.13: It shall be among the nations, as when an olive tree is beaten...as at the gleaning: Compare 17.5,6 and see note on 17.3. In all these passages the writers were using picture-language about everyday things which people would understand, to strengthen the effect of their message. The meaning is that very few people would survive the 'vintage' or harvest time of God's judgement.

24.14–16: They shout from the west...in the east give glory...to the Righteous One...but I say...woe is me: These directions, i.e. westwards and eastwards from Jerusalem, suggest that the writer was referring to Jews of the diaspora (dispersion), i.e., living in countries scattered around the Mediterranean and in other parts of the Near East. These survivors who have escaped the destruction sing praises to God. But the prophet is too overcome by his sense of doom and his belief that there is more terror to come, to share in their joy. The title used for God in this passage 'the Righteous One', is unusual, but it appears again in Isa. 45.21, and also in Acts, where it is used for Jesus.

24.17–20: Terror, and the pit, and the snare are upon you, O inhabitant of the earth!...the windows of heaven are opened...the earth staggers... its transgression lies heavy upon it: The compiler of this chapter cleverly adds to the 'terror' described in each succeeding section. From the internal breakdown of society we move to the battered ruin caused by war, here to the terror of natural disaster, and then on in vv. 21–23 to a darkening of the sun and moon (see notes below). Although the RSV has 'inhabitant' in the singular (v. 17), the prediction is clearly addressed to *all* the people, as other versions show. Verse 18b is an almost exact quotation from Gen. 7.11b: 'The windows of the heavens were opened', describing the prolonged and violent rainstorms which caused the Flood. And the last line of v. 20 echoes the 'fall' of Israel, 'no more to rise', described in Amos 5.2. We see here how later writers quoted from earlier stories and texts, which would be familiar to the people, to describe their own time and the likely consequences of people's actions.

24.21: On that day the LORD will punish the host of heaven: Some scholars say that these verses belong with 25.6–8, rather than here in chapter 24. Like most true apocalypses, both passages are about the 'day of the Lord' (see note and interpretation for 2.11). And both refer to strange happenings which will affect the sun and moon. But true apocalypses relate such events to the end of the world, whereas here the chief idea seems to be the hoped-for time when the God of Israel will rule all the nations of the earth.

Readers are sometimes puzzled because the English phrase 'hosts of heaven' seems to mean different things in different passages. This is because the Hebrew phrase translated 'hosts of heaven' in the RSV (and NEB) is used variously to mean: (a) angels and/or other spiritual 'powers' (1 Kings 22.19); (b) the stars in the sky as such (Jer. 33.22); (c) the stars in the sky as representing protective spirits or the pagan 'gods' of foreign nations (Deut. 4.19,20; 2 Kings 17.16); and, some interpreters would say, (d) by association, the armies of the foreign enemies themselves as used by God to punish His people (34.2,4 and perhaps here in 24.21).

We can see from this that the word 'hosts' (like the word 'armies') can have a good or a bad meaning according to whose army we are talking about and what it consists of. Some other English versions use other words to translate this phrase, which show more clearly whether soldiers, angels, powers, stars, etc. are meant. See also notes on 1.9 and 6.3.

24.21,22: The kings of the earth...will be gathered together as prisoners in a pit...shut up in a prison: Compare 14.15. The idea of 'locking up' evil powers is expressed in both chapters, but in 24 further punishment is expected 'after many days'. Later apocalypses refer to Satan's being bound for 'a thousand years' (see e.g. Rev. 20.2). These ideas may have been influenced by Persian thinking, but they become important for the Jews only in later apocalyptic writings. Here they are merely mentioned in passing.

24.23: The moon will be confounded, and the sun ashamed;...for the Lord...will reign on Mount Zion: Like the stars, the moon and sun were objects of worship in many parts of the Near East. When the God of Israel reigns, His great power and glory will outshine their feebler lights, and, like the nations who worship them, these 'gods' will become powerless.

Before his elders he will manifest his glory: This last line of v. 23

introduces the scene in heaven as God is enthroned and shows His glory
to the people. The description is interrupted by the hymn of thanksgiving
at the beginning of chapter 25, and is only completed in 25.6.

**25.1,3,5: O LORD...I will praise thy name; for thou hast done wonderful
things...therefore strong peoples will glorify thee...the song of the
ruthless is stilled:** Verses 1–5 form a hymn of praise for what God has
done, and of hope for what He will do in the future. As in 24.14–20
we find many words and phrases clearly reflecting the style of earlier
scriptures, which would be familiar to the people from being read,
recited, and heard in worship services, and used in study and prayer.
Notice in vv. 1 and 4 e.g.: 'wonderful things', 'the city of ruin', 'a
stronghold to the poor', 'aliens', 'a shelter' (and see e.g. Psalms 9.5;
6.9; 77.11,12,14; 105.5; also Isa. 4.6 and 25.10,12 below).

**25.2: Thou hast made...the fortified city a ruin; the palace of aliens...will
never be rebuilt:** This may well refer to a historical event, perhaps the
destruction of Nineveh or the fall of Babylon and the consequent
liberation of subject peoples (see 13.19; Nahum 1—3; Jer. 51.37).
Compare also the very similar description of the fate of Damascus
(17.1,2a). The NEB, however, translates v. 2 in general terms without
reference to 'aliens', and although the hymn must originally have been
composed to celebrate the fall of a particular town, it seems to be
inserted here as a suitable tribute to the *power* of the Lord as described
in chapter 24 and the 'enthronement' oracle which follows.

**25.6: On this mountain the LORD...will make for all peoples a feast...of
fat things full of marrow, of wine on the lees well refined:** Verses 6–8 seem
to continue the theme of 24.23, where the Lord took His throne on
Mount Zion (see note on 2.1–4). Here the idea of the 'feast' on the
mountain can be understood as an allusion, not only to Jerusalem as
the place of God's presence among His people, but also to that other
mountain which the people would think of as a symbol of His presence
in earlier times, i.e. Sinai. Both were places where God manifested
Himself and gave His people the nourishment they needed. 'Marrow'
refers to the choicest joints of meat, and 'wine on the lees' would be
the best wine, long matured. Throughout the Bible meals symbolize
good community relationships, and many writers link the idea of a
sacrificial feast with the day of the Lord (see e.g. Zeph. 1.7). Compare
this with the 'marriage supper of the Lamb' (Rev. 19.9), and with the
words of the Lord's Supper (e.g. Mark 14.25). We may notice also the
direct contrast to 24.7–11.

**25.7,8: He will destroy...the veil that is spread over all nations...swallow
up death forever...wipe away tears from all faces and the reproach of
his people he will take away from all the earth:** Here the mountain idea
is developed and interpreted in new ways. The revelation on Sinai, and
the Law there given, were for the instruction and strengthening of the

142

Israelite nation only. Here it is for *all* nations that the veil of ignorance is to be lifted. All people who are willing to receive the 'instruction' God offers will enter into a new and life-giving relationship with Him (see 29.24). The 'death' which separates from God will be at an end for his disobedient people and for the whole earth.

25.9: It will be said on that day, 'Lo, this is our God: we have waited for him': See 8.17 and note on 30.18. Some scholars suggest that this verse was added by a writer wishing to claim 'priority' at the feast for the Jews, who considered themselves to be in a special way God's people, or at least that they should give special praise for the promised salvation they had long waited for.

25.10–12: Moab shall be trodden down...he will spread out his hands... but the LORD will lay low his pride...the high fortifications of his walls he will...cast to the ground: This sudden introduction of a named enemy may seem out of place, especially in comparison with chapters 15 and 16 where some sympathy for the fate of Judah's old enemy Moab is expressed. But the writer seems to be using this oracle chiefly as an example, to show the fate of the Lord's enemies in general.

Christians may take it as a reminder that whilst God offers a place at His banquet to all people, He does not *force* them to come in. Those who remain His enemies and refuse His invitation are also refusing the 'life' described in v. 8.

We should note that people in Old Testament times were not deeply concerned about death as such, except when life was cut short by accident or disease (see note on 38.10–13). Verse 8 is not about death itself, and does not suggest the idea of an 'eternal soul', nor of the resurrection of the dead as it is understood in the New Testament. It simply describes the life-giving consequence of faith in the living God.

STUDY SUGGESTIONS

WORD STUDY

1. Match each word in the left-hand column below with the word or phrase in the right-hand column which explains its meaning in chapters 24, 25 or in the Guide.

   (a) apocalypse   (g) ruin
   (b) symbolize   (h) Sheol or place of the dead
   (c) pit   (i) represent or illustrate
   (d) desolation   (j) revelation
   (e) languish   (k) distant nations bordering the sea
   (f) coastlands   (l) droop, lose strength

2. The idea of 'gleaning' is used symbolically in 17.6 and 24.3. What is gleaning, and what does it symbolize in each of these two verses?

REVIEW OF CONTENT

3. What did the writer mean by the list of opposites in 24.2?
4. What is meant by the reference to 'laws', 'statutes', and 'covenant' in 24.5?
5. In what ways, if any, does the 'pollution' described in chapter 24 resemble or differ from the idea of 'pollution' as commonly used today?
6. In 24.23 it is stated that the sun and moon will be 'ashamed' and 'confounded'. Why?
7. The main idea of 24.21–23 is not the end of the world. What is it?
8. What is meant by each of the following?
   (a) city of chaos (24.10)   (b) kings of the earth (24.21)
   (c) inhabitants of the earth (24.6)   (d) windows of heaven (24.18)
9. In 25.1–5 three different terms are used to mean the enemies of God and of His people. What are they?

BIBLE STUDY

10. Read Matt. 24.29–34,41; Mark 13.24–27; Luke 21.25–28; Rev. 8, and compare these passages with Isa. 24.4,21–23a. What do all these passages describe, and what are the chief similarities and differences between them?
11. 'He will swallow up death for ever' (25.8). What can we learn from the following passages about people's ideas on the subject of death in Old Testament times?
   Gen. 3.22–24   Deut. 30.15–20   Job 5.25,26   Pss. 6.4,5; 88.3–5, 10–12   Isa. 38.10–13   Dan. 12.2   Amos 5.4–6

APPLICATION, OPINION, AND RESEARCH

12. The term 'apocalyptic' is used for writings which reveal the meaning of what is happening in the world through pictures of great disaster and of salvation for God's people at the end of time. Are there any writings of this sort in the traditional literature of your country? If so, how do they compare with the apocalyptic parts of the Bible? How far, if at all, do they help people to understand the meaning of what is happening in the world today?
13. What ideas and beliefs do most people in your country hold, about the end of the world, or the end of time? What do you yourself really believe on this subject?
14. Chapter 24 describes various ways in which the world was, or would be, 'polluted' as a result of the people's sin. Today some say that the chief cause of pollution is ignorance. Others say it is chiefly caused by people's greed and avarice; yet others say by carelessness.

What is your opinion? What steps, if any, are being taken in your country, and by whom, to prevent pollution and over-exploitation of the land, and to 'conserve' natural resources for the benefits of future generations? What part, if any, do the Churches take in the work of conservation?

15. In 24.7–13 the 'lack of wine' is used as a symbolic way of describing a time of disaster and distress. Would it be a suitable way to describe such a situation in your country? If not, what sort of symbols would you yourself use to describe a distressful situation today?

16. Read again 24.7–13; 25.6,7; and also 5.1–7,11,12, 22; 27.2–5; 28.1–3,7,8; 36.16. What are the two chief conclusions we can draw about the writers of these passages, and about people's attitudes towards the drinking of alcohol in Old Testament times? What lessons can we find in them for Christians today?

26.1—27.13
Visions of the Future

OUTLINE

26.1–6: A song about the City of God, praising Him for His support.

26.7–15: A psalm, asking for God's help against adversaries.

26.16–21: A prayer in time of distress: waiting for the coming of the Lord.

27.1 God will punish 'Leviathan the fleeing serpent'.

27.2–6: A song about God's 'vineyard', Jacob (i.e. Israel).

27.7–11: A song about God's judgement of Jacob.

27.12–13: A prose note: God will bring the exiles back to Jerusalem.

NOTES AND INTERPRETATION

26.1,2: In that day this song...in Judah: 'We have a strong city...Open the gates, that the righteous nation...may enter in': Like 25.1–5, 26.1–6 is a 'city-song', but it is obviously positioned here to show the contrast between the city of the 'righteous' on the one hand, which God protects with the 'bulwark of salvation' (v. 1), and the 'cities of the ruthless' on the other hand, whose walls He will bring down (25.3,12). The introductory 'In that day' shows that the whole hymn refers to a time when the expectations and the hopes of the suffering Jewish people will have been fulfilled.

145

26.3,4: Thou dost keep him in perfect peace, whose mind is stayed on thee...he trusts in thee...for the LORD is an everlasting rock: Compare 9.6,7; 25.9; and 17.10. To 'stay' one's mind on something or someone is much the same as to 'wait' for them. With vv. 1,2 this sums up the hope of the Jewish people for the time when, as a righteous nation trusting only in God, He will keep their city strong and at peace. The passage 26.1–6 as a whole seems to be a liturgy, probably used for a triumphal procession (compare Ps. 24).

26.5: He has brought low the inhabitants of the height...the lofty city: Compare 2.12–15; 16.6,13. This verse and those which follow reflect the 'wisdom' teaching found in Proverbs and in many of the Psalms, which is also the theme of much apocalyptic writing. This teaching emphasizes the difference between wordly wisdom which seeks riches and power, and God's wisdom which brings down the rich and proud and raises the humble and meek, the poor and needy (v. 6 and see Phil. 2.8–11; Mark 10.42–45).

26.7,8: The way of the righteous is level...in the path of thy judgements we wait for thee: See note on 2.3. Some versions have 'straight' rather than level, which perhaps gives a clearer idea of the 'honesty' and 'justice' which God demands. The writer could hardly have meant that the path of the righteous is 'level' in the sense of being smooth or easy! **Thy memorial name:** That is, the sacred name 'Yahweh' (see note on 3.1).

26.8,9: ...Our soul...My soul: The change from 'our' to 'my' here is not important. The whole of vv. 7–15 and 16–19 consists of short psalms and petitions put together to form a single prayer of entreaty and trust, which adds further detail to the themes suggested in vv. 1–6. Just as in many present-day liturgies, there are some prayers which use the plural 'we', while in others the singular 'I' nevertheless stands for the whole worshipping congregation.

26.11: O LORD, thy hand is lifted up, but they see it not. Let them see thy zeal for thy people, and be ashamed: See notes on 1.25; 9.12; and 9.7b. 'Them' means 'the wicked' (v. 10).

Let the fire for thy adversaries consume them: The idea of fire is used by Old Testament writers to express two rather different aspects of God's relationship with human beings: (a) the way in which He shows His presence (see e.g. Exod. 19.16–20), and (b) the intensity and power of His nature and His activity in the world (see e.g. Deut. 9.3). In (b) the idea of heat is often used to describe the strength of God's jealousy or wrath (see e.g. Ezek. 36.5; Ps. 79.5). In the New Testament too, fire is sometimes used as a symbol of punishment by God, i.e. hell, see e.g. Matt. 18.8: 'It is better to enter life maimed...than to be thrown into the eternal fire'.

26.13–15: Other lords besides thee have ruled over us, but thy name alone

we acknowledge. They are dead...they are shades...but thou hast increased the nation: 'Other lords' means the victorious enemy nations and the gods of those nations. Judah as restored after the Exile was a very small and unimportant country compared to its former size and status, and no doubt the people hoped it might one day regain some of its lost territory and power.

26.16: In distress they sought thee, they poured out a prayer: The Hebrew here is uncertain. NEB has 'we sought thee', linking up with the use of 'we' in the verses which follow, describing the people's suffering.

26.17: Like a woman with child, who...cries out in her pangs...so were we because of thee, O God: The important words to notice here are 'because of thee'. Although in earlier passages the prophets had emphasized the disobedience of leaders and people as the cause of Judah's distress, the leaders and people themselves refused to accept that accusation. But here they seem to recognize their suffering as God's punishment of their guilt.

26.19: Thy dead shall live, their bodies shall rise. O dwellers in the dust, awake and sing...for thy dew is a dew of light, on the land of the shades thou wilt let it fall: Some Hebrew manuscripts have 'my body' instead of 'their bodies'. 'Dew' and 'light' are both frequently used in the Old Testament as symbols of life (see 9.2; 18.4). Partly for this reason many Christians have held the view that v. 19 actually refers to the resurrection of individuals in the same sense as in the New Testament (e.g. John 11.17–22 or 1 Cor. 15.12–19).

However, the verse should not be interpreted out of context. It seems to have been carefully positioned here to provide a 'positive' contrast to the hopelessness described in the preceding verses, and to lead on into vv. 20,21 by giving expression to the people's hope for a new future in their own land and with their own life-giving ways of worship.

26.20: Enter your chambers...hide yourselves for a little while until the wrath is passed: Although there is no direct connection, this call to the people to be patient while God deals with their enemies may remind us of Isaiah's withdrawal to 'wait' while God fulfilled his threat to punish the disobedient. These last two verses of chapter 26 lead straight into the oracle of assurance and encouragement at the beginning of chapter 27.

As the notes have shown, the two main themes of the hymn in 26.1–6 are, first the importance of *trusting* in God, and secondly the principle of religious 'wisdom' which turns worldly wisdom upside-down (see note on v. 5). We should notice also the teaching about righteousness and justice in vv. 7–10. Christians sometimes mistakenly assume that Israelite religion (and modern Judaism) were and are a 'religion of law'. But this is not true. It is a religion which teaches what God's 'justice' demands of His people in order that they may become 'righteous'. And

'The earth lies polluted...they have transgressed the laws, violated the statutes...a curse devours the earth' (24.5, 6).

In some industrial areas polluting factory smoke is such a threat to health that besides warning notices to motorists, schools are ordered to close when the smog descends.

What sort of 'laws' and 'statutes' could prevent this from happening?

His justice is not 'law' in the modern sense of the word. It is not a set of rules, but guidance about how to *live* in such a way that all our relationships, as individuals, families, communities, nations, are in accordance with God's will. God's justice is not legal justice, but a deep concern that all people should give each to other, and receive from each other, the love, care, and protection which is rightly due to them. This is what Jesus was explaining to His disciples, when He told them that their righteousness must *exceed* that of the Scribes and Pharisees (Matt. 5.17–48).

There is a message for some present-day Christians, too, in the call to 'hide yourselves' (v. 20). We must note that this was *not* a call to hide themselves *from* God (in the way that Adam and Eve hid because they were ashamed of their sin – see Gen. 3.8–10). It was a call to 'lie low' in times of judgement and great danger. It is not always easy to wait passively in this way, or to keep our trust in God in times of persecution. But there are situations today where no other sort of waiting is possible. The experience of the Church in China in recent years, for example, shows very clearly the need for such waiting, and the way in which it can bring eventual release to new freedom.

27.1: In that day the LORD... will punish Leviathan the fleeing serpent... he will slay the dragon that is in the sea: Compare Ps. 74.12–14 and Isa. 51.9,10. These apocalyptic passages use the language of early Ugaritic and Babylonian creation myths, in which the gods fight against dragons and monsters that symbolize the forces of chaos. In these stories the sea was always seen as a great danger, especially by peoples like the Israelites who were not seafarers (compare the references to 'the deep' and 'waters' in Gen. 1.2). And gradually the 'dragon' or 'serpent' came to represent the idea of the 'evil power' which opposes God and must be destroyed (see Rev. 12.7–9).

27.2–4: In that day: 'A pleasant vineyard, sing of it! I, the LORD, am its keeper... I guard it... would that I had thorns and briars to battle': Compare 5.1–7. Here too the vineyard is Israel, but this poem emphasizes the *good* relationship between God and His people, and the protection He offers against their enemies.

27.4,5: I would set out against them... burn them up... or let them make peace with me: This verse makes the important point that not only God's people, but His enemies too, will be included in the peace of the Kingdom if only they willingly submit themselves to His power.

27.6: In days to come Jacob shall take root, Israel shall blossom... and fill the whole world with fruit: See note on 2.3,5. This seems to be an addition inserted as a reminder of God's promise to Abraham that through his descendants the whole world will receive blessing (Gen. 12.1–3).

27.8: Has he smitten them as he smote those who smote them... Measure

by measure, by exile thou didst contend with them; he removed them with...the east wind: Much of the Hebrew in vv. 7–11 is unclear. The switch from third person 'he' to second person 'thou' and back again suggests that this passage too consists of short fragments from different sources and different times, put together as a reflection on the meaning of Israel's suffering. Where the RSV has 'measure by measure' some other versions refer specifically to 'punishment', though the meaning of the Hebrew word is not known. In Palestine 'east wind' means the hot dry 'Sirocco' blowing from the Arabian desert, which scorches the land and is often used to symbolize God's judgement on the wicked (see Jer. 4.11–13).

27.9: By this the guilt of Jacob will be expiated...when he makes the stones of the altars crushed...no Asherim will remain: See 17.8 and note on 17.7–9,11. Israel had suffered heavy blows, death, and exile, but the sin of the people will be fully 'removed' only when they stop worshipping foreign gods and destroy their altars. Some interpreters take this verse to mean that God's forgiveness of Israel depends *only* on the destruction of those places of worship. But the rest of the passage suggests that the people's suffering as such is also part of the 'payment' for their sin (compare 40.2).

27.10,11: The fortified city is solitary...deserted and forsaken...for this is a people without discernment; therefore he...will not have compassion on them: Some scholars think that 'city' here means Samaria, and that the 'people without discernment' means the non-Israelites living there – the despised Samaritans. If so, then probably the whole passage would refer to the Northern Kingdom, and v. 11 may have been added by a compiler who wished to exclude non-Jews from the promises made to 'Jacob'.

27.12: From the river Euphrates to the Brook of Egypt...you will be gathered...O people of Israel: 'Brook of Egypt' means the Wadi el-'Arish (Num. 34.5), the traditional southern border. So this verse refers to the peoples – both Jews and non-Jews – living in the countries which lie in Palestine, *between* the two great rivers.

27.13: In that day a great trumpet will be blown, and those who were lost in the land of Assyria, and those who were driven out...to Egypt, will come: Here the reference is to Jews of the diaspora living outside Palestine, *beyond* the rivers.

Taken together, vv. 12,13 conclude the reflection about the future of the Jewish people with the apocalyptic assurance that God's promises of salvation are for all Jews, wherever they may be, and that *all*, however 'lost' they may have been, will return to their own land and join in worship of God on His holy mountain (see Rev. 21.10,11 and 22.1–5).

Scholars have supposed that the 'vineyard song' in chapter 27 was composed in a time of peace, especially as it suggests that non-Jews have a share of God's care and will have a place in the Kingdom. But it must have been in less peaceful times that it was given apocalyptic significance, as a future hope rather than a present experience.

Christians, however, need to avoid thinking of the Church as a safe and cosy 'vineyard' in which they can isolate themselves from the pressures of the world. The prayer of Jesus for His followers recorded in John 17.14–19 makes this very clear (see especially John 17.15: 'I do not pray that thou shouldst take them out of the world, but that thou shouldst keep them from the evil one').

In the same way, the reference to the 'lost' Israel, i.e. the people of the Northern Kingdom, and the promise of eventual reunification of those who had been scattered by war and exile, has a message for the divided Church of today. Too often we become so involved in our own work and our own problems, and so frustrated by what we see as the weakness of others, that individual Churches go their own ways. They close their minds, and allow even the links which do exist with other Churches to break down, instead of opening themselves to the wider ecumenical community of the people of God as a whole.

The return of the diaspora promised in 27.12,13 is still the expectation and hope of Jews all over the world today. Since the state of Israel was established in 1948 some have actually been able to return to Palestine, but some orthodox Jews believe that the 'return' can only happen when their Messiah appears. In many ways this hope is the same as the Christian hope for the coming of the Kingdom of God when all of God's people will live in unity and peace. In one important sense, of course, God's Kingdom has *already* come, and in Christ we are all His subjects. But we have to admit that it is not yet complete. Too many of us fail in our loyalty as God's subjects, and much of the world has still to recognize Him as King. Too many of us fail to accept that the scope of God's kingdom is wide enough to include the whole world, the whole of humankind in one family.

There is another aspect of apocalyptic thinking, too, which we have to beware of, and that is the assumption that God will 'take sides' *for* 'religious' people and *against* the others. It is only too easy to regard ourselves as 'goodies' and the rest of the world as 'baddies'. But we need to see all of humankind, the world, and nature as an integrated whole, and to recognize other people's troubles and blessings as our own. In fact we have to recognize, and act upon, the responsibility God has given us for what happens in our world now and in the future.

STUDY SUGGESTIONS

WORD STUDY

1. Match each word in the left-hand column below with the word or phrase in the right-hand column which explains its meaning as used in chapters 26, 27 or in the Guide.

   (a) diaspora   (g) places or objects of idol-worship
   (b) Asherim   (h) universal
   (c) discernment   (i) withdraw and wait
   (d) ecumenical   (j) understanding
   (e) hide   (k) atone or pay for
   (f) expiate   (l) scattered people

2. What does the word 'shade' or 'shades' mean in (a) 25.5; (b) 26.14, 19?

REVIEW OF CONTENT

3. 'Parts of chapters 24—27 are clearly apocalyptic in character' (p. 137). Give verse references for *four* such passages in these chapters, and say which particular phrases suggest that the passages you have selected are meant to be apocalyptic.

4. What is meant by each of the following?
   (a) inhabitants of the height (26.5)
   (b) dwellers in the dust (26.19)
   (c) a people without discernment (27.11)
   (d) the Brook of Egypt (27.12)

5. What do 'wine' and 'vines' chiefly symbolize in chapters 24—27, and why?

6. What is the chief difference between the two 'songs of the vineyard', in 5.1–7 and 27.2–5?

7. What 'new' idea about the relationship between God and His enemies is expressed in 27.5?

8. Who were the peoples described in (a) 27.12, and (b) 27.13?

9. In earlier chapters we have discussed the importance of Mount Zion in the history and religion of the Israelite people. Which other mountain was of special importance to them, and why?

BIBLE STUDY

10. What link or links can you find between the 'hymn' in 26.1–6 and each of the following passages?
    Psalms 18.27–32; 24; 48; 52; 100.4,5; 147.6

11. The symbolic references to 'threshing' and to the blowing of a trumpet show that 27.12,13 may be regarded as apocalyptic. In

which of the following passages are references to these activities *not* to be regarded as having an apocalyptic significance?
(a) 2 Sam. 15.7–12   (b) Ps. 81.1–5   (c) Dan. 2.31–35
(d) Joel 2.1,2   (e) 1 Cor. 9.1   (f) 1 Cor. 15.52   (g) Rev. 8.1–7

APPLICATION, OPINION, AND RESEARCH

12. (a) 25.8 'does not suggest the idea of "resurrection" of the dead as it is understood in the New Testament' (p. 143).
   (b) 'Many Christians have held the view that 26.19 actually refers to the resurrection of individuals in the same sense as John 11.17–27. But it seems chiefly to give expression to the people's hopes for a new future in their own land.'
   What evidence for these two statements can you find in the text of chapters 25 and 26, or in the discussion of them on pp. 143 and 147?
13. In 27.1 'Leviathan...the dragon that is in the sea' is used as a symbol of the evil powers in the world. What symbol or symbols would you use to describe such forces to the people of your country today?
14. Some of the descriptions of the end of the world in the apocalyptic books of the Bible seem very like the scientists' description of what would happen in the event of nuclear war today. Some Christians even say that there is no point in trying to prevent such a war, since the prophets have 'foretold' that it will happen. Do you think that is the right way to interpret apocalyptic writings? Give reasons for your answer.

28.1–29
Leaders who Fail to Lead

OUTLINE

Chapter 28 is the first of a series of so-called 'woe complexes' or sets of oracles, each prophesying disaster for one group of people or another, and running through to chapter 33. Except for chapter 30 they are mostly poetry, and most though not all seem to have been spoken originally by Isaiah.
Vv. 1–4: A 'woe word' threatening punishment for the drunken leaders of the Northern Kingdom, and evidently first spoken shortly before the Assyrians' final siege of Samaria in 726 or its capture in 722.

Vv. 5,6: Promise of strength and a crown to the 'remnant' of God's people.

Vv. 7,8: A description of the religious leaders in Judah, who are too stupefied with drink to do their job properly.

Vv. 9–13: These leaders who resent and reject the prophet's message will 'therefore' learn from the foreign enemy what the cost of their refusal to 'rest' in God will be.

Vv. 14–22: An oracle condemning the rulers of Judah for rejecting the prophet's advice, and for taking refuge in an alliance with Egypt which will be annulled and 'beaten down' by the Lord's judgement.

Vv. 23–29: A parable in the style of the 'wisdom' writers, comparing the relationship between God and His people to that between a wise farmer and the land he cultivates.

NOTES AND INTERPRETATION

28.1,3: Woe to the proud crown of the drunkards of Ephraim... the fading flower... on the head of the rich valley: 'Crown' may refer to the leaders, the garlands they wore, or the city itself. But the oracle must first have been pronounced before the fall of Samaria, when the rich and proud leaders of the Northern Kingdom imagined that military strength would keep their city and nation safe, and spent their time in drunken feasting. The reference to a 'valley' is uncertain in the Hebrew, and some English versions have 'perfumes' (NEB, GNB); but the general sense of an irresponsible and self-indulgent leadership is clear.

28.2: The Lord has one... like a storm of hail, a destroying tempest... mighty overflowing waters: Compare 10.3; 17.12,13; and notes on these verses. Here too the prophet was warning of danger from Assyria, but more important is the teaching that whoever the 'one' may be, it is the *Lord* who will *use* the 'mighty and strong' to punish Israel (see e.g. 7.17; 8.7,8). The destructive forces of raging storm, flood, and tempest were traditionally used to symbolize approaching death and the idea of 'Sheol'.

28.5,6: In that day the LORD will be a crown of glory... to the remnant of his people... a spirit of justice... and strength to those who turn back the battle at the gate: In some translations this oracle of promise is set in prose (as in the Hebrew), thus adding to the contrast it provides with the prophetic tirade against the leaders in the preceding and following verses. It may be a later addition. Isaiah chiefly used the idea of the 'remnant' in a negative way, as a warning (see e.g. 7.3); whereas to later writers it symbolized their hope of a return to their own land under the righteous rule of God. The 'battle at the gate', suggesting a siege, may point to a later date.

**28.7: The priest and the prophet reel with strong drink...err in vision...
stumble in giving judgement:** We cannot tell which nation is addressed.
But vv. 7,8 may be positioned here as a link-passage, to point out the
contrast between the ideal 'remnant' as described in vv. 5,6 and Isaiah's
sad description of what remained of God's people after Ephraim had
been snatched like fruit from the tree – that is, Judah. It also leads on
to Isaiah's sharp exchange of words with the befuddled 'scoffers' who
ruled in Jerusalem (v. 14).

**28.9,10: 'Whom will he teach...explain the message? Those who are
weaned from the milk?...For it is precept upon precept, line upon line':**
V. 9 quotes the sarcastic remarks of religious leaders who reject Isaiah's
stern message: 'Does he think we are children, to need teaching about
God's will?' Translations of vv. 10 and 13 vary, but they agree in
conveying that Isaiah's opponents were treating his message as nonsense.
JB simply transliterates the Hebrew, which suggests meaningless sounds
like the prattle of children, unintelligible jargon, or the slurred mumbling
of the drunk – 'hocus-pocus' or 'gobbledygook'.

**28.11–13: Nay...with an alien tongue the LORD will speak to this
people...he has said, 'This is rest'...yet they would not hear. Therefore
the word of the LORD will be to them precept upon precept, etc.':** The
impatient tone of Isaiah's words in this passage may remind us of his
words to King Ahaz in 7.10–20 (see notes on 7.11,13,15,18,20). When
Ahaz rejected God's offer of a sign, a sign was given conveying in
another way the message that the rejection would be punished. In the
same way, the 'scoffers' (v. 14) who rejected as meaningless Isaiah's
message that they should 'rest' in God, would receive the message again
in a language that would really be meaningless to them. This would be
the alien language of the invading Assyrians, whom God would use to
punish 'this people' as he accusingly called them (see e.g. 6.9,10 and
compare the warm 'my people', e.g. 1.3). Then they would 'fall back'
and be broken (v. 13, and compare 8.15).

**28.14,15: Hear the word of the LORD, you scoffers who rule...in
Jerusalem! Because you have said, 'We have made a covenant with
death...when the overwhelming scourge passes through it will not come
to us':** 'Jerusalem' here shows that whilst the oracle in vv. 1–4 related
to the Northern Kingdom, from v. 5 onwards the prophet was
addressing Judah. Although Isaiah referred from time to time to the
covenant which God made with Moses, when He laid down the law for
His people, this passage is the only record of Isaiah's actually using the
word. And here it means a military alliance or agreement with another
power, which he compared to an agreement with death. In vv. 14–17a
the prophet clearly speaks as God's messenger; v. 15 explains the reason
for the message; vv. 16,17 bring the message itself. The leaders had

responded with defiance, thinking that their pact with Egypt would save them, but this was a false hope – as they would find out when the 'scourge' of the Assyrians actually came.

28.16: Therefore...I am laying in Zion for a foundation...a precious cornerstone, of a sure foundation: 'He who believes will not be in haste': A cornerstone must be well laid if a building is to stand firm. 'He who believes' refers to a faith which cannot be moved. Such faith was the only secure foundation for Judah.

28.17: Justice the line, and righteousness the plummet: Translations of the words in vv. 16,17 vary. But 'line' and 'plummet' refer to the string with a weight on the end, which builders use to ensure that the walls of a building stand straight and firm. V. 17 clearly continues the picture of a well-built house, meaning the sort of leadership that is built on a steady trust in God's presence and power (see 7.9b and compare Amos 7.7,8).

28.17b,18: Hail will sweep away the refuge of lies...then your covenant with death will be annulled...when the overwhelming scourge passes through: The false security claimed by the 'scoffers' will not stand against the flood of Assyrian strength. Compare 8.7,8.

28.20: The bed is too short...the covering too narrow: This may have been a popular proverb. There are other such sayings describing the suffering in Sheol which those who reject God's word will experience (compare 14.11).

28.21,22: The LORD will rise up as on Mount Perazim...in the valley of Gibeon...strange is his deed...alien is his work!...a decree of destruction: A reminder of the great victories which God had given the Israelites under David and Joshua (2 Sam. 5.17–25; Josh. 10.9). Only this time – strange! alien! – the Lord would be *against* his disobedient people, not for them. The oracle ends with a reminder that the Lord stands in judgement over His people, measuring them according to the 'plummet' of righteousness (see 3.13). Judah would be found guilty, the sentence: destruction (compare 10.22,23).

28.23–29: Does he who ploughs for sowing plough continually?...does he not scatter dill...put in wheat in rows?...for he is instructed aright; his God teaches him: The Hebrew of this parable is very uncertain, but the various translations agree to the extent of showing what it teaches. A good farmer learns from experience that if he wants to reap a good harvest he must care for the land, and treat each crop 'in its proper place', according to the laws God has laid down for His creation. So, in the same way, the leaders and people in Judah must follow the laws laid down for them by the Lord, who cares for and tends His people as a good farmer tends his land. This is the only firm foundation for a country's peaceful and prosperous survival.

Like the parable of the vineyard in 5.1–7, this passage is an example of the way in which the Bible writers used parables or picture-language, based on people's everyday experience of nature in the world around them, to express profound ideas. Jesus himself did so, as a way of making sure that people would understand and remember his teaching. And we find such parables also in the Qur'an, in Buddhist and Hindu scriptures, and in the writings of Chinese philosophers. We do not know exactly *when* Isaiah used this parable, but it aptly stresses the truth from which all his messages spring: that unless people are willing to trust themselves to God, and build their lives on the 'sure foundation' of faith, disaster of one sort or another is inevitable. In Judah this close relationship with God was lacking. The political and religious rulers, who should have built the national life on such a foundation, had not the faith or the courage to do so, and drank themselves into a stupor to escape from their responsibilities.

We saw in studying chapter 5 that Isaiah did not condemn the drinking of wine as such, only drinking too much. He recognized that people get drunk for many different reasons: to suppress conscience, escape reality, or hide from the mistakes they have made. But people who do this are deceiving themselves, and others often get hurt in the process.

Drunkenness among the rich and powerful in positions of responsibility, as among the poor who seek to 'drown their sorrows in drink', is a serious problem in many countries today. It undermines peoples' ideals, principles, and public and private discipline, in the newer nations of Asia and Africa and the so-called 'developed countries' alike. In Britain the quantity of alcohol drunk has more than doubled in recent years, and the 'gap' between the rich upper and middle classes and the poor and destitute grows wider instead of narrower.

The leaders in Judah, as in other small nations in Palestine, had deceived themselves into thinking that Egypt could help them to withstand the coming Assyrian invasion. But their confidence was based on empty words only, not on fact: according to chapter 19 there was drunkenness and confusion among the leaders of Egypt also.

This does not mean that Christians should always oppose the policies of government as a matter of principle; simply that we should try to look at reality with an open mind. When Jesus exhorted His followers to be 'wise', He did not mean that they should blindly support the existing political leaders simply to avoid oppression. Over the centuries many brave Christian groups have taken a stand on what they believed to be God's will for their nation, and there are many whose firm foundation of faith and close relationship with God enables them to continue doing so today.

According to Isaiah and many other witnesses this relationship with God is a source of renewal which is not only for individuals but for the whole community, the whole world. This chapter also suggests that Christian participation in government and politics is important, and in some circumstances may even be essential to the well-being of the country.

Of course there are many leaders in the world who bring great love and commitment to their work, but who are not Christians. One such who immediately comes to mind is Mahatma Ghandi. They too are surely good messengers of God's love and care for the world, and are close to God themselves. Some may even be closer to God than some leaders in so-called 'Christian countries', who show by their words and actions that they reject the gospel and the teaching of the Church, just as the rulers and religious leaders in Israel and Judah rejected the word of the Lord and the teaching of Isaiah.

Where this happens, Church leaders, pastors, and Christian educationalists today sometimes think that they themselves are failing to teach or preach the gospel in ways that are effective in the modern world. They say that perhaps other, more forceful and more attractive methods are needed to make people accept what is good for them.

It is true that we sometimes fail to communicate the gospel message, perhaps because we are not committed enough, or tend to separate ourselves from those to whom we speak. But the prophets, the disciples of Jesus, and Jesus himself, all experienced rejection by political and religious leaders who had separated themselves from God and followed the 'secular' ideologies of power, nationalism, and selfishness. The prophets and apostles believed in the power of God, so they called on people to commit themselves to Him in faith, and warned them of what would happen if they would not hear. But as we saw in discussing chapter 25, God never forces people to obey Him. He warns us about the consequences of refusing to listen, but we all have to decide for ourselves whether we will follow Him or not.

STUDY SUGGESTIONS

WORD STUDY

1. The following words and phrases are used in chapter 28 with secondary or symbolic meanings. What do they symbolize in each case? (You may find it helpful to start by using a dictionary to confirm your understanding of their primary meaning.)
   (a) proud crown   (b) scourge   (c) foundation   (d) decree
   (e) reeled with wine   (f) cornerstone   (g) rest
2. Who were the 'men of strange lips' (v. 11)?

REVIEW OF CONTENT

3. As shown in the Outline (pp. 153, 154), chapter 28 consists of six separate oracles: vv. 1–4; 5,6; 7,8; 9–13/14; 14–22; 23–29. For each section say:
(a) Who was speaking to whom? (b) What was the mood of the speaker (e.g. scolding? threatening? promising?); (c) What was the main subject or idea in the oracle?

4. Who was the prophet referring to as 'the remnant of his people' in v. 5?

5. What was the 'covenant with death' (v. 15) which the rulers in Judah had made, and what three other phrases did the prophet use to describe it in that verse?

6. For what chief reason or reasons did Isaiah condemn:
(a) the drunkenness of 'the priest and the prophet'?
(b) the scoffing of the priests and the prophets?
(c) the making of an alliance with Egypt?

7. What did the prophet mean by his reference to 'Mount Perazim' and 'the valley of Gibeon' (v. 21)?

8. What was the basic teaching that the prophet was trying to convey by means of the parable in vv. 23–29, about the farmer ploughing and sowing and harvesting his crops?

BIBLE STUDY

9. Isaiah accused the rulers in Judah of drinking themselves into a stupor to escape from their responsibilities. Compare Hosea 4.11–13, 17–19; Amos 6.4–7; Micah 2.8–11. For what chief reasons was each of these prophets speaking against drunkenness?

10. In v. 2 Isaiah was using the symbols of storm and tempest to describe the coming of the Assyrians and the death and destruction they would bring. List the symbols for approaching death or destruction used in the following passages, and where possible say what was or would be the actual cause of the conditions they describe.
(a) Ps. 55.4–8 (b) Jer. 47.1,2 (c) Ezek. 13.8–16
(d) Ezek. 26.19,20 (e) Ezek. 38.18–23 (f) Nahum 1.2–8.

11. Read again 11.2–4,9 and then 1 Sam. 2.3; Isa. 40.1–4, 21–23; Jer. 3.14,15; 31.31–34. In what ways are the ideas about 'knowledge' and 'understanding' in these passages like or unlike those in Isa. 28.9–13? What sort of knowledge do they describe, and what is the relationship between that knowledge and faith? What is the relationship between knowledge and faith among people in your own Church? Which do they consider most important?

APPLICATION, OPINION, AND RESEARCH

12. Look again at the list of symbols for death and destruction you made under Q. 10 above. How suitable are they for Christian preachers and teachers to use today? What alternative symbols might be better?

13. 'The priest and the prophet reel with strong drink' (v. 7). Addiction to drink and drugs is a big problem for many people today. Some governments ban the sale of alcohol and certain drugs, and some Churches and other religious authorities forbid their members to drink alcohol or to smoke. How effective in dealing with the problem do you think such prohibitions can be?

14. What did Isaiah feel when people rejected his messages, according to 28.9,12,22, and why? Some people say that when a message or warning is rejected, it is the speaker who is at fault, not the hearers. What is your opinion? The Greek philosopher Plato, living about 400 years after Isaiah, said, 'A poor democracy is better than a rich dictatorship.' Do you think he was right? How easy or difficult is it for 'prophets' in your country today to take a stand against what they believe to be wrong government policies?

15. Compare the sorts of crop and the farming methods described in 28.23–28 with those used in your country today. If there is much difference, rewrite the parable for a present-day audience, remembering the symbolic meanings which each part should convey.

29.1–14
Distress and Deliverance of Ariel – Part 1

INTRODUCTION

As we study chapters 29, 31, and 36—39 we need to remember the 'Mountain of God' tradition (see 14.24–27 and 17.12–24), because the prophet on the one hand, and the leaders and people on the other, held differing views as to whether the Lord would specially protect Jerusalem.

Isaiah, and other prophets such as Micah (3.9–12), Jeremiah (7.1–20; 12.7–13), and Ezekiel (11.1–12; 12.1–11,17–20), warned again and again that God would punish the city for its sins and not protect it. Later compilers and editors of the words of these prophets, however, living after the destruction of the first Temple, and of Jerusalem itself, found it difficult to accept this harsh attitude. They had understood the mistakes of the past, and hoped that in the future God would protect their city. And they expressed this hope in the words and ideas of those ancient 'Mountain of God' and 'City of God' traditions about Jerusalem. See note on the dating of chapter 17, pp. 120, 121.

Some scholars assume that Isaiah himself was uncertain about God's attitude to Jerusalem/Zion, and so may have made contradictory statements. Others point to Isaiah's apparent belief that God's promises to David would one day be fulfilled. They suggest that his continuing references to a remnant of the people, purged by suffering, who would survive to rebuild the nation, show that he changed the emphasis of his preaching as time went on. However, we must weigh these interpretations against the weight of Isaiah's harsh words in many passages in chapters 1, 5, 23, and 28, as well as here in chapter 29 and in the summing up of his experiences in chapters 6—8. Taken together, these seem to provide clear evidence of his belief in the Lord's 'decree of destruction upon the whole land' because of the people's continuing refusal to repent and 'return' – though 10.5–11 is often quoted as evidence to the contrary.

All the same, Isaiah's belief about the fate of Jerusalem did not stop him from criticizing enemy nations as well. This is what 10.5–11 shows, as does his criticism of Egypt in 19.1–14; 30.1–7; and 31.1–3.

OUTLINE

Chapter 29 has eight parts, of which the first two, vv. 1–4 and 5–8, are linked by the word 'But' to form a single unit.

Vv. 1–4: A 'woe word' against 'Ariel', that is, Jerusalem, and

Vv. 5–7 and v. 8: A promise of deliverance, with a parable about the fate of Jerusalem's enemies.

Vv. 9,10: A command in sarcastic terms, echoing God's word to Isaiah recorded in 6.9,10.

Vv. 11,12: A later reader's note about Judah's lack of understanding.

Vv. 13,14: An oracle of accusation and threat.

NOTES AND INTERPRETATION

29.1: 'Ho, Ariel': This is in fact the second 'woe' of the series (see NEB, NIV, which have the word 'Woe' instead of 'Ho', and notes on 28.1–4). The Hebrew word '*Ariel*' has several meanings. As used in Ezekiel 43.15 and elsewhere, it clearly means 'altar', and it is also a personal name, e.g. in Ezra 8.16. Here in Isaiah 29 it is used in a symbolic sense, and with two distinct meanings. In vv. 1 and 7 it refers to Jerusalem and its Temple, a place of sacrifice. In v. 2b the meaning is reversed: the city itself will become an altar. 'You' (v. 3) is addressed to the whole city, i.e. *all* the people will suffer.

29.1–3: The city where David encamped...I will distress...she shall be to me like an Ariel. And I will encamp against you: This sorrowful reminder of how David had conquered Jerusalem and made it his royal city has the force of an accusation (see 1.13,14). Now God will conquer Jerusalem just as David did, and will turn the idolatrous city into a sacrificial altar, a place of slaughter and burning. Many of the prophets predicted that God would use the military power of Judah's enemies to punish his people (see 10.5; 7.17,18; 8.7,8).

29.4: Then deep from the earth you shall speak: That is, like a spirit in the underworld (compare 8.19). The whole city will be without hope. In Old Testament times people referred in this way not only to the dead, but also to those who were very sick, or in great danger or despair (see e.g. 38.10–15; Ps. 88.3–9).

In some of his earlier oracles Isaiah did hold out some hope, as we have seen, if only the people would repent (see 1.5,6; 18.19). Other accusations, too, must be seen as urgent calls to 'return' (e.g. 5.3,4,7 and 8.1–8). But Isaiah soon became convinced that Jerusalem could not avoid her doom, and his later words, as here in vv. 1–4, were much more final (see also 22.1–14 and the Introduction above).

In studying this development we must always remember that the Book of Isaiah has come down to us through the hands and minds of many generations. We must not be misled by the frequent 'promises' into assuming that Isaiah's threats were not to be taken seriously. Many of the promises were added by those who put the book together later on for reading in synagogue worship. In 29.1–3, as in 22.5,11b, it is God who causes Jerusalem's distress. The enemy and the enemy's army are only the tools God uses. This seems to have been Isaiah's view during the greater part of his ministry, even if not at the very beginning (see again 1.4–8; 6.9–12; 7.17,18).

29.5: But the multitude of your foes shall be like small dust: The ideas expressed in vv. 5–8 are the reverse of those in vv. 1–4. In this section the 'Mountain of God' motifs are used to describe how God will *save* Jerusalem.

Woe to the multitude of the ruthless: See note on 17.12,13 and also Ps. 46.3,6; Ezek. 38.14–23.

29.6: You will be visited by the LORD of hosts with thunder: See 33.2,3; Zech. 14.1–3; and especially Exod. 19.10–19 and 20.18–20.

29.8: As when a hungry man dreams: Here a later writer describes the hope of deliverance in terms of a dream, but from the point of view of the attackers, who will in the end be disappointed. In vv. 1–4 the threat against Jerusalem was quite certainly spoken by Isaiah himself. Verses 5–8, however, do seem to belong to a later time when people expected

God to defend Jerusalem rather than to attack it. Indeed, the main theme here: 'The enemy cannot conquer Jerusalem', reflects the general belief held after the Exile, that Jerusalem was under God's special protection.

Many peoples hold this sort of belief, which today we call nationalism, and which the American naval hero Stephen Decatur summed up in the year 1816 in the phrase: 'Our country, right or wrong.' This belief may cause leaders to deceive themselves and others with boastful lies about the success and power of their own nation, and despise other nations, especially their enemies. Such beliefs are very strong before and during wars, and they tend to confuse people, so that no-one sees clearly what the situation really is (see 29.9,10). They are reflected in such customs as the 'blessing of arms' which is still practised today, and in the symbols carried by or given to soldiers. During both World Wars, German soldiers wore belt-buckles inscribed with the words 'God With Us' (a translation of 'Immanuel' — see 7.14 and 8.8), suggesting that God would take their side in the conflict, as He is described as taking the side of 'Ariel' in 29.6,7.

29.9,10: Stupefy yourselves...be blind...be drunk...for the LORD has poured out upon you a spirit of deep sleep: These two verses are a new and separate saying by Isaiah; compare 28.7. Verse 9 describes what the people were doing to themselves; v. 10 is about what God will do to them. Other Bible writers, too, used the expression 'deep sleep' to describe occasions when God acts in ways which people do not feel or notice (see e.g. Gen. 2.21; 15.12; 1 Sam. 26.12). The words 'prophets' and 'seers' were probably added as explanations.

After many years of serving as God's mouthpiece, Isaiah saw that the fate which awaited Jerusalem would result from what the people were doing to themselves, or what their leaders were doing but which they allowed or even welcomed. In the Jerusalem of Isaiah's time both leaders and people failed to recognize their true situation, because they were blinded by a combination of fanatical nationalism, greedy commercialism, and hypocritical religiosity (see note on 1.10).

This should prompt us to think about our own situation, and to consider what it is that leads people into 'fanaticism' (i.e. excessive and mistaken enthusiasm). Are we too blinded by nationalistic, racist, ideological, or religious feelings? We may also ask ourselves who, if anyone, has the wisdom to see through this mist of confusion and misunderstanding, or the courage to lead the way and decide what role the Churches and individual Christians should play in such situations.

In many countries the political leaders, including some Christians, think that religion and politics should be kept separate. They say that nationalism is a good thing in all circumstances, and that Church leaders should not interfere in questions of military policy affecting

'They err in vision, they stumble in giving judgement...their hearts are far from me' (28.7; 29.13).

Unemployed dockworkers in Djibouti hang about the shipping offices hoping for a job – but there are no jobs. Burnt-out vehicles stand smoking outside a gutted pub after a night of rioting by gangs of youths in a London suburb.

Can the Churches hope to improve people's economic and social conditions where governments have failed to do so?

national security. This was certainly not the view of the Old Testament prophets, nor is it the view of some of the Independent Church movements which have arisen during this century in Africa and elsewhere.

At first most of these movements were strictly religious in character, but they became more nationalistic and political in their aims as a result of persecution in countries still under colonial rule. It has been said that the prophetic and charismatic nature of their leadership fulfills the need for national heroes which people feel in times of oppression. And in some parts of the world such 'prophets' have spoken out not only against unjust political regimes, but also against the support which some existing Church authorities have given to those regimes.

29.11: Like the words of a book that is sealed: In ancient times all 'books' were in manuscript (from the Latin '*manu*' meaning 'by hand' and '*scriptum*', 'written'; i.e. hand-copied), so it can be very difficult to discover what is original in them and what may have been added later. Words or lines omitted by mistake when the manuscript was copied may be added in the margin or between lines by a later copyist, and readers sometimes inserted comments of their own. The prose passage in vv. 11 and 12, falling between sections of poetry, was probably added in this way; and vv. 11b and 12 may even have been inserted at different times, as they both relate to v. 11a and give two different reasons why the vision was impossible to 'read'. The two reasons are not meant to be taken literally. They mean that some people may fail to receive the message because the prophet has hidden it in the symbolic language of his vision, while others merely lack the necessary understanding.

29.13,14: Because this people honours me with their lips while their hearts are far from me...therefore...I will again do marvellous things... wonderful and marvellous: See notes on 28.11. The formal introduction and structure, 'And the Lord said...because...therefore', is common in messages about the coming time of God's judgement. Words like 'wonderful' and 'marvellous' were traditionally used to describe God's saving acts, e.g. the liberation from Egypt (see Exod. 15.11: 'glorious deeds...wonders'; and also Ps. 77.11–15; Micah 7.15). The repeated use of such words here, and the sarcastic application of them to emphasize the stupidity of trying to deceive the Lord, shows that this oracle was certainly pronounced by Isaiah himself.

In v. 14 he was contrasting the tradition(s) of God's saving acts and the 'marvellous things' which He does for His people, with the 'wisdom' of their so-called 'wise men' which would turn out to be as perishable and useless as the people's shallow acts of worship. The words 'wise men' may seem puzzling, but Isaiah was speaking sarcastically to men who thought themselves wise because they were advisers to the kings and helped to decide the policies of the government (compare 31.1–3).

STUDY SUGGESTIONS

WORD STUDY

1. Match each word or phrase in the left-hand column below with the one in the right-hand column which is nearest to it in meaning, as used in 29.1–14.

   (a) deep from the earth   (f) passing chaff
   (b) stupefy yourselves   (g) cover your head
   (c) blind yourselves   (h) like a ghost
   (d) small dust   (i) Mount Zion
   (e) Ariel   (j) be drunk

2. What is meant by the word 'sealed' in v. 11?

REVIEW OF CONTENT

3. Why did Isaiah refer to Jerusalem as 'the city where David encamped', and what event was he referring to?
4. 'And she shall be to me like an Ariel.' About whom did Isaiah say this, and what did he mean?
5. 'Like a dream.' What was the writer comparing to a dream?
6. 'Learned by rote.' What does this mean, and why did Isaiah say it was a wrong thing to do?
7. The words 'wonderful and marvellous' have a sarcastic meaning as used in v. 14. Why was the prophet being sarcastic?
8. What sorts of people were meant by 'one who can read' and 'one who cannot read'?

BIBLE STUDY

9. In 29.13,14 Isaiah was being sarcastic when he spoke of the 'wisdom' of the so-called 'wise men' in Judah. According to the following passages, what is the proper role of 'wisdom', and what is the relationship between 'true wisdom' and 'faith'?
   Prov. 1.7; 2.1–15; Isa. 5.13; 33.6; 58.2; Jer. 2.8; Hos. 4.6; 6.6.
10. Compare Isa. 29.4 with
    (a) Exod. 22.18;   (b) Lev. 19.26b,31;   (c) Lev. 20.6,7;
    (d) Deut. 18.10–14;   (e) 1 Sam. 28.8–14;   (f) 2 Kings 23.24.
    In each of these passages:
    (i) What is the role or function of 'ghosts' or 'spirits'?
    (ii) Does the writer approve or disapprove of dealing with ghosts or spirits, and what are the reasons for his attitude to them?

APPLICATION, OPINION, AND RESEARCH

11. In 1 Cor. 2.6,7, Paul distinguished between the 'wisdom of this age' and the 'secret and hidden wisdom' of God. Which sort of wisdom

was the prophet referring to in 29.14? In the light of your study under Q. 9 above, what are your own ideas about the role of faith as compared with that of 'wisdom' as it is described in those passages.

12. 'Blind yourselves, be drunk, stagger' describes what the people of Judah were doing to themselves (p. 163). What are some of the ways in which Christians and others 'blind themselves' today, and are 'drunk, but not with wine'?

29.15–24
Distress and Deliverance of Ariel – Part 2

OUTLINE

Vv. 15,16: A 'woe word', similar to 28.1.
Vv. 17–21: A prediction of eventual salvation, which we may compare to 'the desert shall bloom' (see 35.1,2,6b,7).
Vv. 22–24: A prediction that the 'house of Jacob' will eventually overcome their failure to understand what God does (24).

NOTES AND INTERPRETATION

29.15: Woe to those who hide from the LORD their counsel: This third oracle of woe, too, is by Isaiah himself. The word 'counsel' suggests that he was referring to the policy which he so often condemned, of making treaties with foreign nations for military protection (see 20.5; 30.1,2; 31.1). The question he quoted, 'Who sees us?', echoes the words of the evil-doers who thought they could hide their wrong actions from God (see Ezek. 8.12,13; Job 22.13–15).

29.16: You turn things up-side-down! Shall the potter be regarded as the clay?: As in 5.20, Isaiah was criticizing the leaders' reversal of moral values (see also Amos 5.7; 6.12).

A century or so later Jeremiah used this same idea of God as a potter and His people as the clay (Jer. 18.1–12), and so, many centuries later still, did Paul (Rom. 9.19–22). In these two later examples the 'clay' symbolized the whole people of God, and though Isaiah was addressing the leaders in Judah, he included the people also in his accusations.

The important point about this parable is that it describes God's people as one indivisible unit. Isaiah was emphasizing two truths which both leaders and people had forgotten:

167

1. God is the *creator* of His people, and He intends them to live in an intimate relationship with Him;

2. The leaders of God's people (and thus the leaders of the Church) are *responsible*, and therefore accountable, to God for the people whom they lead. Isaiah attacked the leaders in Judah precisely because they were not fulfilling their responsibility, and as a result people suffered because their relationship with God had been destroyed.

The closest modern comparison to the political activity which Isaiah was condemning is probably the ideological-political intrigue of our own time – the sort of distorted 'wisdom' which leads people to believe and do the reverse of what is true and right. As Christians we should certainly not point in accusation to any particular nation or group, but put our own house in order first. The most serious and frightening aspects of this sort of activity are that: (a) it completely disregards God, as a matter of principle; and (b) it does the greatest possible harm to God's creation, and especially to human beings.

29.17: Is it not yet a very little while until Lebanon shall be...a fruitful field: This begins another of the so called 'eschatological' oracles. It gives a feeling of urgency and suggests that the expected salvation described in vv. 17–20 would happen very soon. For 'Lebanon' compare 14.3,7–9. Elsewhere Isaiah predicted the destruction of Lebanon's famous cedar trees by the enemy. But here the prediction is full of promise, and this oracle is almost certainly by a writer living after the Exile.

29.18,19: In that day the deaf shall hear...the blind shall see...the meek shall obtain fresh joy...the poor...shall exult: See note and interpretation on 2.11 and compare 11.4. It is not altogether clear whether 'deaf' and 'blind' here refer to the healing of physical disability, or to the eventual 'return' to obedience of those who had so far refused to heed Isaiah's message (see 6.10 and compare e.g. 35.5,6). But the promise of rejoicing for the meek and poor clearly refers to a time when oppression is ended, whether oppression by corrupt and unjust leaders or by a harsh and cruel enemy. Because the downfall of Judah in 586 BC not only led to exile, but meant that the people continued to suffer under alien rulers, these words were often used to describe the Jews in general. And in time they came to be used as meaning 'virtuous' or 'righteous', not merely humble and poverty-stricken (see 25.3,4; Ps. 37.8–17).

29.20,21: For the ruthless shall come to naught...who lay a snare for him who reproves in the gate...who turn aside him who is in the right: The word 'ruthless' came to mean not just wicked and cruel generally, but more particularly the 'enemy' of God's people (see e.g. 29.5). In this verse, however, it means the false witness or unjust judge in a court-case, rather than an enemy in war (see note on 3.26).

In studying this passage we shall find it helpful to read Genesis 2.4b—

3.24 and re-read Isaiah 11.6–9, which tell us something of the people's hopes and expectations at that time about what we call 'paradise', i.e. a perfect state in which all nature and human beings live in total peace and harmony. By contrast this also tells us what people were suffering or fearing they might suffer, and so wanted to bring to an end forever (see vv. 17–19 and 20,21).

Verses 20,21, like 1.21–23 and 5.22, refer to one sort of evil which must end before paradise can come, namely corruption. Evidently the writer was thinking of the law-courts, and today, also, bad administration of the law affects the well-being of the whole community. Too few people realize that the evil of corruption has its roots in the ways in which ordinary people treat each other in their daily lives. A 'small evil' easily becomes a 'big evil'. People who themselves give short weight or sell damaged goods in the market are less likely to blame officials who accept bribes. Those who tell 'white lies' to their neighbours to gain some small personal benefit are more likely to perjure themselves in the law-courts if there is some financial advantage to be gained from doing so. Too many people fail to take a serious view of corruption unless it affects them personally.

29.22: Therefore thus says the LORD...Jacob shall be no more shamed: This introduction echoes the oracles of 'Second' or 'Deutero' Isaiah, the prophet of the Exile, in Isaiah 40—66, who referred to the exiled Jews in captivity as 'Jacob' and 'Israel' (40.27; 41.14), and also reminded them of their descent from Abraham (51.2). So 'therefore' in v. 22 can be taken as a simple continuation of the preceding passage, probably by another writer living some time after the Exile.

29.23: For when he sees his children: Compare with 49.20–22 and 54.1–3.

29.24: And those who err will come to understanding: The two parts of this verse may have the same meaning. See also 35.8 and Ezekiel 14.11; this last passage expands the idea in an important way: 'That the house of Israel may go no more astray from me' (i.e. from God). The word 'murmur' is also used in this way to mean 'grumble' or 'complain' (e.g. Deut. 1.27). Here in Isaiah 29.24 it emphasizes the people's lack of faith and of understanding.

Notice the development of thought in this passage. From the question in v. 22a: 'Who is this God?', the writer goes on in v. 22b to remind people of God's promise to Jacob. Then in vv. 23,24 he describes how and why Jacob will change his attitude, and explains that by 'Jacob' he means the people as a whole. Like Jeremiah and Ezekiel he reminded the people of God's saving act by which they were to be changed (Jer. 31.31–34; Ezek. 36.26,27).

This same idea is also found in the New Testament, where God's action is described by the word 'grace' (see Acts 15.11; Rom. 3.24). In 29.24 the writer raises a very important question: How do we distinguish between right and wrong ideas about God? He sums up the answer in two words, by 'understanding' and 'instruction', both of which are connected with the idea of learning, of going to school. To the prophets Hosea and Jeremiah, and to the Jews of later times, the object of this learning was Yahweh, the God of Israel, and the instruction which He had given to Israel, e.g. in the Ten Commandments (see Hos. 4.6; Jer. 2.8).

To 'err in spirit' (v. 24) means to turn aside from what is known as God's good will for the people (see 30.9–11). It does not mean being possessed by a bad spirit, as was thought to be the case with disturbed or insane people. In Old Testament times people did find it difficult to distinguish between those who merely lacked understanding, and the mentally sick or those whom they regarded as 'obsessed'. And in any case all are equally in need of an understanding of what God is and does. We may note the story of the man who was possessed by a 'demon' in Mark 5.1–20. When the man had been freed by God's grace from the demon who possessed him, Jesus sent him to tell others: 'how much the Lord has done for you'.

STUDY SUGGESTIONS

WORD STUDY

1. Match each word or phrase in the left-hand column below with the one in the right-hand column which is nearest to it in meaning, as used in 29.15–24.
   - (a) sanctify
   - (b) murmur
   - (c) the ruthless
   - (d) learned by rote
   - (e) the Lord
   - (f) who watch to do evil
   - (g) with their lips
   - (h) stand in awe
   - (i) err in spirit
   - (j) the potter
2. 'Meek', 'poor' and other words like these refer to suffering, oppressed people in general. In the following passages, which are the words which refer to such people?
   (a) Ps. 9.12 (b) Ps. 22.24 (c) Ps. 82.2–4 (d) Ps. 140.12
   (e) Prov. 31.20 (f) Zeph. 2.3 (g) Ezek. 34.4,16 (h) Jer. 5.28
   (i) Amos 8.4

REVIEW OF CONTENT

3. Explain what Isaiah meant by 'potter' and 'clay', and why the people were wrong to turn the function of each 'upside-down'.
4. What are the shortcomings of people who are deaf and blind? Why did the prophet compare the Judeans with such people?

5. What did the writer of the prediction in vv. 17–21 mean by 'lay a snare for him who reproves in the gate'?
6. 'Who err in spirit...who murmur' (v. 24). What does this verse tell us about the people's difficulties and wrong-doing?

BIBLE STUDY

7. (i) What do vv. 19b and 23b tell us about the people's attitude towards 'the Holy One of Israel'?
(ii) In which of the following passages is the people's attitude similar to that described in 29.19b and 23b? In which is their attitude different, and in what ways?
(a) 1.4   (b) 5.19–24   (c) 17.7   (d) 30.11,12,15
(e) 31.1   (f) 41.14–20   (g) 45.11
(iii) What differences can you see between the ideas about God in those passages listed in (ii) above which belong to the 8th and 7th centuries BC, and the ideas in the later passages belonging to the 6th century BC? That is, why did Isaiah himself say that the Lord sent prophets to *accuse and warn* the people, whilst the later prophet(s) of the Exile said that He sent prophets to *comfort* them and call them to return to Him?
8. (a) In Rom. 3.23,24 Paul used the word 'grace' to describe salvation as a *gift* from God. In what ways is this idea like or unlike the ideas expressed and implied in Isa. 29.22–24?
(b) In what chief ways are the ideas expressed in 29.22–24 like or unlike the ideas expressed in each of the following passages?
(a) Jer. 31.31–34   (b) Ezek. 36.26,27   (c) Acts 15.11
(d) 2 Cor. 8.9,10   (e) Eph. 2.4–8   (f) Titus 3.5–7

APPLICATION, OPINION, AND RESEARCH

9. 'In that day...' (v. 18). In the traditional beliefs of people in your country, are there any expectations of a day of salvation or judgement which can be compared to those described in Isa. 29.17–21? Do many people laugh at such expectations and hopes, and if so, for what reasons? In what ways, if any, can such traditional expectations be used to express expectations which are part of the Christian faith?
10. 'One sort of evil which must end before paradise can come is corruption' (p. 169).
(a) What particular sorts of corruption were the leaders in Israel and Judah guilty of, according to chapter 29? (See also Exod. 23.6–8 and Deut. 16.18–20.)
(b) If present-day leaders and others in your country are tempted to practise corruption, in what ways, if any, does it differ from the

corruption in Isaiah's time, and why. What do you think is the best way for governments to prevent corruption from being practised today?

30.1–17
'Egypt's Help is Worthless'

OUTLINE

Chapter 30 falls into two main parts. The first, a fourth 'woe complex' consisting of poetic oracles of accusation and warning by Isaiah about God's judgement against alliance with Egypt, runs through from v. 1 to v. 17.

Vv. 1–5: A 'woe word' against the rulers in Jerusalem.

Vv. 6–7: An oracle against seeking help from Egypt.

Vv. 8–11: Words of instruction from God to the prophet.

Vv. 12–17: Two formal accusations by Isaiah, each followed by a threat of destruction.

NOTES AND INTERPRETATION

Some scholars believe that the whole of chapter 30 was written by the prophet Isaiah himself, rather than partly at a later time. In studying it we shall look especially at certain words, themes, and theological ideas which seem to provide evidence that later writers added words of promise (as they did to other chapters).

30.1,2: Woe to the rebellious children, who...add sin to sin: Compare 28.14–16; 29.15–17, and also 19.11,12; 24.6. To the sin of relying on human help instead of trusting in the Lord, the leaders in Judah were adding the sin of rejecting the prophet's repeated message. Notice the words 'refuge', 'protection', and 'shelter' which the faithless leaders of Judah were seeking from Egypt in spite of Isaiah's warnings. Compare Pss. 31.1; 91.1–4.

30.3: Therefore shall the protection of Pharaoh turn to your shame: This would be the direct result of their faithlessness.

30.4: Zoan...Hanes: The Egyptian city of Zoan is thought to have been the capital of the Hyksos kings, and thus a reminder of the time of the Israelites' captivity and oppression in Egypt, as described in Exodus. Hanes was further to the south.

30.6: The beasts of the Negeb: This verse describes the dangerous journey, by way of the wilderness, which was taken by Judah's envoys carrying tribute to Egypt in return for the promised help.

172

Asses…camels: These animals were (and still are) the normal means of transport in the sandy desert regions of Southern Palestine and Egypt.

30.7: Egypt's help is worthless…therefore I have called her 'Rahab who sits still': Egypt would fail and deceive Judah as Rahab had deceived the King of Jericho (see Josh. 2.1–21). In describing Egypt as 'a people that brings neither help nor profit' (v. 5), and her aid as 'worthless and empty', Isaiah was emphasizing the message he had so often repeated: that turning to other sources of strength than God would not help the people at all.

30.8: And now, go, write it before them…inscribe it in a book, that it may be…as a witness forever: Compare 8.16. Here again Isaiah wrote down his message to serve as proof that he had spoken the truth. Written words could also be read out to remind people of the message, and to spread it more widely.

30.9: Sons who will not hear the instruction of the LORD: See note on 1.23. The Hebrew word translated 'instruction' is '*Torah*', which as we have seen means the first five books of the Scriptures: Genesis–Deuteronomy, which deal with the Law God gave to His people. Parts of this Torah were read out in the Temple during the great festivals, as a way of teaching people about the will of God. The same word was also used for instruction given by a priest or prophet (see 5.24b; 28.9,12–14; Hag. 2.11).

30.10: Who say to the seers, 'see not': As in 28.9, the prophet was ironically quoting the words of those who refused to hear his message (see Micah 2.6,11). There are even clearer descriptions in 1 Kings 22 and Jeremiah 26—28 of the continuing conflict between prophets and the political and military leaders who disliked being accused of dangerous policies.

30.11: Leave the way…let us hear no more of the Holy One of Israel: What the leaders wanted to hear was the opposite of what God willed. See notes on 1.4; 2.3; and 30.23.

30.12: Therefore…because you despise this word: This sums up the opposition to the prophet's words, and its results. Notice the direct connection between 'despise' and 'trust in oppression'. In 5.18–24, also, Isaiah describes evil-doing as the direct result of despising the Torah. *Because* 'they have rejected the law…and despised the word of the Holy One of Israel', *therefore* the inescapable consequence is the 'woe' to come.

30.13: Like a break in a wall: This reflects the idea of faith in God as a building whose foundations are firm and whose walls are straight and true (see notes on 28.16–18). Where there is no such faith and trust, the building will fall. The 'break in the wall' is more than picture language. It predicts what will actually happen when Judah becomes the next victim of Assyria because of its alliance with Egypt: the walls of many cities will indeed be broken, and the whole structure of society will collapse.

30.15: For thus said the Lord... 'In returning and rest you shall be saved; in quietness and in trust': See 7.4; 14.3,5; 28.12. These key words: 'returning', 'rest', 'quietness', 'trust', as well as 'be saved', can be understood in both a spiritual and a political and military sense. 'Be saved' means both to be saved from war, and to remain in relationship with God. To achieve this, two things are necessary. The first is a 'returning', i.e. the turning away from the alliance with Egypt, and a coming back to the 'way' of listening to God's commands. The second is 'rest' (NEB: 'keep peace'), i.e., refraining from doing anything which might cause the Assyrians to make war. Since Judah was a vassal of Assyria, the prophet's advice was that the kingdom could only be saved by remaining so. Judah's present weakness could be overcome not by leaning on Egypt (36.6), but by waiting in 'quietness' (see 7.4 and note on v. 18 below), meaning active restraint and 'trust'. This in turn meant absolute reliance on and obedience to God's will as proclaimed by the prophet. It would call for self-discipline and commitment, but it was the only way in which Judah could become strong again.

30.15,16: And you would not, but you said 'No!': Because of the way the poetry is set out and punctuated in RSV, some readers find it difficult to make sense of the transition from v. 15 to v. 16. The NEB translation is clearer: 'These are the words of the Lord...come back, keep peace...there lies your strength. But you would have none of it; you said No.' Notice how Isaiah follows the typical style of Hebrew poetic form in describing the attitude of Judah's leaders and its result, using twin words and repetition: 'We will speed...therefore you shall speed... We will ride...therefore your pursuers will be swift.'

30.17: Like a flagstaff...a signal: This picture-language may remind us of 1.8, which also describes defeat and desolation in symbolic terms: 'The flagstaff stands, but the soldiers have taken down their flag and fled.'

The whole meaning of the woe word in vv. 1–5 is summed up in v. 1, addressed to the 'rebellious children' who 'add sin to sin'. We have already discussed Isaiah's teaching about sin in 5.8–23, where he singled out particular groups of people whom he condemned for specific sorts of wrong action. Here in 30.1 the word 'sin' is used in a rather different way from that in chapter 5, and from the way it is often used today.

Most of us have a fixed idea of what sin means: e.g. breaking the Ten Commandments or the rules of our Church, disobeying our elders or the customs and traditions of our country, wrong sexual behaviour, telling lies, losing our temper – and for some people, smoking, drinking alcohol, dancing, or going to the cinema, etc. Not all Christians agree on the subject, and different Churches in different parts of the world have different ideas of what sin actually is and what its results are.

Here, as in 1.4, Isaiah was pointing to the wrong actions of the leaders in Judah as being the *result* of their sin, that is, of their turning away from God and rebelling against Him. A 'rebel' is a person who refuses allegiance, or fails to support an existing relationship. The leaders in Judah had destroyed their relationship with God by making decisions and carrying them out without regard to His will for them or to the Law He had given them. According to this view there are no different sorts of sin, but the one sin of separating oneself from God may have many different *results*.

We have seen, too, that Isaiah often used the language of the lawcourts to stress the seriousness of sin – as he did in saying he would provide written 'witness' of his words. Many Bible writers used the word 'witness' to emphasize God's faithfulness or His justice. Isaiah, however, was so concerned about the broken relationship between God and His people, that he spoke more often about their 'rebellion' than about their 'sin' as such. As a true prophet (see Special Note 3) he felt bound to proclaim what he believed to be 'right'. A true prophet does not proclaim his (or her) *own* ideas, however important these may be, but has to witness in direct accordance with 'the instruction of the LORD' (v. 9, and see Jer. 32.33; 35.13).

Both messages of accusation which follow in vv. 12–17 are about the refusal of leaders and people to receive and follow this 'instruction', and to the 'crash' (v. 13) which would be the inevitable result of their failure to do so. In fact, considering the political situation in Palestine at the time, and especially in Judah, it is not surprising that the people found it difficult to accept Isaiah's message. He purposely used words such as 'refuge', 'shelter', 'salvation', which were familiar to them from the Psalms and prayers which were commonly used in the Temple. But the way he used these words in connection with their 'secular' ideas and activities must have surprised and shocked them.

The religious leaders would never before have thought of their action in advising the king as being 'rebellion' against God. And although it was usual for the kings to consult with the religious leaders, the military leaders were not accustomed to linking their own personal religious practice with practical decisions about national policy or military strategy. Isaiah was confronting chiefly the leaders, but also the people as a whole, with the question of politics.

This same question confronts the Church in many countries today. How seriously do we – as ordinary Christian farmers or traders or factory workers or teachers or housewives – take what we understand as the will of God when we read the Bible or listen to sermons, and apply it to the decisions we have to make in our everyday lives? How seriously do Christian pastors and teachers take the task of interpreting what they understand as the will of God in their preaching and teaching, so that their hearers will have no doubt about what they believe to be right?

Many people today feel helpless to change the circumstances or direction of their own lives, let alone the decisions of the leaders whose actions affect the life of the nation as a whole. And for some people this is true. But in countries where ordinary people have the vote they *can* use it to bring about changes in government policy. And religious leaders *can* speak out against political decisions they believe to be wrong.

Isaiah was speaking at a time when the leaders' wrong use of their power was throwing the whole nation into a dangerous crisis. He spoke of military strength in terms of 'horses' (v. 16), as we today might speak of nuclear submarines or missiles. He was trying to convince the people that having faith in God's purpose meant believing that peace should be founded on goodwill and not on armaments. Today many people believe this, even though they are not Christians, and may not even believe in God.

Some people, however, even some Christians, claim that according to such Old Testament books as Deuteronomy, Joshua, and Judges, warfare is actually 'the will of God'. But these books which seem to glorify the victories won by the Israelites in their struggles to establish themselves as nations, were not written down till much later, when Israel and Judah had been defeated, and the longing for a return to former strength and glory was very strong.

In the New Testament we find no such concern. Jesus Himself declared that He had 'not come to bring peace, but a sword' (Matt. 10.34). But He made it very clear that He was not referring to physical warfare: the whole of His teaching was directed towards reconciliation and peace-making. And St Paul and other New Testament writers were concerned with *spiritual* warfare against the power of evil, not against enemy nations.

STUDY SUGGESTIONS

WORD STUDY

1. For each of the words listed (a)–(g) below find the definition from those listed (h)–(n) which best explains it, as used in 30.1–17.

   (a) perverseness   (h) alliance
   (b) illusions   (i) disobedience
   (c) profit   (j) untruths, fantasies
   (d) smooth things   (k) evidence or proof
   (e) league   (l) support, aid, benefit
   (f) witness   (m) trust
   (g) wait   (n) false hopes, flattery, false promises

2. (a) What does the expression 'speed on horses' refer to?
   (b) What do the words 'flagstaff...signal' describe? What other words might be used today to describe the same sort of thing?

REVIEW OF CONTENT

3. 'Woe to the rebellious children...who make a league...to take refuge...therefore everyone comes to shame' (vv. 1–5).
   (a) Who were the 'rebellious children' to whom this 'woe' would come?
   (b) With whom did they 'make a league'?
   (c) From what did they seek to take refuge?
   (d) What sort of 'shame' did Isaiah have in mind?

4. Why did the prophet refer to Egypt's help as 'worthless' (v. 7)?

5. 'Who say to the prophet: "See not...prophesy not what is right"' (v. 10). Why did the leaders and the people reject the prophet and his message?

6. 'Leave the way, turn aside' (v. 11). What 'way' is meant here?

7. 'This iniquity shall be like a break in a high wall' (v. 13). What was so serious about this 'iniquity'?

8. 'In returning...shall be your strength' (v. 15). Returning where to? And to whom? And where from?

9. Compare 8.1,2 and 8.16 with 30.8. What are the similarities and differences between the circumstances described? Why did Isaiah need witnesses in each case?

BIBLE STUDY

10. (i) What is meant by 'asking for my counsel' (30.2)?
    (ii) Compare Isa. 30.2 with (a) Judges 20.18–28; (b) 1 Sam. 23.2,3; (c) Isa. 58.2–9; (d) 65.1–7. According to these passages what were people 'inquiring of God', or 'asking God' to say or do?
    (iii) In the Isaiah passages the prophet seems to disapprove of the way in which the people were 'asking God'? Why was this? What did he suggest as the 'right' way of asking God?

11. (a) What is the full meaning of the word 'despise' as used in 30.12?
    (b) Compare 30.12 with 1 Sam. 15.21–26; Isa. 5.24; 8.6; Jer. 8.5–10; Ezek. 5.5–8. In what ways did individuals or the people as a whole in each place show that they despised and rejected God's word?

12. (i) What are the attitudes shown by those who have faith in God, according to 30.15?
    (ii) What other attitudes essential to faith does each of the following passages suggest?
    (a) Isa. 7.9b   (b) Hos. 4.1,6

APPLICATION, OPINION, AND RESEARCH

13. 'The leaders' misuse of their power was throwing the whole nation into a crisis' (p. 176). Collect as many examples as you can from books, newspapers, radio reports, etc., of people who misuse their

power. Why and for what purposes do people chiefly seek power? Suggest at least two examples of what you would consider the *proper* use of power.

14. What is the attitude of people generally in your country to the 'seers' and 'prophets' of today? What is the attitude of Christians and Churches – are they eager or reluctant to 'hear the instruction of the Lord'?

15. What is the policy of your country's leaders on international relationships – do they chiefly rely on 'quietness and trust', or on the modern equivalent of 'swift steeds'? Do the majority of the people agree with government policy in this matter? What are your own views about it?

30.18–33
'The Lord Waits to be Gracious'

OUTLINE

The second part of chapter 30, after a brief transition passage in v. 18, is in sharp contrast to the first part. It is mainly prose in the RSV, and probably of later date. Consisting of two sections, vv. 18–28 and 29–33, it promises future blessing when God restores His people after the eventual overthrow of Assyrian power.

Vv. 18–22: A word of comfort and promise, followed by predictions, from the period after the Exile, that God will send prosperity and healing when the people repent and return to true worship.

Vv. 23–26: A description of the 'ideal' conditions they will enjoy.

Vv. 27–28: A poetic oracle against 'the peoples', also from a later time.

Vv. 29–33: A new section predicting a return of rejoicing for God's people when He turns His anger against the Assyrians, smiting them with the rod and preparing their funeral pyre.

NOTES AND INTERPRETATION

30.18: Therefore the LORD waits to be gracious to you...the Lord is a God of justice; blessed are all those who wait for him: Although the word 'therefore' seems to link this and the following verses with the preceding passage, it introduces oracles of promise in a very different style, probably written after the time of Isaiah. We can see the difference between Isaiah's thinking and that of later writers in their differing ideas of God's 'justice'. Both firmly believed that the God of Israel was a just

178

God, but while Isaiah and other prophets claimed that God's 'justice' was the reason for the punishment of Israel and Judah (see e.g. 3.14; 5.7,17), the Jews of later times saw it as the reason for God's gracious acts of mercy towards them. Notice also the two meanings of 'wait' in 8a and 8b, which are like the two sides of a single coin. God 'waits' patiently and faithfully for the people to 'return' in repentance and once again 'wait' in faith and trust for His word.

30.19: O people in Zion...you shall weep no more...at the sound of your cry...he will answer you: The Jews who had experienced the sufferings of the Babylonian conquest which preceded the Exile could appreciate this promise (see also e.g. Lam. 1.1–6). The claim expressed in v. 19b is very common in the Psalms (see Pss. 22.24; 30.2; also Isa. 41.17).

30.20: The bread of adversity and the water of affliction: These expressions are also used by other writers to symbolize suffering, bread and water being the diet of prisoners – that is, the least which people need to keep them alive (see e.g. Ps. 80.5; 1 Kings 22.27).

30.20,21: Your Teacher will not hide himself any more, but your eyes shall see...your ears shall hear a word...saying 'This is the way': The Hebrew word translated 'teacher' is plural, but most scholars agree that it means God. At last a time will come when the people no longer refuse to listen, but accept and obey God's teaching (see 29.18; 35.5 and compare 6.8–11; 29.9–11). Verse 20b must refer to understanding rather than physical eyesight or visions (see note on 1.5). For 'way' (v. 21), see note on 2.3. God revealed His will for His people through the Law which He gave to Moses. But for those who will listen He continues to provide guidance when they stray from the right road.

30.22: Then you will defile your...graven images: Compare 2.20, describing how people threw away their idols which gave them no help in the day of terror, and 17.8,9. When the people accept God's teaching they will no longer respect idols nor need them (see also 42.16,17).

30.23–26: He will give rain for the seed...the produce will be plenteous... oxen and asses will eat salted provender...there will be brooks running with water...the light of the sun will be sevenfold: Though set as prose in RSV, these verses may have originally been a poem, describing the restoration of the land and nature generally from desolation and drought to riches and prosperity, from wilderness to well-watered garden (see e.g. 2.14; 6.11; 7.23–25; 24.4–6 and compare 25.6–8). Compare the reference to an extraordinary increase of light (v. 26) with the 'great light' of salvation described in 9.2 (see also 42.16; 60.19; Rev. 21.23).

30.26: When the LORD binds up the hurt of his people, and heals the wounds inflicted by his blow: When God punishes His people He does so because of His love for them, and the punishment is matched by His mercy (see Hos. 6.1,2; Ps. 147.2,3). This teaching is emphasized in the

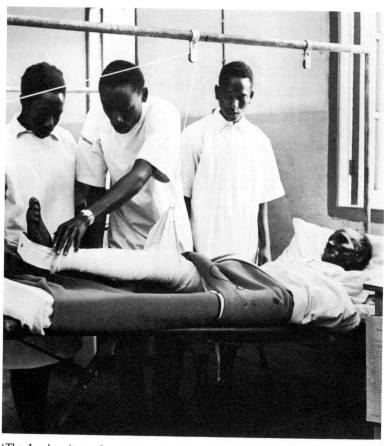

'The Lord waits to be gracious to you... and heals the wounds inflicted by his blow'... 'blessed are all those who wait for him' (30.18, 26).

Doctor and dressers in a Kenya hospital bind up the leg of a patient who 'waits' for his broken bone to be healed.

What *more* is involved in waiting to be healed by God, than in waiting for the relief from suffering that human healers can give?

New Testament. As Paul wrote: 'When we are judged by the Lord, we are chastened so that we may not be condemned along with the world' (1 Cor. 11.32).

30.27: The name of the LORD comes from far: See note on 24.15. Clearly the meaning is that the Lord himself comes 'from far'.

His lips...his tongue...like a devouring fire; his breath is like an overflowing stream: We must not take these references to mean that the prophet thought of God as having a body like a human body. The comparison of the Lord's 'breath' with water rather than wind is unusual, but the idea of overflowing floodwater was often used to describe invading armies (e.g. 8.6–8; 7.12,13; 28.2). And in describing how the Assyrians themselves would eventually be destroyed the prophet wanted to make it clear that this would be the work of the Lord. So he spoke of the heated battle-cries and the fury of the 'stream' of armies coming against the 'terror-stricken' Assyrians as being the voice and power of God Himself.

30.28: To sift the nations with the sieve of destruction...a bridle that leads astray: The Hebrew of this verse is uncertain (as is much of vv. 27–37), and translations vary. Instead of 'sieve' NEB for example has 'yoke', which was used by other Bible writers to symbolize slavery or subjection. Taken with 'bridle' in the next line (or 'bit', see also NIV, JB), this seems the best choice, as meaning that God will drive the nations of the Assyrian empire to their ruin.

30.29: You shall have a song...as when one sets out to go to the mountain of the Lord...the Rock of Israel: See notes on 2.2 and 17.10. Coming at the beginning of a new section describing God's action against the enemies of His people, the title 'Rock of Israel' is used, as it is in many of the Psalms and other poetic texts, to express gratitude for His help and protection, for salvation, and for His faithfulness (see e.g. Pss. 18.46; 19.14; 31.2–4).

30.30,31: The LORD will cause the descending blow of his arm to be seen...with a cloudburst and tempest...when He smites with his rod: See notes on 1.25; and also Exod. 6.6; Isa. 40.10 (arm, hand); 28.2 (tempest); 10.5 (rod); and also 10.15–17. Some scholars believe that vv. 27–30 were spoken by Isaiah, but the style, and the way in which these words are used, do not seem to support this.

30.31: The Assyrians will be terror-stricken: This raises the question we have already discussed about whether Isaiah himself predicted the downfall of the Assyrians. See Introduction to chapter 29 and note on 29.8. For almost 250 years, from the reign of Shalmaneser III in the 9th century BC to the conquest of Nineveh in 612 BC by the Babylonians, the Assyrians were the most dreaded enemies of Israel and Judah. They were also the most cruel, and the way in which the name 'Assyria' and 'Assyrians' appears in texts of a much later time, from the Dead Sea, shows that Assyria had come to be regarded as a typical 'enemy', who would be defeated by God Himself in 'the day' that was to come (see note on 2.11).

30.32: Sound of timbrels and lyres: Translations of this verse vary because it is not known exactly what the ancient instruments were like. But the general meaning is clear, and echoes the description of what has been called a 'Holy War' in 2 Chronicles 20.1–30, and especially vv. 28,29. The Hebrew of the last line of the verse, too, is uncertain, but it is obviously about God's fight against the enemies of His people, and the people's rejoicing over His victory.

30.33: A burning place has long been prepared...for the King it is made ready: The Hebrew word translated 'burning place' in the RSV is 'Topheth' (NEB, JB, AV). This seems to refer to a place in the Valley of Hinnom, south-west of Jerusalem, where human sacrifice was made to the Canaanite God Molech or Moloch, which can also mean 'king' (compare 22.1,2). So the prophet was predicting death for the Assyrians like the death of those sacrificed at Topheth. The prophet Jeremiah condemned the cult of Molech (Jer. 32.35); and the fact that the prediction was directed against the Assyrians suggests it was made at a later time, when the words of Isaiah and Jeremiah against Jerusalem were no longer understood as a threat (see e.g. 29.1–4; Jer. 19.3–9).

Like a stream of brimstone: Compare v. 28 and 11.4. 'Brimstone' is another name for the mineral sulphur, used in making gunpowder and other explosives.

The vocabulary and style of writing, as well as the actual theme in 28.18–26 suggest very strongly that this passage comes from a date after the events of 598 and 586 BC, when Nebuchadnezzar had besieged and finally taken Jerusalem and carried the people away into exile in Babylon – though, as we have said, some scholars would disagree.

If we look for: (a) words describing God's kindness, mercy, and love towards His people (e.g. in vv. 18,19,26), and (b) phrases pointing to the contrast between the people's present suffering, affliction, and want and their hopes for future healing, happiness, and plenty (e.g. vv. 19,20,23–26), we shall find many similarities with passages of hope, encouragement and comfort known to have been written after those disastrous days, e.g. in Isa. 40—66.

The references to what is sometimes called the 'condition(s) for grace', though not identical with later passages, are strikingly similar. Compare for example 30.18, 'the LORD waits to be gracious' [the promise] '...blessed are all those who wait for him' [the condition]; with e.g. 40.31 'they who wait for the LORD' [the condition] 'shall renew their strength; shall not be weary' [the promise]; or 45.22 'turn to me' [the condition] 'and be saved' [the promise]. To 'wait' means to have 'hope' (see notes on 8.16,17 and v. 16 above), and in the Bible this means to believe in God and to trust the promises He has given.

We find this same teaching in the New Testament as well as the Old Testament. According to the Gospels, Jesus himself in several parables emphasized the need to *wait* for good things to come from God (e.g. Matt. 13.24–30; Mark 4.26–29; Luke 13.6–9; and see also Acts 1.1–5; Rom. 8.22–25). Such waiting is not a passive attitude; it requires faith and strength and courage. Many Churches and individual Christians throughout history, and especially today, are striking illustrations of this faith, and of the hope which enables people to continue to work for peace, justice, and human dignity for others as well as for themselves, in spite of disappointments, oppression, and much suffering.

In complete contrast, the theme of the oracles in vv. 27–33 is one familiar to us from the Psalms, that is, the pouring out of God's wrath upon His enemies, who are the enemies of His people, in response to the people's prayers. This Isaiah passage does not in fact contain the word 'enemies' or 'enemy', but many Psalms refer to personal enemies, or to the enemies of the king, or of the Jewish people, or of God. They even express the hope that God will not only defend His people, but destroy and ruin those who are against them. As Christians we may even feel shocked and embarrassed by the fierceness and cruelty of some of the feelings expressed in such Psalms (e.g. Ps. 137.9).

We may compare the attitude shown in 30.27–33 with the attitude towards Judah's traditional enemy Edom in 34.5–15, or that towards Gog and Magog in Ezekiel 39.1–6. This attitude continued on to some extent in later Jewish writings of the last century BC and first century AD, and was eventually reflected in the passages against the 'great city' and the 'great harlot' in Revelation 16.19 and 17.1,15–18.

But, of course, this was not the only way in which Bible writers described the treatment of enemies. As we know, Jesus's teaching on the subject as summarized in Matthew 5.43,44 was very different: 'I say to you, Love your enemies and pray for those who persecute you'. And Paul passed the message on to the Churches: 'If your enemy is hungry, feed him' (Rom. 12.20); 'When reviled, we bless' (1 Cor. 4.12). Some Old Testament writers too, including Isaiah, described a love which overcomes hatred and enmity (see Exod. 23.4,5; Prov. 25.21; Isa. 2.1–4; 42.1–4).

The very harsh and cruel attitudes towards enemies are easier to understand if we remember that most of such passages, in the New Testament as well as in the Old Testament, were spoken or written at times of extreme suffering and want. The conditions which the exiles experienced so affected them that they came to believe that their own enemies and oppressors must also be God's enemies, and as such had no right to live. It was this belief which caused some Jews to become very exclusive – as they have remained to this day, and gave them the idea that anyone thinking differently from themselves must be treated not only as wrong, but as enemies of God. This is not to say that such attitudes and ways of thinking are to be excused, but it may help to explain them.

We may also recognize in these passages some of our own present-day intolerances and prejudices against those we believe to have injured us, or whom we simply think of as 'different' from ourselves (and hence as inferior!). And in present-day situations of great injustice, oppression, and suffering, people's hopes and expectations are likely to include, as a matter of course, the punishment and destruction of the oppressor/ enemy. Only genuine and selfless love can overcome such attitudes and enable us to 'make friends' (Matt. 4.25) rather than enemies.

STUDY SUGGESTIONS

WORD STUDY

1. For each of the words listed (a)–(f) below, find the one from those listed (g)–(l) which is nearest to it in meaning.

   (a) gracious   (g) downward
   (b) affliction   (h) idols
   (c) images   (i) adversity
   (d) wound   (j) hurt
   (e) plenteous   (k) merciful
   (f) descending   (l) abundant

2. (a) Explain what the prophet meant by the word 'waits' as used in v. 18a: 'The LORD *waits* to be gracious.'
   (b) Explain what he meant by the word 'wait' as used in v. 18b: 'Those who wait for him.'

REVIEW OF CONTENT

3. What were the chief differences between Isaiah's ideas about God's 'justice', and the ideas of later writers on the subject?

4. Describe in your own words:
   (a) The 'rich and plenteous' conditions promised to those who 'wait' for God;
   (b) The punishment threatened for the Assyrians when the Lord 'comes from far, burning with his anger'.

5. Which words and phrases in vv. 18–33 suggest that these oracles belong to the period of the Exile, rather than to Isaiah's lifetime?

6. For what reasons would the people 'defile and scatter' their 'graven images' (v. 22)?

7. Who was the 'Teacher' mentioned in v. 20?
8. What do we learn from v. 26 about the relationship between God and His people?

BIBLE STUDY

9. We have seen that v. 18 points to 'the conditions for grace'. What are those conditions according to:
   (a) Paul in Romans 3 (especially 3.19–31)?
   (b) James, according to James 1.12; 2.8–26?
   (c) Jesus, according to Mark 8.34–38?
   What differences are there, if any, between the conditions suggested in these New Testament passages and those described in Isa. 30.18–26?
10. What teaching about the nature of God found in 30.18–33 is also found in Hos. 6.1,2; Ps. 147.2,3?

APPLICATION, OPINION, AND RESEARCH

11. What differences, if any, do you think there are between the 'conditions for grace' described in 30.18–26 and in the New Testament passages studied for Q. 9 above, and those required of Christians in their everyday lives today?
12. How would you answer someone who asked: 'If God's demand for "faith" and "waiting" means that patient endurance of suffering is a condition of grace, why should Christians try to reduce the suffering in the world? Should we not welcome it, for others and for ourselves?'
13. What sort of 'images' or other idols might people who repent and turn back to God in your country today chiefly need to 'scatter' and say 'begone' to?
14. Many people today, even in times of peace, feel that they are confronted by 'enemies', whether at work, in business, or in other circumstances of their daily lives. Describe any such situation you can think of, and the sort of 'enemy-image' people are likely to have in their minds in each case. Do you yourself feel that any individuals or groups of people are your 'enemies', and if so, for what reasons? What is the best way to get rid of such feelings of enmity?

31.1–9
Messages of Threat and Salvation – Part 1

OUTLINE

Chapters 31 and 32 each consist of four separate messages, all set as poetry in the RSV except for 31.6,7.

Vv. 1–3: A 'woe word' and threat by Isaiah against the leaders in Judah and Jerusalem.

Vv. 4,5: A promise that God will bring salvation to Jerusalem.

Vv. 6,7: An exhortation to return to God, probably a later addition.

Vv. 8,9: An oracle against Assyria.

NOTES AND INTERPRETATION

31.1: Woe to those who go down to Egypt for help...rely on horses...trust in chariots: This fifth 'woe' begins in much the same way as chapter 23 (see notes also on 28.16; 31; 30.15). Notice that the word 'trust' here means 'believe in', rather than 'rely on' as in 30.12.

Those who...do not look...or consult the LORD: Compare 30.2: 'Who carry out a plan, but not mine...without asking for my counsel'. Bible writers often used the word 'seek', 'consult', 'ask', to mean worship or pray (see e.g. 1.16,17; 9.13; Amos 5.6: 'Seek the Lord and live').

31.2: 'He is wise and brings disaster': Isaiah and Jeremiah both emphasized that God alone is truly wise, and that He sends disaster to silence political and religious leaders who rely on their own wisdom (see 5.21; 29.14; Jer. 8.8; 9.12). As we have seen, the fact that it is God Himself who 'brings the disaster' (and not merely the enemy who is God's instrument), was an important insight of the prophets. It is expressed in many passages, e.g. Deuteronomy 28.15–24: 'If you will not obey the voice of the LORD...all these curses shall come upon you', and 1 Kings 9.6–9: 'If you...go and serve other gods and worship them, then I will cut off Israel from the land.'

He does not call back his words: The people had already been warned, so God's judgement was inescapable. (Compare 5.25b: 'His anger is not turned away.')

Will rise against: Compare 28.31. Many writers used this phrase as part of a request that God would fight against His people's enemies (e.g. Ps. 3.7). But here 'against' means against the leaders and people of Judah (compare Amos 9.7).

31.3: The Egyptians are men, and not gods...flesh, and not spirit: We must not confuse this statement with passages in the New Testament which contrast flesh and spirit, e.g. Rom. 7.14–25 and 8.1–17. Isaiah was comparing faith and trust in the divine Spirit of God who will not let the people down, with reliance on fallible human helpers. Paul on the other hand was referring to moral values, and the weaknesses which individual people must learn to control in order to do what is right.
When the Lord stretches out his hand: See notes on 1.25. Here the phrase is a threat against Egypt, whom the Israelites now look to as a helper. This time Judah 'who is helped' will perish.

Isaiah was again emphasizing the uselessness of seeking security by military means while neglecting the genuine trust and faith in God essential for true security (see 30.12,15–17). By 'look' and 'consult' (v. 1) Isaiah did not mean formal acts of worship, but an attitude of faith, the lack of which would cause God to 'bring disaster' so that the hoped-for security would crumble like dust (see note on 30.15).

Of course Isaiah could only speak in this way to people who knew God, and who had been taught that all their actions and the actions of their political leaders should be in accordance with the relationship between them and God Himself.

Responsible national leaders in any so-called Christian country, who are concerned with problems of international political and military security, have to face the question whether it is practical in the modern world to try to formulate national policies in accordance with what is understood as God's will. No doubt such leaders do, to some extent, consciously or subconsciously recognize this problem. But many point out that we live in much more complicated situations today than was the case 2,000 or 2,500 years ago. They claim that we cannot possibly apply the principles which the prophets demanded (or which Jesus proclaimed in the Sermon on the Mount), without endangering national safety.

It would certainly be a mistake to try to 'apply' any message or call of Isaiah's directly to our own time. But we have to recognize the *spirit* of what the prophets were talking about and what Jesus was teaching. The clear demand Isaiah was making here, was that people's relationship with God should be the decisive factor in all questions of importance. This applies to individual Christians, just as it does to groups and to the Church as a whole, and it places a heavy responsibility upon us all.
31.4,5: As a lion...like birds hovering...so the LORD...will come down: These verses clearly promise that God will protect Jerusalem. However, the pictures of the lion and the hovering birds are confusing, because elsewhere in the Bible they are used with the opposite meaning. Hosea uses the idea of the lion as a threat that God will 'rend' and 'devour' Israel and Judah (Hos. 5.14; 13.8). And 'shepherds' (v. 4) is used here

not as a symbol of gentle care, but as in Jeremiah 6.3, where it means foreign armies.

The idea of 'coming down' may remind us of the time when God 'came down' to Moses on Sinai (Exod. 19.18–20). That event too was meant for the salvation of Israel. The suggestion that God 'will come down to fight' in this context means 'fight *for* Jerusalem'. However, the prophets often used this phrase as a threat *against* Israel, Judah, and Jerusalem (see especially Jer. 21.5,13; 2 Kings 21.12,13).

The picture of 'birds' to describe God's actions also appears in e.g. Ruth 2.12; Ps. 17.8; Matt. 23.37. The 'hovering' certainly means protection, as parent birds hover over their nests to protect their young from predators.

The use of these various terms, and especially the emphasis on Jerusalem's need for protection, suggest that this message can hardly have been spoken by Isaiah himself. The view expressed in these two verses, that God is offering His people an 'unconditional' act of salvation, is based on what is often called 'popular' theology. This is the idea that 'no matter what happens, or what we do, if Jerusalem is attacked by any enemy, God will save us!' (See Introduction to Chapter 29.) This stands in clear contrast to the reprimand in vv. 1–3, and to Isaiah's implicit demand for faith and obedience as the *condition* for salvation.

31.6,7: Turn to him...for in that day every one shall cast away his idols: See notes on 10.20–24; 19.22; 30.15. 'Turn' here has the same meaning as 'return' in those passages, that is, 'stop rebelling and turning *away* from God to idols' (e.g. 30.1–3,9–13 and see Jer. 4.1,2). These two verses combine Isaiah's familiar demand that people should 'turn' with a promise that there will be an end to the worship of idols, which was considered the most serious sin during the Exile and after. The editor who put this chapter together seems to have taken the 'popular' view of vv. 4,5, and so added an exhortation and expectation of his own. 'Turn to him...' states the obvious condition for salvation, i.e. repentance. And v. 7: 'For in that day...' expresses the expectation of what God will accomplish for His people only in the future. Compare 2.20 where the 'terror of the Lord' and 'glory of his majesty' lead people to overcome their disobedience to God's will.

Both Jeremiah and Ezekiel expressed this same expectation, but in a very broad way as concerning the whole life of the people (Jer. 31.33,34; Ezek. 36.22–28). Here in Isaiah 31 it is narrowed down to idol-worship as the chief sin which will be brought to an end.

Many people today, in so-called Christian countries at any rate, probably think of idol-worship as something practised only by people in undeveloped areas of the world, or by those involved in certain forms of witchcraft. But there are many different sorts of 'idols' in the modern

'Every one shall cast away his idols' (31.6). 'Many different sorts of idols in the modern world may tempt people to turn away from God' (pp. 188, 190).

Poor slum-dwellers in the Philippines gamble away the little money they have, trusting in 'Luck' to bring them a fortune.

Teen-age fans in Britain lavish all their devotion on the star who is this week's 'top of the pops'.

How easy or difficult is it for people to 'cast away' such idols?

world which may tempt people, including Christians, to turn away from God. Some of these are 'objects', like those which the pagan nations in Old Testament times hoped would protect them and bring prosperity. Others are more abstract, such as status or riches, or even *ideas* which people follow blindly rather than seeking to do God's will.

31.9: His rock shall pass away: See notes on 17.10; 26.9; 30.29. Here 'rock' seems to mean security in general.

Desert the standard: See note on 11.10–12. Those who 'desert' are those who run away from the fight and leave the flag behind for the enemy to capture (compare 30.17).

Whose fire is in Zion: See 29.1 and the note on 'Ariel', also 30.33.

These verses continue the theme of v. 7 regarding foreign affairs: God will conquer the enemy – something else which the people could not do for themselves.

We may think it would follow naturally that once the main cause of God's anger was removed, He would not hesitate to help His people (compare 1.16–20; Jer. 4.1,2; also Matt. 5.21–26). However, we must be careful not to assume that God's help can be *bought* in any way. Salvation comes only in God's own time. Even when people recognize that their own sin is the cause of their sufferings, they need to understand for themselves, and to teach their children, that although God's help and blessing is always available to us, we can only receive it when we submit ourselves to His will.

We may notice too that different sorts of sin were assumed to be the cause of God's wrath or displeasure by the people of different times. Isaiah and other earlier prophets pointed to many different sorts of disobedience, including false standards of worship. But they only rarely mentioned 'idols' as such. It was later, after the Exile, when many of the Jews became dispersed, and formed communities outside Palestine, that the pagan religions of the people around them, involving the worship of idols, became a serious cause of temptation for God's people. Being far from Jerusalem they set up their own synagogues in every place. This was often a cause of friction between them and the local people, and the question of 'idols' became a matter of great concern to those who wanted to play a full part in the local community, yet still to remain faithful to the God of Israel.

STUDY SUGGESTIONS

WORD STUDY

1. Explain the meaning of each of the following phrases:
   (a) he does not call back his words (v. 2)
   (b) a sword, not of man (v. 8)
   (c) desert the standard (v. 9)

REVIEW OF CONTENT

2. (a) In what chief ways is Isaiah's accusation against the leaders in Judah in 31.1–3 like or unlike his accusation in 30.1–5?
   (b) What differences are there, if any, between the political and military concerns described in each of these two passages?
3. Who were: (a) 'the helper' who would stumble, and (b) 'he who is helped' who would fall, according to 31.3?
4. What evidence can you find in the Bible text to support each of the following statements?
   (a) 'Isaiah 31.4,5 can hardly have been spoken by Isaiah himself.'
   (b) '31.6,7 is probably a later addition.'
5. Read again 31.4,5, and also 5.26–30 and 15.9—16.4, where the writers use the picture of young lions and of birds to illustrate the subject of their message. Explain the meaning of the message in each case, and say whether it was a promise, a threat, or a lament.

BIBLE STUDY

6. In 31.3 Isaiah contrasted flesh and spirit as a way of describing the difference between relying on human helpers and trusting in God who does not let people down.
   (i) In which of the following passages do the words 'flesh' and 'spirit' describe this same difference between human beings and God?
   (ii) What difference or differences do the words 'flesh' and 'spirit' describe in each of the other passages listed?
   (a) Joel 2.27,28   (b) Mark 14.37,38   (c) Luke 24.36–40
   (d) John 3.5–8   (e) Gal. 5.16,17
7. Isaiah himself and later prophets spoke of 'turning *to*' God and also of 'turning *from*' Him. New Testament writers more often spoke of 'repenting'. What differences, if any, can you see between the ideas of Old Testament writers and those of New Testament writers on this subject, as expressed in the following passages?
   OT: Isa. 30.9–11; 31.6,7; Jer. 17.5,13; Ezek. 33.10–20; Hos. 11.5–7
   NT: Matt. 11.2–24; 12.38–42; Mark 1.4; Luke 5.27–32; 13.1–5; Acts 26.12–18; 1 Peter 2.24,25
8. What is the meaning of 'rock' or 'Rock' in each of the following passages?
   (a) Ps. 40.2   (b) Ps. 42.9   (c) Ps. 89.26   (d) Isa. 8.14,15
   (e) Isa. 17.10   (f) Isa. 22.16   (g) Isa. 30.29   (h) Isa. 31.9
   (i) 1 Cor. 10.4   (j) 1 Peter 2.6–8

9. There are many sorts of 'idols' which tempt people today to 'turn away from' God. But they are not all 'religious' in character. Give examples of three different sorts of 'secular' idols to which people devote themselves today, and say what sort of benefit or protection they expect to receive as a result of their devotion.
10. Isaiah condemned the leaders in Judah who failed to 'consult the Lord' (v. 1). People often try to excuse their failure to obey God's will by saying they don't know how to discover what His will is. How would you answer someone who said: 'How can I obey God's will when I don't know what He wants me to do?'?
11. 'We can have security or we can have freedom: we cannot have both.' How far do you think Isaiah would have agreed with this statement? How far do you agree with it, and why?

32.1–20
Messages of Threat and Salvation – Part 2

OUTLINE

Vv. 1–5: A prophecy about a future time of peace and salvation.
Vv. 6–8: A 'wisdom' saying, contrasting the godless and the righteous.
Vv. 9–13: A message to complacent women, predicting great disaster.
Vv. 15–20: An oracle addressed to 'my people' (v. 18), about a time of salvation to come.

NOTES AND INTERPRETATION

32.1: Behold a king will reign: Many of the prophets, and especially those of the Exile (in Isa. 40—45, Jeremiah and Ezekiel) began their messages 'Behold', in order to draw attention to some special subject, such as the greatness of God and the smallness of 'nations' (40.15), or the idea of the 'Servant' (42.1).
In righteousness...in justice: See notes and interpretation on 9.6,7; 11.4; 16.5; 28.17. Not only are these the qualities of God Himself, they are also qualities which He demands of His people (see e.g. 1.17, Ps. 9.8; 72.1,2; Jer. 4.1,2; Micah 6.8).

32.2: Like a hiding place...a covert...a stream...a shade: This symbolic description of the help and protection God will bring reflects the longing of people who live in countries as arid as Palestine was then, and is even more today.

32.3: The eyes of those who see: Compare 6.9 and 29.9,10. This promise is for the time when the punishment of those who 'did not look' to God (22.11) will be over, and God's chosen King rules.

32.4: The rash...the stammerer: Compare 35.4: 'Those who are of a fearful heart'. In both cases the NEB translation is 'anxious'.

32.5: The fool...the knave: This refers to people who do not *want* to obey God's will (see 5.18–23; Deut. 32.5,6; Ps. 14.1).

Verses 1–5 are very similar to other passages belonging to the period after the Exile. This type of writing is often called 'religious wisdom', and is characteristic of early Judaism. There is much of it in the Book of Job (e.g. 28.12–28), in the Psalms (e.g. Pss. 1; 14; 37), and especially in Proverbs and Ecclesiastes.

Like chapters 9 and 11, these verses refer to the expectation of an ideal King who will reign in righteousness and justice. When we compare passages in the Old Testament referring to the Kingdom or Rule of God as one which will be 'righteous' and 'just', with New Testament passages on the same subject, we may find some differences in the meaning that the writers give to these words.

As here in Isaiah, the Old Testament prophets were clearly talking about the need for right and just social conditions. This was an important expectation among the people up to the time of Christ's coming. But already in Jewish teaching 'righteous' was also used to mean 'obedient to God's Law', since those who truly obey that Law are not likely to oppress their fellow citizens or treat them unjustly.

However, the meanings of words change, or their emphasis does. In the New Testament, added to the idea of justice we find the idea of 'justification'. This means that, through God's grace, sinful people can be *made* 'righteous', that in Christ God will treat them as if they had always obeyed His law – that is, He will *forgive* them (see Rom. 3.19–26). So writers came more and more to use these words with this meaning only. Paul, however, pointed out, as Jesus had done, that those whom God 'justifies' are in duty bound to obey Him (Rom. 6 and see Matt. 5.6,10,20).

This change in the meaning of the word 'righteousness' has caused much misunderstanding between Jews and Christians. There is a traditional saying that: 'If only all Jews would perfectly do God's Will, i.e. observe the teachings of the Torah, for one day, the Kingdom of God would come.' And again, Jews question the Christian claim that God's Kingdom has already come. 'Why then' they ask, 'is there so much injustice everywhere, even in so called Christian countries?'

Righteousness and justice are at the very heart of the biblical expectation of the Kingdom. The picture-language in Isaiah 32.2 emphasizes the people's understanding of these two words, which in many Psalms express the protection and help people hope for when they turn to God.

'The rash' and 'the stammerers' (v. 4) almost certainly meant those whose lack of understanding results in anxiety, rather than people with actual physical disabilities. In either case God will overcome the uncertainty and anxiety of people suffering these handicaps, and mentally weak people will become whole (see 31.24). The people described in v. 5, however, who *consciously* oppose God's will and disobey God's law, will *not* receive his protection. In the Kingdom their stupidity and sin (v. 6) will be shown up, and they will never again be falsely called 'noble' and 'honourable' (see Prov. 19.3; Job 12.4–6).

32.6,7: For the fool speaks folly...plots iniquity: These verses seem to have been added at a later time to explain in greater detail the reasons for what was said in v. 5. They list the evil deeds of the 'fool' and the 'knave' who *intend* to 'practise godlessness' (JB), and actually 'plot' to do evil (GNB, and see 9.17).

Even without the detailed explanation, the use of the words 'fool' and 'knave' side by side shows that 'fool' must here mean someone who is more than just foolish or silly. Like 'knaves', these 'fools' know very well what is right, but choose to do wrong, and are stupid enough to think they can get away with it. They may deceive others, and even themselves, into thinking they are noble and honourable. But they cannot deceive God. This is what Paul meant when he accused the Galatians of falling from grace and failing to 'obey the truth which he had taught them': 'O foolish Galatians!...Having begun with the Spirit, are you now ending with the flesh?...Do not be deceived; God is not mocked' (Gal. 3.1,3; 6.7).

The evil and ungodliness of these fools and knaves are of three main sorts:

(a) They are dishonest and untruthful (v. 6a); NEB translates: 'A liar even to the LORD'; and GNB: 'What he says (is) an insult to the LORD'. (See also 19.13,14: 'Lead astray'.)

(b) They are selfish and uncaring (v. 6b; compare Job 22.5–7).

(c) They are greedy and corrupt (v. 7; compare Amos 2.6–8; Ps. 14.1–6).

32.8: But he who is noble devises noble things: that is, in contrast to the knave, he does his best to obey God's law. The word 'noble' formerly meant people of high birth, leaders, those holding an official position (and in some countries, e.g. Britain, still means people with hereditary titles). But today we chiefly use the word to mean the responsible and unselfish way of life expected of such leaders. In Job 21.28 the 'noble' (translated 'prince' in RSV) is contrasted with the 'wicked', and Old Testament writers continued to use the word 'noble' to describe the way people *ought* to behave (see Prov. 8.12–16; and Prov. 17.26 where it has the same meaning as 'righteous').

The standards of noble behaviour described here are those which God laid down for His people. But this passage shows that His people are not to be identified with any particular human group or nation. Among the Jews themselves, there were both fools and knaves as well as those who were noble. This must mean that the 'people of God' can include everyone who decides to follow God's standards (see Exod. 20.1–20; Matt. 5.1–12).

True religion is expressed in the Bible in very practical terms. It is not merely a 'philosophy', or set of ideas. It is a commitment to *live* and behave in a particular way (see notes on 2.2,3 and 35.8). The Jews of Bible times knew this, and so did the early Christians. And although Paul rejected 'justification' by works alone, he explained in detail the ethical demands which are the visible side of faith.

To understand this we may find it helpful to read the following passages in the order suggested: Rom. 12.19–21; Gal. 5.13–26; James 1 and 2; Matt. 5—7 and then Exod. 20.1–17,23; 23.4–12; and Job 31; Prov. 1—3; Isa. 1.5; Jer. 4.1–4; 7.1–11.

Although these passages are by different writers living at different times and in different situations, their demands agree, and they show very clearly what standards God expects His people to follow. The most comprehensive summary of them is to be found in the Ten Commandments (Exod. 21.17). Paul's list in 1 Corinthians 13, properly understood, in no way contradicts the Commandments, but sums them up as Jesus did when the Scribes asked Him which was the most important of God's commandments. 'The first', He said 'is, "Hear O Israel: The Lord our God, the Lord is One; and you shall love the Lord your God with all your heart, and with all your soul, and with all your mind, and with all your strength." The second is this, "You shall love your neighbour as yourself." There is no other commandment greater than these.' (Mark 12.29–31.) This is what commitment to God is all about.

32.9: Rise up...hear my voice...give ear: These commands, and the fact that they are addressed to women and not to the whole people, mark the beginning of a separate section.

32.10: In little more than a year: The date of the coming event is given as the next harvest time. The prophets did not often give such exact dates (but see Jer. 28.16). Even when they did, their date predictions were not always fulfilled (see e.g. Amos 7 and Jer. 28.11).

32.11–13: Tremble you who are at ease...shudder you complacent ones; strip, and make yourselves bare...Beat upon your breasts for the pleasant fields...for the soil of my people: Compare Nahum 2.7b; Luke 23.48.

As the following verses (12–14) show, this is a warning to those who were so prosperous themselves that they gave no thought to the future or to the poverty of others (vv. 6,7). They should already be in mourning because of the threat to the city and to the country as a whole. Baring part of the body, e.g. the breasts, was a common symbol of mourning, as it still is in some countries today, like the custom of wearing sackcloth. Compare Isaiah's symbolic action as described in 20.2–4, and that of King Hezekiah and his officers in 37.1–3; also 33.9, where the prophet describes the land itself and nature as 'mourning'.

32.14: For the palace will be forsaken: Compare with the description of desolation in 5.17; 13.20–22.

Isaiah and other prophets spoke directly to women on a number of occasions (see e.g. 3.16–26; Ezek. 16; Hosea 2; Amos 4.1–3). Some of these passages are clearly symbolic in meaning, and the 'woman' or 'women' means the inhabitants of Judah or Jerusalem, or God's people as a whole. Some, including the first two we have listed and also 32.9–13, have a double meaning. So the prophets may have been thinking of individual women, but also of the people or nation or city to which they belonged.

The words 'at ease' and 'complacent' may remind us of 3.16—4.1, and are similar to Amos 6.1–6. Both of the Hebrew words thus translated are used in 'political' passages (such as 30.15 and Jer. 30.10) to describe either the attitude the prophet was calling for, or a promised time of peace. But here in 32.9–11 (and in Amos 4.1) they express criticism of uncaring and selfish attitudes, especially concerning social injustice and *wrongful* political activity, i.e. politics without God (see 30.31).

It seems that Isaiah was also criticizing the women of his time for not playing a much more active role in the community. Because they were unconcerned about the welfare of others, they would soon have nothing to do but to mourn 'for the soil of my people...for all the joyless houses...the populous city deserted' (vv. 13,14). He seems to have felt that the women could have done more to save the country from the fate which was looming: the loss of statehood, of freedom and of their own land.

Today too, many peoples are faced with this sort of loss, and may be experiencing much of the suffering described in these verses. This oracle will help us to understand that such suffering is not willed by God, but happens when people *fail* to do God's will. To the people of Israel and Judah especially, 'land' meant much more than just the place where they happened to live. It provided them with their food and their livelihood; to be driven from their land meant certain death (Gen. 4.14). And they also learnt to see their land in a second way; theirs was the land which God had given to their forefathers, and which was now to be taken from them in punishment (see 28.25–28; Lev. 18.25–28; Deut. 5.31,32).

32.15: Until the Spirit is poured upon us: The RSV and NEB both show the beginning of v. 15 as a direct continuation from v. 14, but 'until' actually begins a new section. A later writer has followed up the prediction of disaster and the call for mourning with a word of comfort, and a promise of peace to come when God's Spirit is poured from on high (compare 29.13–21; Ezek. 39.29; Joel 2.28,29).

32.19: And the forest will utterly go down, and the city: Some readers may find this verse puzzling as it follows directly upon the description of the restoration of the people to peace and 'secure dwellings'. But we may compare it with 25.1–5 which, as we saw, combines thanksgiving for God's help with praise for His destruction of the enemy. As 'forests' and 'city' are used in the same way in both parts of the verse, they probably mean the same thing, i.e. an enemy, in both cases.

32.20: Happy are you…: The people to whom vv. 15–20 are addressed are being congratulated, so they cannot be the same as those addressed in vv. 9–14. The link-word 'until' in v. 15 indicates that the wilderness described in vv. 9–14 will become a fruitful field only at a later time, when God's promise of salvation through righteousness and justice is fulfilled.

In vv. 17,18 ideas expressed by Isaiah himself (e.g. in 30.15) have been combined with later ones in which the words 'quietness' and 'trust' are used to describe peace as the effect or result of righteousness. In 30.15 Isaiah said that people must *actively* cultivate those attitudes and qualities within themselves in order to preserve peace. Here in 32.17 the words have a more *passive* meaning: The people will *experience* 'quietness and trust' when the Lord gives it to them. This suggests that the writer was probably familiar with Isaiah's words, but in his own time and situation they meant something different to him.

The same is true of the words 'righteousness' and 'justice'. In this passage they are not meant as general moral values, but rather as standards which people can achieve by *living* in accordance with God's will. They may even be used instead of the word '*Torah*', e.g. in v. 16, where 'justice' translates the Hebrew word translated as 'ordinances' in Deut. 6.1 and Ps. 19.7–9. Similarly, the words 'effect' and 'result' (v. 17) mean 'work' or 'deeds'. The Torah has to be acted upon, obeyed; this is the only way in which peace can be achieved.

This whole way of thinking about God's purpose and promise for His people was developed during and after the Exile, and was the beginning of what is now called 'Judaism', the religion of the Jews.

The promise in v. 18 is related to the promises about the future King (see 32.1). In Deuteronomy the word 'rest' refers to the time in history when the Israelites received their land (see Deut 12.9 and 25.19, where it is part of a promise, and Deut. 33.28 where the promise is fulfilled). Here in Isaiah 32.1 and 32.18 it refers to the *hope* of a people who were no longer in 'secure dwellings', but in constant danger and fear.

These and other promises may lead us to wonder how far this sort of religious hope is based upon faith, or whether it simply arises from the experience of insecurity and frustration. But we should note that the writer formulated this particular verse as a word from God Himself: '*My* people...'. This must mean that he at least saw such hope as an act of trust in God.

In v. 20 it is not very clear who was being congratulated.

(a) Was it the Jewish community exiled in Babylon (see Jer. 51.13)? Jeremiah encouraged the exiles to settle down and not think of an early return to Palestine (Jer. 29.4–7). And Babylon certainly had 'fruitful fields' and plenty of 'waters', as it was situated on the River Euphrates. In fact, for many centuries it was the most important centre of Jewish culture and religious learning outside Palestine.

(b) Or was the congratulation meant for the people who would be living in the future time of salvation? 'Waters' may simply indicate blessings and a fruitful, prosperous country (e.g. as used in 30.25; Pss. 65.9–13; 104.14–16). But water was also used by Bible writers as a symbol for the renewal of life which comes through doing God's will (see Ps. 1.3; Jer. 17.8; John 4.14).

STUDY SUGGESTIONS

WORD STUDY

1. Explain the meanings of the words 'quiet' and 'quietness' as used in 32.17–18. What are the meanings of these words as used in each of the following passages?
   (a) 7.4 (b) 14.7 (c) 18.4 (d) 30.15 (e) 33.20

REVIEW OF CONTENT

2. What evidence can you find in the Bible text to support the statement that 32.6–8 seems to have been added at a later time?
3. Who were:
   (a) those who 'see' and those who 'hear' (v. 3)?
   (b) the 'rash' and the 'stammerers' (v. 4)?
   (c) 'us' (v. 15)?
4. Compare and contrast Isaiah's criticism and warning to women in 32.9–13 with those in 3.16—4.1. What particular groups of women was he addressing in each case?
5. What were the chief characteristics of the 'restored' land, as described in chapter 32?

6. Summarize the messages addressed to women in each of the following passages. In what ways, if any, are they like Isaiah's message in 32.9–14?
   (a) Jer. 9.20   (b) Ezek. 13.17–23   (c) Amos 4.1–3

APPLICATION, OPINION, AND RESEARCH
7. Some readers of 32.1,2 say that the prophet was describing an 'impossible dreamland' which no government could ever bring into being. Does this mean that we should give up all efforts to change and improve society so as to come nearer to such an ideal? If not, what can either the Churches or individual Christians do to help achieve it?
8. Isaiah criticized the women of Jerusalem for their uncaring and selfish attitudes. Do you think women generally are more, or less, 'uncaring and selfish' than men are, in regard to questions of social justice, poverty, etc.? Some people say that women fail to play a more active role in the community only because men will not allow them to do so. What is your opinion?

33.1–24
Present Destruction and Future Deliverance

INTRODUCTION

Not only the five books of the Torah (Genesis to Deuteronomy), but most of the Old Testament Scriptures were read aloud in the Temple worship services. The form of many of the Psalms shows that they were written for singing, and parts of the prophetic books have been arranged in such a way as to make them suitable for use in worship. Because chapter 33 seems to fall into two parts, vv. 1–6 and 7–24, each following what could be an order of worship, some scholars think it consists of two ancient 'liturgies' put together, with some added material at the end. Others, however, see in it just a collection of prayers, oracles, and thanksgivings with no particular pattern to it.

OUTLINE

V. 1: A 'woe word' and curse against a treacherous oppressor or enemy.
V. 2: A prayer for salvation.
Vv. 3,4: An oracle about the 'peoples'.
Vv. 5,6: A hymn praising the Lord for His care for Zion and her people.
Vv. 7–9: A lament for people who suffer, and for their land.
Vv. 10–13: An oracle in which the Lord declares His forthcoming act of judgement and deliverance.
Vv. 14–16: A dialogue describing the distress to come and what the faithful must do in order to survive.
Vv. 17–22: An oracle proclaiming that the Lord will be King in Jerusalem.
Vv. 23,24: Three additional sentences which seem to belong to vv. 21,1, and 20 respectively.

NOTES AND INTERPRETATION

33.1: Woe to you, destroyer...you treacherous one...you will be destroyed: This sixth 'woe complex' does not name the cruel and deceitful oppressor who stands condemned. Perhaps the Babylonian conqueror is meant, suggesting that the passage is of later date, rather than the corrupt exploiters in Judah whom Isaiah himself chiefly accused. The accusation is followed by a prediction that the destroyer will be paid back in his own coin (compare Hab. 2.5–8). Notice the typically poetic form of this verse, the prediction in the second half being an exact parallel with the accusation in the first.

33.2: O LORD be gracious to us...be our arm every morning...our salvation in the time of trouble: This is the petition of people who have suffered much from their enemies (compare e.g. Ps. 123.3; Lam. 3.19–23). For 'arm' see notes on 9.12; 30.30; here the meaning is obviously 'protection'. 'Every morning': the emphasis is on continuance; i.e. protection *always*, though it also carries the idea of hope and renewal (see note on 21.11,12 and compare e.g. 2 Kings 3.20; Exod. 14.24). Early morning was a good time for defeating an enemy by surprise attack, and many ancient peoples believed dawn to be a special time of divine activity. (It was probably this which led to the practice of early morning prayer.)

33.3,4: Thunderous noise...the lifting up of thyself: See note on 17.12,13 and compare 29.1–4. For 'the lifting up', which is set as a parallel for the 'noise', NEB has 'thunder' and 'rumbling', the traditional terms for God's 'voice' (see Ps. 29).

33.4: Spoil is gathered: See notes on 8.4; 10.6. Those who had suffered so much 'despoiling' would enjoy plundering their enemies (see e.g. Exod. 3.21,22).

33.4: As the caterpillar gathers, the locust leaps: This description of the looting to come would have been specially vivid for people only too familiar with the devastation of their crops by such insect plagues.

33.5,6: The LORD is exalted...he will be the stability of your times...the fear of the LORD is his treasure: This brief hymn of praise concludes the first 'liturgy'. Many such hymns are included among the Psalms. The Hebrew of v. 6 is uncertain and the varying translations are confusing. The NIV has 'he will be the sure foundation...the fear of the LORD is the key of this treasure', i.e. to the 'abundance' of salvation, wisdom, and knowledge. This is probably the clearest, as emphasizing God's steadfast love, and the 'fear', or 'reverence' (GNB), which should be our response to it.

Compare 11.2, which shows the close link between this sort of 'fear' and the 'knowledge' of God (see notes on 5.12; 8.12; 11.2; and also Hos. 2.20; and 3.5).

33.7,8: The valiant ones cry without...envoys of peace weep...covenants are broken: Words of great sadness introduce the lament in vv. 7–9. The Hebrew word translated 'valiant ones' in RSV is uncertain, and JB has 'Ariel', suggesting it means the inhabitants of Jerusalem (see notes on 29.1,2). But this hardly agrees with 'envoys of peace', which seems to relate the whole lament to a war-time situation. 'Without' means 'outside', and v. 8 certainly describes the disruption and destruction caused by war, at least for the losers. 'Covenants' probably refers to broken treaties (see NEB, JB, NIV), though it can also mean social and inter-personal relationships.

33.9: The land mourns and languishes...Lebanon...Sharon...Bashan... Carmel: A further description of the devastation war brings. Compare 22.2–5 and especially 24.4, and see note on 2.12–14. Bashan was also noted for its fat cattle (Ps. 22.12; Amos 4.1), and Carmel and Sharon as well as Lebanon for their rich vegetation and forests, now destroyed.

33.10: 'I will arise' says the LORD: The oracle in vv. 10–13 is introduced with words reported as being spoken by God Himself: '*I* will arise'. Priests as well as prophets often used the formula 'Thus says the Lord' or similar phrases when speaking to the people. In the Temple worship also, the priest or prophet would announce God's answer to people's prayers and petitions with what is often called an 'oracle of salvation' in this form. The same form of words was used for many of the oracles of the prophet of the Exile, e.g. Isa. 45.1,2: 'Thus says the LORD..."I will go before you"'; 49.22: 'Thus says the LORD..."I will lift up my hand"'. Some of Isaiah's early messages, too, were reported in this way, see e.g. 1.24: 'I will vent my wrath'; but those were reprimands and threats against Israel and Judah.

33.11,12: You conceive chaff...your breath is a fire: Translations of this verse vary as to detail, but the general meaning of accusation and threat against God's enemies, 'far and near', is clear.

33.12: Burned to lime: This means 'burned completely', i.e. finished forever. Compare Amos 2.1, where the punishment for burning the King of Edom's bones was death. At that time some peoples believed that the spirit of a dead person lived on in the corpse, so that to destroy the bones was to destroy the spirit also – as people in some parts of the world still believe today. Most Christians, too, believe that the bodies of the dead should be allowed to rest in peace, though cremation is becoming the custom in many countries today.

33.13: Hear, you who are far off...what I have done; and you who are near: In the RSV v. 13 is set as the start of a new section, but the reference to 'what I have done' suggests that it is the conclusion of the preceding oracle (as set in JB). As such it may be interpreted as a 'call to the nation'. In Isaiah 40—66, we find many similar calls addressed to the exiled Israelites 'far off' in Babylon, so the oracle in vv. 10–13 may have been intended to comfort and give new hope both to the defeated who remained in Judah and Israel under alien rule, and also to the exiles (compare 26.16–21; 49.1–4).

33.14: The sinners in Zion are afraid...who among us can dwell with the devouring fire?...He who walks righteously...he will dwell on the heights: This short section seems clearly to be arranged for worship. God is not the speaker, but His action upon Zion is described as fire (meaning the same as 'Ariel' in 29.1). In a time of fear, worshippers ask: 'Who can survive the judgement and the punishment He sends?' And the answer (given by priest or prophet) is both teaching and promise: The righteous, those who are honest and just; they will 'dwell on the heights', that is, with God (see note on 2.2).

This passage strongly resembles some of the Psalms, especially Pss. 15 and 24.3–6, which are sometimes called 'entrance liturgies', because they are thought to have been recited as people entered the Temple area. They may also have been used as a sort of short 'catechism' or summary of the law, rather like the Ten Commandments.

33.16: Place of defence...fortresses of rocks...bread...water: These are all symbols of the 'salvation' promised for the righteous and upright who 'fear' and obey God: safety with Him in His Holy Place, a plentiful harvest, and a year-long water supply – a special blessing in a country like Palestine where many streams flow only after rain (see notes on 17.10; 30.23–26).

33.17: Your eyes will see the king in his beauty: vv. 21 and 22 indicate that this oracle is about God as King. If v. 17 is taken literally this raises again the whole question of whether God *can* be seen by human eyes (see notes on 6.1,5). Some Bible passages do suggest that God can be seen (e.g. Exod. 24.10,11; Pss. 11.7; 17.15); but those in the Psalms may refer to dramatic presentations in the Temple by priests wearing masks. Some scholars consider that this oracle carries on the promise of the *ideal* king who will come to rule God's people as His vice-regent (see notes on 9.6,7). In any case, these verses are not concerned with a 'theophany' or visionary experience of God in worship, but with the 'day' of God's final judgement and His rule over the world (see Rev. 22.3,4).

33.18,19: Your mind will muse on the terror: 'Where is he who counted...weighed the tribute?'...You will see no more the insolent people...of an obscure speech: Here again, as in vv. 14,15, the people, remembering the time of fear, ask the question which interrupts the recital of the Lord's action 'What has become of our overlords?' And the answer comes, describing what God has done: The occupying forces of Babylon with their foreign speech and alien religion have gone; God's people can return to the way He prepared for them.

33.20,21: A quiet habitation...immovable...a place of broad rivers and streams, where no galley can go, nor stately ship can pass: – that is, no hostile ships – a symbolic promise of safety and salvation (compare vv. 6 and 16 and see 32.17,18). Actual ships cannot have been meant as threatening to Jerusalem!

33.22: The LORD is our judge...ruler...king; he will save us: Further details reminding the people of their relationship with God by using traditional titles for Him (compare e.g. Judges 11.27; Pss. 94.2; 95.3; 103.19).

33.23,24: Your tackle...cannot hold the mast firm...spoil will be divided...the people will be forgiven: As noted in the Outline above, the content of these two verses does not hang together, but seems to have been added to provide extra detail for earlier verses: v. 23a for the reference to ships in v. 21; v. 23b about looting for v. 1 (or possibly v. 4?); and v. 24 perhaps for v. 20, describing the place where God rules (see e.g. 35.5; 65.18–23).

We have already noted the harsh and cruel attitude towards enemies expressed in 30.27–33 (p. 183). The same element of hate is very strong in 33.1–16, and for the same reason. The writer's experience of reality was of a powerful and successful enemy who had destroyed the nation and deceived the people. In pointing to the future destruction and betrayal of that enemy, he was merely confirming the popular idea of 'justice' as expressed in the Torah: 'As he has done it shall be done to him: eye for eye, tooth for tooth' (Lev. 24.19,20; Deut. 19.21 adds 'life for life').

Some Old Testament writers rejected such an attitude of revenge (see Exod. 23.4,5; Job 31.29,30). The Book of Jonah teaches that God will be merciful even towards the Assyrians. And the earlier prophets, including Isaiah at the start of his ministry, taught that enemy attacks were to be seen as evidence of God's wrath and as the instruments of God's will (see Isa. 10.5; 51.17–20). But even though Jesus and the

New Testament writers condemned the idea of revenge, and preached forgiveness of enemies, people in general had – and still have! – great difficulty in overcoming the idea that 'an enemy is an enemy', and always to be treated as such.

One difficulty about the second liturgical sequence (if it is one) in vv. 7–33 is that it is not always clear who the words are addressed to. It starts, as the first one did, with the writer's experience of a nation in defeat. The roads are dangerous, travel is disrupted, the countryside devastated, administration of the law has broken down. But here there is no threat or curse against the destroyers. Indeed there was no need for threats, since the next few verses suggest that the enemies will, as it were, destroy themselves ('as if burned to lime').

Then, in the dialogue passages, the terrified people ask: 'Who will survive this holocaust, and how?' And the answer, both for those who remained in Jerusalem and those in exile, was the answer which Jesus gave to the man who asked what he must do to 'inherit eternal life'. 'You must obey God's law – stop running after money and turn to me'; then your enemies will melt away, you will have 'treasure in heaven' (see Mark 10.17–21). Or, as the prophet put it: 'you will see the king in his beauty...you will see Jerusalem...there the LORD in majesty will be for us...he will save us (33.17,20,21 and see Jer. 7.5–7; Ezek. 18.5–9).

This whole passage deals with the question of salvation – of 'justification': is it by 'works' or by 'faith'? Jesus in the passage we have quoted told the man what he must *do*. But on other occasions He emphasized the importance of *faith*: 'Whatever you ask in prayer, *believe* that you have received it, and it will be yours' (Mark 11.24). And when Paul was asked the same question by his jailer at Philippi: 'What must I do to be saved?' he told him simply to have faith: '*Believe* in the Lord Jesus' (Acts 16.25–34). In his letter to the Romans Paul discussed this whole question of faith and works more fully: 'No human being will be justified by works of the law...since all fall short of the glory of God, they are justified by his grace as a gift'. And 'a man is justified by faith apart from works of law...do we then overthrow the law?...on the contrary we uphold the law' (see Rom. 3.9–31).

There is no real contradiction here. What Paul was talking about, and what Isaiah 33.14–22 is about, is the *continuing* relationship between God and His people. The Israelites were *already* God's people (see Exod. 22), and this passage, like many others, is a call to them to 'return'. Their 'fear and trembling' were both the basis of their obedience and faith in God, and also the consequence of their sin which would make them seek Him again. And the 'works' described in 33.15 are not the 'conditions for salvation', but, as we saw in 32.6–8, the visible signs or *results* of faith. God's people had thought they could show their faith by their many religious observances – 'sacrifices...solemn assembly...

appointed feasts' (see 1.11–14). But the signs of a proper relationship with God are proper relationships with other people. When the Scribe responded to Jesus's summary of the Law by saying that to love one's neighbour is much more than burnt offerings and sacrifices, Jesus told him 'you are not far from the Kingdom of Heaven' (see Mark 12.28–34). In 33.17–22 the prophet was not only describing the eventual physical 'return' of the exiles – the 'remnant' – to Jerusalem. He was sharing his vision of what God offers to all who return to a right relationship with Him: a time when God's glory, peace, and security will replace the fear and trembling. That is, the healing, forgiveness, and 'salvation' of the Kingdom of Heaven. And this is not something we can achieve for ourselves by our faith or our works alone, though it is only when we turn or return to God that we are able to receive the grace which He offers.

STUDY SUGGESTIONS

WORD STUDY

1. What is meant by each of the following phrases as used in chapter 33?
   (a) be our arm   (b) the lifting up of thyself
   (c) the stability of our times   (d) burned to lime
   (e) fortresses of rocks   (f) an obscure speech.

REVIEW OF CONTENT

2. For what reason do some scholars suggest that chapter 33 is based on two liturgies or 'orders of service' as used in worship?
3. What was the chief message of 33.1–6?
4. In what chief way do vv. 7–9 resemble v. 1? In what chief way are they different?
5. Why did the prophet refer particularly to the places mentioned in v. 9?
6. Who were (a) those who were 'far off', and (b) those who were 'near', whom the prophet was addressing in v. 13?
7. What were the six qualities or attitudes which the prophet listed as necessary in order to live through ('dwell with') and survive the sufferings which the Israelites were experiencing?
8. Who were the 'insolent people' and what did they 'count' and 'weigh' (vv. 18,19)?
9. What did the prophet mean by saying that the Lord would 'be' the place of broad rivers and streams (v. 21)?

BIBLE STUDY

10. Compare 33.10–12 with the following passages. To whom were these passages addressed, why were these words spoken to them, and in what circumstances?
    (a) 1.28–31 (b) 5.24 (c) 9.19 (d) Hos. 13.2,3
    (e) Mark 9.43 (f) 1 Cor. 3.10–15

11. What do the following passages describe? Compare them with 33.15 and with Exod. 20.13–17. In what chief ways do any of these passages differ from 33.15, and what conclusions, if any, do you draw from your study of them?
    Pss. 15; 24; 50.16–20; Isa. 58.6,7; Rom. 13.8,9

12. What do the following passages have in common with 33.2?
    Pss. 7.6–8; 44.23–27; 123.2; Lam. 3.19–23

APPLICATION, OPINION, AND RESEARCH

13. In this chapter the writer uses many traditional ideas and sayings to describe situations and express emotions; for example, 'thunder' for the noise of battle, 'caterpillars and locusts' for looters, etc. Throughout history writers, artists, musicians, and architects have used traditional forms of expression to communicate religious ideas and messages.
    (a) Give examples of some of the ways in which Churches in your country have used traditional art-forms of earlier times to communicate the gospel, and consider what further use might be made of them.
    (b) What traditional ideas, if any, would you use in your country today to describe the situations and emotions found in chapter 33?

14. The main themes of chapter 33 are the experience of suffering and the hope of future relief. What are the chief causes of suffering in your country today from 'acts of God' (i.e. natural disasters), human carelessness, intentional human action? What organizations exist to prevent such suffering? Suggest any further realistic ways to prevent or reduce that suffering.

15. Consider how the hopes and expectations of the Jews for a better future arose out of their experience of suffering in exile, and compare them with the hopes and expectations of different groups of people today. How far do you think their hopes are likely to be fulfilled?

16. 'Actual ships cannot have been meant as threatening to Jerusalem!' (p. 203). Draw a rough sketch map to show why not.

34.1–17
'Judgement upon Edom'

INTRODUCTION

Chapters 34 and 35 together read like a collection of apocalyptic messages. They contain many familiar thoughts and expressions, not only from earlier chapters in Isaiah, but which also echo chapters 40—66 and Jeremiah and Ezekiel. So it seems clear that the writer lived and wrote at a much later time than those from whom he borrowed (see Special Note 2).

This writer and the people for whom he wrote were probably looking forward to the time when God would execute judgement over the peoples whom they had regarded as their enemies, of whom Edom was one of the most feared (34.5,9 and see 63.1). But this judgement was only the prelude or introduction to a much more important event: the coming of God's rule.

Some scholars suggest that this unknown writer was experiencing the defeat of Edom by the Nabateans, an Arabian tribe who had settled on Edom's eastern border around or before 350 BC. Chapter 35 could thus be a description of his expectation of a great reversal of past historical experiences, and the renewal and restoration of peace which would result.

OUTLINE

Vv. 1–4: The nations are called as witnesses; God's judgement is announced.
Vv. 5–8: The judgement is upon Edom; Zion will be avenged.
Vv. 9–12: Consequences of the judgement for Edom's countryside.
Vv. 13–15: Consequences for Edom's fortified places.
Vv. 16,17: This judgement had already been announced and recorded in the 'book of the Lord'.

NOTES AND INTERPRETATION

34.1: Draw near, O nations: Compare 31.1,2 with 1.2–4, but notice that, unlike chapter 1, chapter 34 contains no accusation against those who are called to hear.
34.2: The LORD is enraged against all the nations...He has doomed them: Verses 1–4 are addressed to 'all the nations', and seem to form a

'The Lord is enraged against all the nations...he has a day of vengeance...its smoke shall go up for ever' (34.2,8).

After an earthquake in Venezuela a father searches for his missing children among the rubble that was his home.

Are such 'natural' disasters always a sign of God's vengeance upon those who suffer? If not, how should we regard them?

separate oracle predicting a day of general judgement against all nations (compare 26.20,21).

34.3,4: The mountains shall flow with their blood...the host of heaven shall rot...the skies roll up: The language of these verses is like that of the 'apocalyptic' writers, predicting cataclysm and ruin (compare Isa. 24.21–23a; Ezek. 39.4,5; Joel 2.31; Matt. 24.29; Rev. 6.12–17).

34.5: For my sword has drunk its fill...behold it descends upon Edom: NEB has 'the sword of the Lord appears', which translates the version of the Book of Isaiah found in the Dead Sea Scroll. This makes more sense than the traditional version in RSV, because 'appear' leads on to 'behold'.

34.5,6: The Lord has a sword...sated with blood...of lambs and goats...a sacrifice in Bozrah...great slaughter in Edom: In this gruesome passage the writer describes the destruction of Edom (where Bozrah was an important town) as if it were a sacrificial feast, with the burning of 'devotional' objects and slaughter of animals on the altar. It echoes similar passages in Deuteronomy 13.15–17 and 32.41,42.

34.8: A day of vengeance...of recompense for the cause of Zion: The destruction of Edom would be a just revenge or 'pay-back' for the earlier destruction which Edom and other enemies caused to the armies and people of Jerusalem. It seems that having started this chapter with an oracle about the fate of Israel's opponents generally, the writer went on to use the defeat of Edom as an example of what would happen to the other nations as well.

34.9: The streams shall be turned into pitch...her land become burning pitch: This may simply be a way of describing the blood and stench of unburied or burning bodies. However, burning oily substances such as pitch or tar did sometimes 'erupt' from the ground during earthquakes in parts of the Near East. This may be the background to the story in Genesis 19, and writers may well have used such frightening occurrences to describe the ultimate disaster of God's judgement upon His enemies, rather as we use such terms as 'holocaust' and 'devastation' to describe the effects of nuclear warfare today.

34.11: Her land shall lie waste...the hawk and the porcupine shall possess it: Compare NEB, JB, etc. The different English versions give varying translations of the Hebrew names of wild animals and birds mentioned here and in vv. 13–15, who would come to live in the ruined cities and take possession of the land devastated by war.

He shall stretch the line of confusion over it, and the plummet of chaos over its nobles: Compare 2 Kings 21.13; Amos 7.7–9; and also Isa. 28.17. The plumb-line used to measure the straightness of a building would also show the extent of its crookedness, or fitness for destruction.

34.12: They shall name it No Kingdom There: The RSV translation of this verse resembles Hosea 1.9. The NEB, JB, and NIV translations are less symbolic in their language. In any case it is clear that the reference is to the members of the royal family and other leaders in Edom.

34.13: Thorns shall grow over its strongholds, nettles and thistles...there the satyr shall cry...the night hag alight: Compare 7.23–25; 32.13, and other English versions, and see note on v. 11 above. The RSV translation suggests that in addition to wild animals, the devastated land would be haunted by 'demons' and nature gods or spirits either good or evil. This idea may well have been in the writer's mind, as referring to popular belief at the time, just as today we might fancifully refer to 'goblins' or 'witches'.

34.16: Seek and read from the book of the LORD...for the mouth of the LORD has commanded: This probably refers to a book or collection of oracles known by the people for whom this writer wrote – possibly even an earlier version of the Book of Isaiah (see 13.20–22). But it was usual for prophetic oracles to be introduced and/or concluded with some such formula, e.g. 'the Lord has spoken', 'therefore the Lord says...'. So it may mean any prophetic book.

34.17: He has cast the lot: The casting or drawing of 'lots' was often used in order to reach a decision by chance, just as we today toss a coin, use a computer, or draw a longer or shorter straw. It was also used officially in allocating land (see Josh. 18.8–10; Mark 15.24), and here means that God would reallocate the land which had been laid waste, and give it over to wild birds and animals instead of human beings.

The ideas in chapter 34 (and also 35) clearly belong to times when people no longer remembered the concerns of the earlier prophets very well, chiefly because the political situation in Palestine had changed.

As we have seen, the earlier prophets usually directed their accusations against Israel or Judah, and other nations were thought of as 'witnesses'. Here it seems that the other nations themselves are to be judged. The earlier prophets had aimed to awaken the conscience of God's people and persuade them to 'return' to Him. But now that Israel and Judah were vassal states, unable to decide their own policies, the preachers of Judaism were mainly concerned to comfort them. These later writers no longer saw their suffering as punishment from God which they justly deserved in spite of its harshness. Now they saw it as due only to the hatred of the enemy, so that now under God's 'justice' their enemies would be punished instead (pp. 114, 203).

In fact it was probably during this period of suffering, when Israel and Judah no longer existed as independent states, that the idea of Israel as the 'chosen people' of God was born. This may seem puzzling, but over many centuries their leaders, the priests and the prophets, had spoken to the Jewish people and admonished them in ways which suggested they had a special relationship with God. Hosea, for example, had described it first as that of man and wife, and later of father and child (see e.g. Hos. 2.16; 11.1). This seemed quite natural: only the Israelites knew Yahweh. He was the God of their nation, and they were not allowed to 'know', that is, to love and obey, any other God but Him (Exod. 20.1–6). And as they came to understand that there was indeed only one God, they still believed that they alone had this special relationship with Him (Deut. 4.32–39).

Some prophets thought rather differently, e.g. Amos saw God as leading other nations too, and admonished them in the same way as Israel and Judah (see Amos chapters 1 and 2 and 9.7,8). If the Israelites claimed a special relationship, he said, they must expect a special punishment.

At all events, after the Jews had lost everything else, they were determined to hold on to their relationship with God in any way they possibly could. At that time their claim to be God's people had no racist intentions; it was (as it still is) a solemn confession that there is one God only, and they want to be His people forever.

All this is why in 34.5–15, as in 30.27–33, more than merely human feelings of vengeance against a human enemy are expressed. First there is the strong sense of justice imbued in the Jews over a long period. They now turned the prophets' accusations against others who had done wrong. Secondly, there is the remarkable world-view shown here and by other Bible writers of that time, a world-view based on hope, and on the belief that God will not leave the world to its evil fate. These writers were convinced that one day the world will again be as God originally intended it, that all evil will be overcome and God will cause 'a new heaven and a new earth' to come about (Rev. 21.1). How could this not be the will of God for His creation?

Instead of sympathizing with Judah and Israel at the time of the Babylonian attack on Jerusalem, when the city and Temple were destroyed and the leaders and craftsmen were deported, Edom and other neighbouring small nations showed only hostility and greed. So when Edom's turn came to suffer, the Jews could not help seeing it as a punishment from God (see especially Obad. 10–14).

It may seem that the Bible writers of this time and later, such as Daniel, Ezra, and Nehemiah, were concerned only with the sufferings of the Jews, and made little of those of the surrounding nations. But they were of course writing for the Jews, and not for other readers. And the Jews did suffer very greatly during the power struggles of the great nations: Persia, Greece, and Egypt, and later Rome.

In fact, since the days of the Exile until the founding of the State of Israel in 1948, the Jews have been more or less in constant suffering of one sort or another. Sometimes things went well for a while, but again and again they were persecuted, in Spain, in Central Europe, before and during the Crusades, in Eastern Europe and in Russia, and finally during the 12 years of Nazi terror, so that they had to seek refuge elsewhere. But even 2,000 years, and more, of rootlessness and suffering has not destroyed their belief that God will one day found His kingdom of justice and tolerance for them. This explains why the Jews just want to be themselves and nothing else, and why sometimes they seem to be a little too sensitive. Christians especially have an important lesson to learn from this: that 'tolerance' may be the most challenging way for Christian love to express itself.

At no other time in history has the problem of 'minority groups' been such a burning issue as it is today. Oppression and prejudice against refugees, immigrants of other races and other religions, migrant workers, indeed anyone regarded as 'different', is a sad fact in many so called 'Christian' countries. Until recent times, and in some places even now, it has been difficult for Christian minorities, such as Roman Catholics in chiefly Protestant areas or vice-versa, to lead their lives on an equal footing with the majority of the people, in countries like Spain, Austria, and some parts of Central Europe and Latin America. We have still to learn that God's love demands of us 'inclusiveness', rather than 'exclusiveness' in *every* area of human life.

STUDY SUGGESTIONS

WORD STUDY

1. What are the possible meanings of the following?
   (a) host of heaven (v. 4)   (b) pitch (v. 9)
   (c) satyr (v. 14)   (d) night hag (v. 14)
2. What did the prophet mean when he said that the Lord would stretch the 'line of confusion' and the 'plummet of chaos' over the land of Edom?

REVIEW OF CONTENT

3. What events are described in chapter 34, and what possible date has been suggested for them?
4. The reference to lambs, goats, and rams in vv. 5–7 is not about the killing of farm animals in war. What is it about, and what has it to do with the destruction of Edom?
5. What more do we find in vv. 1–5 than 'merely human feelings of vengeance against a human enemy'?

BIBLE STUDY

6. Compare 34.5–7 with Deut. 32.39–42 and Jer. 46.7–12. What are the chief differences between these passages, e.g. who is addressed

in each one, what are the accusations against them, and what action did God take?
7. What do the following passages tell us about 'the book of the Lord' as described in 34.16, and what was in it?
Isa. 1.20; 40.5; Deut. 28.58,59; 30.9,10; 31.24–26; Josh. 1.8; 2 Kings 22.8–13

APPLICATION, OPINION, AND RESEARCH

8. Chapter 34 describes in detail the condition of a country after being devastated by war in Old Testament times. How far would this description fit a country devastated by war today? What other conditions might be found in such a country today?
9. 34.11 refers to 'the cause of Zion'. 2,000 years of suffering have not destroyed the Jewish people's belief that God will one day establish His kingdom of justice and tolerance for them, and tolerance may be the most challenging way for Christian love to express itself. What is the attitude of Christians in your country to Jews? to other minority groups? What practical steps can Christians take to overcome any prejudices they may have against people of other races or nationalities or interests than their own?

35.1–10
The 'Holy Way'

OUTLINE

Vv. 1–4: Prediction of a great reversal of Zion's fortunes; God will avenge and comfort those who are without hope.
Vv. 5–7: Prediction of the healing of the people and the regeneration of nature which will result.
Vv. 8–10: Prediction of the 'Holy Way', leading in safety to Zion.

NOTES AND INTERPRETATION

35.1,2: The wilderness and the dry land shall be glad...the desert blossom...the glory of Lebanon...be given to it: In most apocalyptic writings there are two main themes: judgement and salvation. Here chapter 34 has described the judgement; now chapter 35 describes the contrasting salvation. The contrast does not however refer to the same country: 34 was about Edom, 35 is about Israel/Judah. Compare in chapter 25 the contrast between salvation for 'this mountain' i.e. Judah (vv. 6–9), and judgement upon Moab, the enemy who would be 'trodden down' (v. 10).

Many of the teachers of 'wisdom' in Old Testament times wrote in this way, contrasting the fate of the just and that of the wicked (see e.g. Pss. 1; 9.5–10; Prov. 10.28,29). Many passages in Isaiah 40—55 express the idea that God can and will change barren desert or uncultivated wilderness into a fruitful garden (e.g. 41.17–20; 51.3; 55.13; and see notes on 32.15). And 35.2 directly promises the regeneration and restoration to fertile productivity of the forests and gardens whose destruction was described in 33.9.

35.3,4: Strengthen the weak hands...the feeble knees: This is not meant as a reference to people's physical weakness but describes their fear and hopelessness (compare Jer. 6.24; Ezek. 7.17). Now the words of promise and comfort change to exultation, as in many passages in chapters 40—55 (see e.g. 40.1,2; Deut. 31.6; Josh. 1.6).

35.4: Your God will come with vengeance, with the recompense of God. He will save you: Compare 34.8. The writer sees God's 'justice' in both the destruction of His enemies and the restoration of His people. In Old Testament times people did not see any separation between spiritual and physical weakness, nor any difference in the ways in which they could be healed (see 32.1–5).

35.5,6: Then the eyes of the blind shall be opened...the ears of the deaf unstopped...the lame man leap: Again see 32.1–5; 33.24; and especially 6.8–12. Through all Isaiah's preaching, the leaders and people of Judah had refused to 'see' or 'hear'. But now comes the promise: *they will* 'understand with their hearts, and turn and be healed' (see 6.8–11).

35.6,7: For waters shall break forth in the wilderness: Compare 30.23–26. As we have seen, many passages of promise for Israel/Judah refer to plentiful water – always a symbol of prosperity in a land so much of which was (and still is) arid and subject to drought. Some present-day inhabitants of the State of Israel see their irrigation projects and desert reclamation schemes as the beginning of the fulfillment of this and other promises in the Scriptures.

35.8: And a highway shall be there...the Holy Way: Many interpreters see in this verse, and also in 11.16 and 30.21, a foreshadowing of the words of the prophet of the Exile in 40.3 and 49.11, when he proclaimed the forthcoming return of the exiles from Babylon. He also compared this to the first Exodus (51.10 and see also 19.23). However, v. 8 may have another meaning: like 2.2, 3; 30.11 and 21 it may be a reference to the sort of 'way' described in Pss. 25.4; 37.34 etc. (see also Matt. 7.13; John 14.6). That 'way' is the way to God, hence it is salvation.

35.9: No lion: Compare 11.6–9.

35.9,10: The redeemed shall walk there. And the ransomed of the LORD

shall return, and come to Zion with singing: Verse 10 seems to have been inserted to conclude the hymn of promise which is chapter 35, and perhaps was chosen because the idea of 'the ransomed' seemed to match the 'redeemed' at the end of v. 9. But it refers to the vision of the prophet of the Exile about the return from Babylon to Jerusalem, and does not really fit this context very well.

The words 'redeemed' and 'ransomed' here mean rather more than 'redeemed' in 1.27. In Hebrew law, a 'redeemer' meant a near kinsman who would 'buy back' family property lost through debt, or 'avenge' the murder of a relative or pay to free one taken into slavery. The word is frequently used in Isaiah 44—66, where God is described as the 'redeemer' who will avenge the defeat of His people and free them from 'slavery' in Babylon. It also emphasizes the closeness of God's relationship with His people.

35.10: Everlasting joy shall be upon their heads: This emphasizes the people's rejoicing, as a contrast to the Israelite mourning custom of hiding one's face and covering one's head (see 2 Sam. 15.30).

The Jews always expressed their hopes in concrete terms: as relating to their land, their psychological and physical well-being, and especially the rule of God instead of the corrupt human leadership they knew so well. The importance of their land to them was, of course, largely due to the fact that they had lost it. Even to this day all Jews of the 'diaspora', i.e. those living outside Israel, sing in their *Passah* liturgy: 'next year in Jerusalem'.

In recent years, too, the importance of the land for the survival of the whole human race has come to be understood in ways that were unknown to earlier generations. Over the past 100 years or so, new methods of farming and fishing have been introduced, and new industries have been developed, which could help to make life easier and more prosperous for people everywhere.

But experience shows that unless great care is taken these developments can be dangerous as well as beneficial. If too many trees are cut down too quickly it affects the weather and may cause drought. If too many crops are harvested in quick succession the soil becomes 'sterile' and turns to desert. Chemical fertilizers, pesticides, and the chemical waste from factories can poison water supplies and pollute the atmosphere, causing disease and death. And radiation pollution from the use of nuclear energy carries dangers which are not yet fully known or understood.

Some people care little about such matters so long as they can make a quick profit from the land. But already in many countries those who do care what happens to people in the future are protesting and trying to persuade governments to pass laws to prevent such pollution.

In the light of all this we can perhaps more easily appreciate the

'We can appreciate the passionate hope of the Jewish exiles that their land would again one day "blossom abundantly"' (p. 217 and 35.2).

In Israel today scientists are working on reclamation schemes that will turn desert areas into fertile farmland again.

What chiefly influences people who are 'separated' from God to 'return' to Him and help to make 'the dry land glad' (35.1)?

passionate hope of the Jewish exiles that their land which had been 'laid waste and utterly despoiled...polluted' (see 24.4–7), would again one day 'blossom abundantly' (see 35.1).

After the restoration of the land, the second great theme in chapter 35 is the 'healing' of the people. The word 'healing' is not actually used but as we have seen in 19.22 and 30.26, the idea of 'salvation' included the healing or 'making whole' of those who were suffering either spiritually or physically or both.

In Old Testament times people readily accepted that even such physical handicaps as blindness and deafness could be 'healed' if that were God's will. And we cannot deny that physical healing of this sort does take place today too, both in the Church and in other cultures, through prayer and the laying-on of hands.

But whatever our opinion on that point, it seems clear that in chapter 35 the writer was thinking about spiritual sickness, and about God's purpose. This purpose had led the people from their 'blindness' and 'deafness' *through* the call of Isaiah and their consequent punishment; to their ultimate 'return' from their own evil ways to the 'Holy Way' of the Lord; and so to their ultimate healing and salvation (see again 19.22; 30.15,18–20; note on 35.8 above; Jer. 18.11).

We should also notice that the 'remnant' who returned were not to experience salvation as believing individuals, but as a *community*. People as individuals need to believe in a certain way in order to receive salvation. But in the end God's salvation is His gift to the community as a whole. And the 'Holy Way' is not confined to any one Church or denomination – or even to one religion. It is *God's* Way, and He opens it as He chooses to the whole of humankind.

STUDY SUGGESTIONS

WORD STUDY

1. Match each of the quotations in the left-hand column below and overleaf with the one in the right-hand column which is in most direct contrast to it.

(a) The desert shall bloom abundantly.

(b) He shall stretch the line of confusion over it.

(c) With the recompense of God he will save you.

(d) From generation to generation it shall lie waste.

(g) The LORD has a day of vengeance.

(h) The glory of Lebanon shall be given to it.

(i) Thorns shall grow over it.

(j) Wild beasts shall meet with hyenas.

(e) Her land shall become burning pitch.	(k) A highway shall be there...called the Holy Way.
(f) No lion shall be there, nor any ravenous beast.	(l) The burning sand shall become a pool.

2. Which *four* of the following words are nearest in meaning to the idea of 'vengeance' and 'recompense' as expressed in 35.4?
   compensation   recoupment   replenishing
   retribution   pay-back   recomposition
   vendetta   reparation   pay-off

REVIEW OF CONTENT

3. What evidence is there in chapters 34 and 35 for the statement that 'the writer lived at a much later time than those from whom he borrowed'?
4. What connection, if any, is there between 35.2 and 33.9?
5. In chapter 35 the writer was thinking about spiritual sickness. Which verses in that chapter refer to spiritual sickness, and how did the writer describe it?
6. Explain in your own words what is meant by 'redeemed' and 'ransomed' in 35.9,10, and what ideas the writer was using these words to express.

BIBLE STUDY

7. In chapter 35 the writer describes how salvation will bring (a) new life for the land, (b) new hope for human beings, (c) new health and life for those who have been poor and oppressed. Compare these descriptions with 40.27–31; 41.17–20; 42.18–25; 44.1–5; 55.1–13; Joel 3.17,18; Gen. 1.26–31; Gen. 3.16–19; Deut. 8.7–10; Deut. 11.13–17. In what way(s) are the expectations described in chapter 35 similar to an earlier condition of the land and the people, and why was that condition lost?
8. In studying 35.8 we discussed possible meanings of the words 'way' and 'highway'. Which of these meanings (or any other meaning) do you think each of the following passages is meant to convey?
   (a) Ps. 16.11;   (b) Ps. 18.21,22,30;   (c) Ps. 119.3,14;
   (d) Acts 18.26;   (e) Acts 19.9
9. What difference, if any, do you see between 35.9 on the one hand, and 11.6–9 and Hos. 2.18 on the other?

APPLICATION, OPINION, AND RESEARCH

10. The idea of life as a 'way' which can be either good or evil, is found in the Bible, in Christian teaching, and also in other religions and ideologies. Find as many examples as you can of how this idea is expressed in the Bible, and by Christian writers over the centuries.

Do you think people today still find this idea useful, and if so for what reasons? If not, why not? What is your own feeling about it?

11. The land was specially important to the Israelites because they believed that God Himself had given it to them, and that basically it still belonged to Him.

(a) What do people in your country believe about ownership of land, and what effect does this belief have on the laws regarding land?

(b) Is the present distribution and use of land in your country fair and just to the people as a whole? If not, how do you think the situation might be improved?

12. 'God's "Holy Way" is not confined to any one Church or denomination or religion; He opens it to the whole of humankind.' Would the members of your Church agree with this statement? Do you? What is the official teaching of your Church about relationships with Christians of other denominations? with people of other religions? with those who are doubtful about religious belief altogether?

Special Note 3
Prophets and their Function

Writers of the Hebrew Scriptures used the title '*nabi*' for people who proclaimed, or were 'spokesmen' of, the word of Yahweh, the God of Israel. '*Nabi*' means to 'speak', 'speak out', 'speak to', 'speak on behalf of...'. The word can also mean to 'be called', as a prophet is 'called' by God. And it has yet another meaning: to 'act or speak in a strange manner'.

Because of this last meaning many people have thought that all the prophets in the Bible were 'ecstatics', like the people we call 'mediums' or 'shamans' who prophesy in a state of trance, or like those who 'speak in tongues' today. 'Ecstatic' prophesying of this sort, too, is described in the Hebrew Scriptures, and it seems likely that some at least of the early prophets did prophesy 'in tongues' (see e.g. 1 Sam. 10.5,10; 19.20–24). In some passages they are described as 'madmen', who went about in bands with music and dancing. In many cases they are mentioned in connection with holy places or 'sanctuaries' (see e.g. 1 Sam. 21.13–15; Jer. 29.26–29; Hos. 9.7b).

What we today call 'the prophetic function', or work of a prophet, is a widely known and many-sided activity with a long history. Clay tablets discovered at Mari in Mesopotamia, which date from the 18th century BC, describe prophets who received messages from the god

Dagan in his temple, which they had to deliver to the king Zimrilim. These men were prophesying about 700 years before Nathan and Gad spoke to King David in Jerusalem (see 2 Sam. 7.4–6; 24.11,12).

Among the better known of these 'seers' or 'men of god', as they were called, whose work is described in the Bible, apart from those whom we usually consider the 'real' prophets, were Samuel, Elijah, Elisha, and Micaiah (see 1 Sam. 3.21; 1 Kings 17.1–7; 1 Kings 19.15–19; 1 Kings 22.8–28).

Stories about such people and their words were told in the holy places of Israel, and were handed down from one generation to another. We call these stories 'legends' rather than history, because they were not chiefly meant to be accurate accounts of the way events actually happened. They were told in order to show how important these people had been for Israel, because they spoke the words of Israel's God, and so guided the rulers and people in the right way. Lessons and stories of this sort have been handed down in many countries about national heroes who have led the people to victory over enemies, or guided them well in periods of prosperity and peace. For similar reasons later generations in Israel described Abraham, Aaron, and Moses in this way also (see Gen. 20.7; Exod. 14—17; Numb. 11.16,17).

When we study the prophetic books in the Bible, however, we can see that although the function of the men they describe was much like that of the earlier seers, they were in many ways rather different people. For one thing, most of the accounts in the prophetic books refer to historical events for which there is firm evidence. They are not of the sort we call legends (the account in Isaiah 36—39, or most of it, is an exception). The messages of the prophets Amos, Hosea, Micah, Isaiah, Jeremiah, and Ezekiel (to list them in their probable historical order), show that they spoke out of a deep concern for the people, the kings, and the Jewish nation as a whole. They wanted the people to understand that social conditions and political events, in fact everything that happened in Judah and Israel, was directly connected with their own faith in the Lord, or the lack of it.

In these books, too, the prophets are sometimes described as experiencing dreams and visions (see Amos 7.1–3; Isa. 6.1–8; Jer. 1.4–12; and especially Ezek. 1.1—2.2). But the details of what they saw in their visions were a much less important part of their message than their warnings of what would happen as a result of people's mistaken attitudes and evil deeds. These prophets were deeply committed to carrying out God's will. They were continually reminding kings, leaders, priests, and the people in general that this meant faith and obedience to God's commandments, not injustice and rebellion. It meant a deep trust in God's protection of his people, not reliance on human allies. Because of their own faith in God, and their commitment to His will, these prophets were convinced that anything less on the part of others would bring disaster to Israel and Judah. This was why they felt they must speak out urgently, and lead people not only to understand the word of God which they had been taught, but to obey it. The phrase 'Hear the word of the Lord', which they often used to introduce their messages, was meant as a direct challenge to those who preferred to follow their own ideas.

Many people today think that 'ecstasy' and visionary experiences are an important characteristic of any prophet. And though opinion continues to differ on this matter, it is fair to say that the tradition of ecstatic prophecy has persisted since ancient times, and can be found almost everywhere on earth. The Pentecostal Churches which have grown up during the 20th century, chiefly in North and South America and the British Isles, look for 'baptism in the Holy Spirit'. Speaking in tongues similar to the occurrence recorded in the Acts, and divine healing, form an integral part of their worship services.

In some of the newer 'Independent' Churches of Africa and Asia, especially, the leaders are themselves regarded as prophets. The use of charismatic gifts and the practice of healing are perhaps the most essential part of their work. For them this 'irrational' feature of being a prophet is of fundamental importance. And even within the older Churches of the West, instances of speaking in tongues have recently been occurring (with somewhat upsetting and divisive effects).

But however we look at the matter, the prophets of the Lord in the period before and during the Exile (approximately from the 9th to the 6th century BC), were, as we have seen, very sober-minded people. They mistrusted those who boasted too much about their dreams and visions, and who based their claim to be inspired on these, rather than on the word of God (see Micah 3.5–8; Jer. 29.5–19). This is made clear in the stories of Micaiah and of Jeremiah (1 Kings 22.8–25; Jer. 28.1–11). And although the Book of Ezekiel contains many descriptions of what may seem to be ecstatic experiences, Ezekiel's actual messages are very sobering.

The great prophets of Israel and Judah certainly felt impelled to act and speak in ways which would make people pay attention to their words. It was not their fault if people failed to distinguish between them and the many so-called prophets and 'diviners and soothsayers', who offered advice to the leaders and people. These diviners were more like the fortune-tellers and astrologers whom people consult today (see Isa. 2.6; Amos 7.12–15). The great prophets' messages were quite different, and they spoke with the one overriding purpose of guiding God's people into the way of His will.

Some people today are confused about the true role and function of the prophets, because the words 'prophet' and 'prophesy' are commonly used to mean 'forecast' or 'foretell the future', without any religious significance attached. This shows how easily changes of meaning can occur when Scripture (or any sort of writing) is translated.

In the 3rd century BC, Jews living in Egypt began to translate the Hebrew Scriptures into Greek. This was for the benefit of the many Jews who had settled outside Palestine, in countries around the Eastern Mediterranean, and as a result had lost their knowledge of the Hebrew language.

According to a legend, 72 different rabbis were each set to undertake the whole translation, all at the same time. They were not allowed to communicate with each other, but when they had finished it was found that all their translations were identical. This legend has helped to give their translation the status of 'inspired Scripture' which the Jews had already attributed to the Hebrew version.

More important to us is the fact that the name given to this translation, the 'Septuagint' (meaning 'the 70'), may refer back to that legend. In this first translation into Greek of what are now the books of the Old Testament the Hebrew word '*nabi*' was translated by the Greek word '*prophetes*'. This was very suitable, because at that time it meant someone whose job it was to speak on behalf of another. It was the title given to those who served the Oracles connected with the sanctuaries or temples in Greece, where people received answers to their questions about what they should do or what was likely to happen. The Oracles were actually priests or priestesses stationed in the sanctuary. They did not speak to the people directly, but conveyed replies through the *prophetes*, who spoke on the Oracle's behalf. The word 'oracle' was also used to mean the reply or message itself, as in Isa. 13.1; 15.1; etc.

So it seems that the Jewish translators thought of the prophets in Israel as people who, like the Greek *prophetes*, conveyed messages to the kings and people from a higher authority – in their case, of course, messages from God. But this original meaning of the word was gradually forgotten as the old Greek religion died out and the Oracles no longer existed. People remembered only that the *prophetes* had given warnings about the future. So the word 'prophet' came to mean chiefly 'one who speaks beforehand', i.e. makes predictions, and this is its generally accepted meaning today.

Nevertheless, there are still men – and women too – who feel that God has given them special insight and calls them to speak in His name. Their messages may be of warning or encouragement to the leaders of the nation or the Churches. Or they may be addressed to the people as a whole, awakening them to the truth about themselves and about the inescapable consequences of their actions and attitudes. Always the aim of these prophets is to call people to turn or return to God and try to fulfill His purpose for their lives.

There are also people who feel a similar call, and whom we often call prophets, although they do not attribute their call to God but simply to their own political or philosophical convictions. They too seek to awaken people to what they believe to be the truth, and call upon them to act accordingly. These people speak, often against strong opposition and even persecution, out of their passionate commitment to what they believe to be the truth.

But there are also numbers of people today who are ready to exploit the longing of others for comfort in times of doubt or distress, or for guidance about the 'unknown' future, by 'prophesying' in the popular sense of the word. That is, they make their living as fortune-tellers, astrologers, and the like. Their activities range from that of the gypsy with a crystal ball at a fair or circus, to that of the sophisticated journalist in a Western city writing a daily 'horoscope feature' or 'agony column', answering people's questions in a national newspaper or on a TV or radio programme. Of course they cannot be compared in any way with the true prophets of Israel. As we have said, they are more like the 'diviners and soothsayers', or the 'mediums and wizards who chirp and mutter' (see Isa. 2.6; 8.19).

STUDY SUGGESTIONS

1. (a) Explain the origin of the word 'prophet'. Who used it first and when, and why is it used in the Bible?
   (b) How would you answer someone who asked you 'what is a prophet?'
2. Match each of the words in the left-hand column below with the appropriate definition in the right-hand column.

   (a) *Nabi*   (h) A holy man
   (b) Ecstatic   (i) A person who has visions
   (c) Madman   (j) A person who practises magic and sorcery
   (d) Shaman   (k) A person who acts in strange ways
   (e) Medium   (l) A person who speaks on behalf of someone else
   (f) Seer   (m) A person who is insane
   (g) Man of God   (n) A person who can communicate with the spirits of the dead

3. Do any of the *traditional* religious leaders in your country regard their function as a prophetic one? If so, in what ways are their attitudes and actions like or unlike those of the biblical prophets? What is the attitude of people generally towards them, and what is their status as compared with that of political or other leaders in the community?

4. Find out all you can about the character and functions of the leader or leaders in one or other of the 'Independent' Churches in your own country, or elsewhere. In what ways are they like or unlike those of the biblical prophets?

5. (a) Do you think that God calls the leaders of the Christian Churches today to exercise a prophetic function? If not, why not?
   (b) If so, what sort of people do you think they should be? Which *two* of the following do you think should be their *chief* aims, and which, if any, do you think should *not* be among their aims? Give reasons for your answers.
   (i) To unite all Christians in one body.
   (ii) To found new Churches based on 'pure' biblical teaching.
   (iii) To reform the life and worship of the Church.
   (iv) To preach the word of God to the faithful.
   (v) To gather in as many new converts as possible.
   (vi) To seek political power for the Church.
   (vii) To work for justice, equality, and love amongst all people.
   (viii) To remind sinful people of their duty to God and of the consequences of disobedience.

6. If you live in a country where Christians are a minority, what difference, if any, do you see between the function of the traditional religious leaders of that country and the function of leaders in the Church?

36.1—37.7
A Crisis of King Hezekiah – The First Account

INTRODUCTION

Chapters 36—39 are often referred to as a 'historical appendix' to the collected messages in Isaiah 1—35. They consist of a group of legendary accounts about the deeds of King Hezekiah of Judah (son of King Ahaz) which have been transplanted almost as they stand from 2 Kings 18—20, no doubt because they contain a number of oracles said to have been pronounced by the prophet Isaiah.

These accounts do not appear in chronological order. The first two (in chapters 36,37) are two somewhat differing versions of what happened when King Sennacherib of Assyria attacked and conquered Judah in the course of an expedition against rebellious states in Palestine, and his armies besieged Jerusalem but withdrew without taking the city.

The third and fourth accounts, about King Hezekiah's sickness (ch. 38) and the visit of a delegation from the King of Babylon (ch. 39), clearly relate to the events of a few years earlier, when for two short periods King Merodach-baladan in Babylon rose against the Assyrian overlord, and may have hoped to obtain Hezekiah's support.

In some respects these accounts seem to conflict with other parts of the Book of Isaiah, and there are discrepancies of detail within the Book of Kings itself. But we know from other historical sources that in 701 BC Sennacherib's troops did lay siege to Jerusalem and also lifted the siege before they had actually conquered the city, though possibly for different reasons than those suggested here in Isaiah. And for two short periods, 722—711 and in 703, the Babylonian king did succeed in freeing Babylonia from Assyrian rule, and may well have wanted to persuade the rebellious vassal states in Palestine to form a united front with him.

But also there is little doubt that the writers and editors who put these stories together in 2 Kings, and those who later on included them in Isaiah 1—39, were not chiefly concerned with historical accuracy, but rather with the religious significance of the events and actions recorded. Both books seem to have been compiled by a lengthy process of selecting, combining, and adding to accounts from earlier periods. And the purpose of those responsible for putting the Book of Kings into its final form, probably during (or after) the Exile, was not only to provide an evaluation of the past in the light of prophetic warnings and promises. They wanted to present it in such a way as to comfort and encourage the suffering remnant of a nation which had experienced total collapse, as they began to rethink their future.

As we have seen, Isaiah's attitude to the rulers in Judah had been a very critical one, and his messages to them were of admonition, warning, and the threat of punishment for their disobedience and apostasy. And enemies such as Assyria, though he described them as both cruel and treacherous, were nevertheless shown to be instruments of God's purpose.

These accounts from 2 Kings, however, were clearly written in order to impress the reader with the piety and faithfulness of King Hezekiah who 'had done what was good' in the sight of the Lord (Isa. 38.3); and by contrast, with the blasphemous attitude of the Assyrians and the arrogance of King Sennacherib. They show too how each of these kings met the fate appropriate to his individual character and actions. Furthermore, in transferring these chapters into the Book of Isaiah, care was taken to omit 2 Kings 18.14–16, which shows how at one stage Hezekiah had surrendered to Sennacherib and offered to pay him tribute, whilst a psalm of lament and thanksgiving to God, supposedly written by Hezekiah after his illness, was added (Isa. 39.9–20). Thus, although there is no mention of Hezekiah in the writings attributable to Isaiah himself, the later writers seem to have thought it important to show the prophet's relationship with the 'good' King Hezekiah as having been a favourable one.

(A third and very much shorter version of these stories is also to be found in 2 Chron. 32, where again the purpose was to comfort and encourage the people, by showing how God delivers and saves those who put their trust in Him.)

OUTLINE

In the Outlines for chapters 36 and 37, and in that for 38 and 39 below, the references for parallel passages in 2 Kings are given in brackets following the Isaiah references.

The two accounts in chapters 36,37 vary somewhat in character. The first is a fairly straightforward record of events, probably based more directly on the Assyrian annals, as it gives the Assyrian side of the encounter at greater length than the second one does.

36.1–3 (18.13,17,18): The date of the Assyrian advance and Sennacherib's sending of envoys to meet Hezekiah's representatives.

36.4–11 (18.19–26): The Assyrians sarcastically taunt Hezekiah for relying on help from Egypt, and also for trusting in God. They blasphemously claim that God has commanded them to destroy Judah.

36.11,12 (18.26,27): Hezekiah's officers ask the Assyrians to speak in Aramaic rather than the language of the people.

36.13–20 (18.28–35): The Assyrians speak directly to the people, calling on them to surrender, or suffer like the other nations whose gods have failed to save them.

36.21,22 (18.36,37): The Judeans carry the message to Hezekiah.

37.1–4 (19.1–4): Hezekiah sends for Isaiah.

37.5–7 (19.5–7): Isaiah promises that Sennacherib will raise the siege and be killed on return to his own land.

NOTES AND INTERPRETATION

Before embarking on detailed study of these chapters, it will be useful to read 2 Kings 18.1–12, as providing relevant background to the passages taken into the Book of Isaiah, and also 2 Kings 18.14–16 which was omitted from the material transferred.

36.1: In the fourteenth year of King Hezekiah: Scholars point out that 'fourteenth' is an error, and the true date was probably the 21st or 24th year. But as we have seen, exact dates for these early periods are difficult to determine, and errors may in any case be due to mistakes in copying. **Sennacherib, king of Assyria, came up against all the fortified cities of Judah and took them:** This is the beginning of a historical account which

226

agrees with the official Assyrian Annals of Sennacherib. Most scholars agree that this attack took place in 701 BC.

36.2: Sent the Rabshakeh from Lachish: Lachish was a strongly fortified city which was vital for the defence of Jerusalem. It had already been captured by the Assyrians, so Jerusalem was in danger. 'Rabshakeh' was the official title of a high-ranking official of the Assyrian court. The 2 Kings account adds the titles of two other such officials who came with the Assyrian army to Jerusalem. For 'upper pool' and 'Fuller's field' see notes on 7.3. These locations must have been important strategically for both the attackers and the defenders of the city.

36.3: And there came out to him Eliakim...Shebna...and Joah: For Eliakim and Shebna see 22.15–25. This verse shows that Eliakim had succeeded Shebna as controller of the royal household. These three men went as Hezekiah's delegates to meet the three envoys from the Assyrian side (2 Kings 18.17). For details about such officials in Judah see 1 Kings 4.2–6, and also the various translations of their titles in NEB, JB, NIV.

36.4–6: Thus says the great king...'On what do you rest this confidence of yours?...now that you have rebelled against me...you are relying on Egypt': 'The great king' means Sennacherib, ruler of the Assyrian empire, of which Judah was at that time a vassal. He evidently shared Isaiah's opinion that Egypt's help was worse than useless! (See 30.1–5 and 31.1–3.)

36.7: If you say 'We rely on the LORD our God'...is it not he whose high places and altars Hezekiah has removed?: This is a direct reference to the action for which Hezekiah is praised in 2 Kings 18.3–6. As we have seen, when Hezekiah's father King Ahaz made Judah a vassal of Assyria in return for so-called 'protection', he had not only to pay tribute, but also to introduce Assyrian religious practices and symbolic objects into the Temple (see interpretation of 7.29; and 2 Kings 16.7–18). As a sign of his wish to regain political independence, Hezekiah had removed these objects, though this was explained by the writer of 2 Kings 18.4,22 (Isa. 36.7) as a sign of his faithfulness to God, and it is true that Hezekiah was removing symbols which caused the people of Judah to worship false gods. The Assyrians may have misunderstood this action, and thought that Hezekiah was angry with the Lord because of the defeats Judah had suffered. So they now suggested he could no longer expect help from the Lord anyway.

(There may however be another explanation. Some 100 years later, under King Josiah, the so-called 'Second Book of the Law', Deuteronomy, was discovered, which demanded that God should be worshipped only in the Temple at Jerusalem. Other shrines and 'high places' of worship in Judea had therefore been abolished. Working at a later date still, the writer of 2 Kings 18 may have had this in mind, rather than Hezekiah's earlier action.)

36.8: Come now, make a wager: That is, 'make a bet'. This is the beginning of the Assyrians' boasting (see also 36.19,20). The writer obviously wanted to show how 'wicked' Sennacherib was (see also 37.11–13,23–25).

36.10: Is it without the LORD that I have come...the LORD said to me, 'Go up against this land': Prophets often began their messages with words like these, to show that they were speaking or acting as God had commanded them (see 6.8,9; 8.1; 21.6). By imitating them in this way, Sennacherib seems to have been mocking them, as well as arrogantly claiming that God had sent him to destroy Judah. This was indeed what Isaiah and other prophets had taught earlier on (see 10.5). But by the time these chapters were written, Judah had become a small oppressed country ruled by foreign powers, and the people now looked to their prophets for comfort rather than accusation. They held firmly to the idea that God must always be on their side, so that Sennacherib's boasting was now seen as blasphemy.

36.11: Pray, speak...in Aramaic...do not speak to us in the language of Judah within the hearing of the people: Aramaic was the official language for most peoples in the Near East at that time, and was used for international trade and diplomacy as well as literature. So it is understandable that Hezekiah's officials wanted the Assyrians to use it, rather than let the people overhear the demand for surrender in their own local Hebrew. It may seem more surprising that Sennacherib's spokesmen could speak Hebrew. But the Assyrians had been fighting to and fro against the Palestinian nations, gradually extending their empire to the west, for more than a century. They had already ruled the Northern Kingdom for twenty years by the time of this attempt against Jerusalem. Like the colonial administrators of modern times, the Assyrian officials who had to deal with the conquered areas must have learnt the local languages (even if they didn't always speak them very well! – see 28.11).

36.14,16: Do not let Hezekiah deceive you, for he will not be able to deliver you...make your peace with me...then every one of you will eat of his own vine: Again Sennacherib's message imitates the messages of Isaiah and earlier prophets, who had warned against trusting in human strength, and promised that for at least a remnant of the people who trusted God there would come a time of peace and prosperity (see 28.14–18; 30.1–7; Jer. 7.3,4,8; 29.8,9,11). Of course, these prophets had spoken in a quite different situation, and the allies whom Ahaz and other kings relied on *had* 'deceived' them. So it is obvious that Sennacherib was treacherously trying to tempt the people to trust his assurance and promise. The reference to the 'vine' reflects the idea of fertile gardens and vineyards traditionally associated with salvation. As it turned out, of course, Hezekiah had not deceived the people. For whatever reason it may have been (see 37.5–7,33–38), Jerusalem *was* 'delivered' on this occasion.

36.18,19: Beware lest Hezekiah mislead you by saying 'The LORD will deliver us'. Has any of the gods of the nations delivered his land out of the hand...of Assyria? Where are the gods of Hamath and Arpad... Sepharvaim...Samaria? See notes on 10.10,11 and interpretation. Isaiah had warned the people of his time against the mistaken idea that God would always protect Israel and Judah so long as they continued to attend worship services and observe the rules for religious sacrifices – even though they thought it useful to have human allies as well. Now the later writers were attacking the false belief that God would protect them simply because they were *His* people, whether they obeyed Him or not. Sennacherib's words could be taken to mean that he regarded the gods of the nations as 'nothing', as mere powerless idols. And this was what the writer wanted to convey, so as to comfort his hearers and strengthen their belief in the Lord. Sennacherib himself, if he did use such words, would simply have meant that Assyria's 'national' god Asshur was more powerful than all the others put together, including the God of Israel, and that this was a strong reason for the people to surrender to him, even if – as must have been the case – they did not believe that God was on his side.

36.21: But they were silent: 'They' means both the people and Hezekiah's officials.

36.22: Then Eliakim...Shebna...and Joah came to Hezekiah with their clothes rent: To 'rend' or tear one's clothes was a traditional way of expressing mourning or distress, rather like the wearing of sackcloth (see 37.1,2 and note on 32.11).

37.1,2: Hezekiah rent his clothes...and went into the house of the LORD...and he sent Eliakim...and Shebna...and the senior priests clothed with sackcloth, to the prophet Isaiah: Notice the difference between the attitude of Ahaz, whom Isaiah had to seek out while he was inspecting the city's defences in order to admonish him, and that of the 'good' Hezekiah who is described as going to the Temple himself and politely sending a delegation of important officials to ask for Isaiah's reassurance and prayers (compare 7.3,4,10–12).

37.3: This day is a day of distress. It may be that the LORD your God heard the words of the Rabshakeh...and will rebuke the words...lift up your prayer for the remnant: See 37.20b. Although the people had not responded to Sennacherib's mockery or his call to surrender, Hezekiah wanted Isaiah's assurance and his prayers that God *would* stand by His word and save Jerusalem and the remnant of the people.

37.6,7: Thus says the LORD, '...do not be afraid because of the king of

Assyria... I will put a spirit in him... he shall hear a rumour and return to his own land; and I will make him fall by the sword: The message Isaiah sent back to Hezekiah was certainly one of reassurance, though perhaps a little vague about what was to make Sennacherib break off the siege. 'A spirit' could mean fear, confusion, or actual misleading – like the spirit whom the Lord caused to mislead King Ahab (1 Kings 22.19–23). Verse 9 refers to Sennacherib's hearing that Egypt's army was marching against him, which might be called a 'rumour', but the details are historically inaccurate. A quite different version of Isaiah's message is given in the second account (see 37.32–35). And according to the statement in 37.36,37, it was a sudden outbreak of sickness among Sennacherib's soldiers which made him turn round and go home to Nineveh.

STUDY SUGGESTIONS

WORD STUDY

1. What is the meaning of the word 'spirit' as used in 37.7?
2. Which of the following words would you use to describe the character of Sennacherib?
   treacherous   prudent   misleading   mistaken   godless
   scoffing   cunning   tolerant   haughty   conceited
   deceitful   decrepit   blasphemous   boastful   considerate

REVIEW OF CONTENT

3. (a) What did Sennacherib mean when he spoke of Hezekiah's having removed the Lord's 'high places and altars'?
   (b) What did Sennacherib mean when he asked: 'Where are the gods of Hamath and Arpad?'?
4. Why did Hezekiah's officials ask the Assyrian messengers to speak in Aramaic rather than in Hebrew?
5. What did Sennacherib promise in return for the people's surrender?
6. (a) For what reason did Hezekiah hope that God might 'rebuke' Sennacherib, and thus rescue Jerusalem?
   (b) What did Isaiah prophesy that God would do, to make Sennacherib 'return to his own land'?

BIBLE STUDY

7. Re-read (a) 30.1–5 and 31.1–5, and (b) 36.4–7,10,14,15, and the introduction, notes, and interpretation for these passages. Notice what is said in each set of passages on the subject of 'trust', 'reliance', 'confidence', and make parallel lists of your findings for each set. Note who the speaker is in each case, and what demands,

accusations, and reprimands are made. How far do the two lists agree?

8. Read the following Psalms, and then make a list of their references to 'trust' and 'faith' in the same way as for the passages set for Q. 7. Then compare the results of your study of the two sets of Isaiah passages and your study of Psalms. What similarities or differences are there, if any, between the ideas expressed in the three sets of passages?

Pss. 22.3–5; 33.20–22; 37.1–5; 78.19–22; 115.2–4,8,9; 118.8,9

APPLICATION, OPINION, AND RESEARCH

9. 'The writers and editors who put these chapters together were not chiefly concerned with historical accuracy, but with the religious significance of the events and actions recorded.... These accounts were clearly written to impress the reader with the piety of Hezekiah.' How can present-day scholars discover whether records of events which happened 2,700 years ago are 'historically accurate' or not? It has been said that there is no such thing as unbiased history: what is your opinion?

10. According to 36.16–17 Sennacherib promised the people of Jerusalem freedom and plenty in their own land and a good living if they were 'carried away' into captivity, if only they would surrender. But in fact many nations suffered great hardship under Assyrian rule. Which do you think is worse: (a) to conquer a people by violence and bloodshed in battle, or (b) to trick them into submission by lying and deceitful 'diplomacy'? Give reasons for your answer.

37.8–38
A Crisis for King Hezekiah –
The Second Account

OUTLINE

This second account is clearly intended to emphasize Hezekiah's part in the incident, and includes his prayer in the Temple after receiving Sennacherib's message, as well as an extensive oracle by Isaiah.

Vv. 8–13 (19.8–13): After two verses about fighting elsewhere and the possibility of Egyptian aid for Hezekiah, the second account takes up the point reached in 36.13, with the Assyrians pointing to Sennacherib's successes against the kings of other nations.

Vv. 14–20 (19.14–19): This time the message appears to have been a written one, and Hezekiah takes the letter into the Temple and prays for deliverance.

Vv. 21–29 (19.20–28): Isaiah commends Hezekiah for turning to God, and responds with a long poetic oracle against Sennacherib.

Vv. 30–32 (19.29–31): He adds a prediction that in three years' time Judah will be saved.

Vv. 33–35 (19.32–34): A further prose oracle: God will protect Jerusalem.

Vv. 36–38 (19.35–37): A conclusion which fits both accounts: fulfillment of the prediction in 37.33–35 and of the promise at the end of the first account: Sennacherib's army withdraws, and eventually Sennacherib himself is murdered.

NOTES AND INTERPRETATION

37.8,9: The Rabshakeh returned...the king heard concerning Tirhakah, king of Ethiopia, 'he has set out to fight against you': These two verses were clearly inserted by a later editor to form a bridge between the two narratives. The reference to Tirhakah suggests that Sennacherib went off to prevent Egyptian help from reaching Judah, and provides a motive for the beginning of the second account: When Sennacherib 'heard of it, he sent messengers'. But it is confusing because Tirhakah, the 'Ethiopian' Pharaoh (see note on 18.1,2), did not come to power till 690 or 689 BC, so either the writer or a later copyist had mistaken the name or the date, or else the two accounts refer to two different attempts by Sennacherib to capture Jerusalem. There is no direct historical evidence either way. However, there is certainly a difference of emphasis as between the two accounts.

37.9,10: He sent messengers...saying, 'Thus shall you speak to Hezekiah: "Do not let your God deceive you by promising that Jerusalem will not be given into the hand of Assyria...have the gods delivered...the nations which my father destroyed?"': Notice that in this account it is God himself whom Sennacherib accuses of deception, not merely Hezekiah. And he points to a whole list of places whose kings had been 'deceived' by their 'national' gods, who were powerless to protect them against the Assyrians (see 36.19 and also 10.9).

37.14,15: Hezekiah received the letter from the messengers, and...went up to the house of the LORD, and...prayed to the LORD: See 37.9b and note on 7.3,4. The 'messenger formula' was also used at the start of letters, which were thought of as 'carried messages'. The location of the Temple was higher up on the Rock of Zion than the old city of David where the king had his palace. The details showing that the king had direct access to the Temple, and went there to pray directly to the Lord himself, suggests that this account comes from an earlier time than when the first account was written (see notes on 37.2,6,7).

37.21: Isaiah sent to Hezekiah, saying, 'Thus says the LORD... "because you have prayed to me... this is the word that the Lord has spoken"': The prophet knew of Hezekiah's prayer and already had a message for him from the Lord. Some interpreters have inferred from this that Isaiah was perhaps attached to the Temple in some regular capacity, as a priest or prophet, but there is no real evidence for this, and few scholars today support this view.

37.22: She despises you, the virgin daughter of Zion... she wags her head behind you, the daughter of Jerusalem: See note on 1.8. In the poetic oracle in vv. 22b–29, the Lord is addressing Sennacherib. The people of Jerusalem despise him and mock him ('wag their heads') behind his back.

37.23: Whom have you mocked and reviled?... raised your voice and haughtily lifted your eyes?... The Holy One of Israel!... You have said 'I have gone up the heights of the mountains... I felled its tallest cedars': We can see in Isaiah's accusations against Sennacherib's attitude to God and his boastful arrogance, a clear reflection of the prophet's accusations against the leaders in Israel and Judah, and also of his warning about the devastation the Assyrians would cause (compare 1.4; 2.12–17; 6.11; 14.8). The Assyrians and Babylonians were always eager to conquer mountainous forest regions in Palestine, not only because they regarded mountains as the home of the gods, but because they coveted the timber, which was lacking in the relatively treeless Mesopotamian plain.

37.25: I dried up... the streams of Egypt: See note on 19.5. This verse implies that the Assyrian army had already conquered Egypt by the time of Sennacherib's attack on Jerusalem. But this was not achieved until 669 BC, under his successor Esarhaddon (see 37.38). Probably the whole of this oracle was spoken (or written) long after the time of Isaiah by someone unfamiliar with the earlier history.

37.26,27: Have you not heard that I determined it long ago... that you should make fortified cities crash into... ruins, while their inhabitants... are dismayed and confounded: Clearly the writer of these verses, and of verse 23, was familiar with Isaiah 10.5–11.

37.28,29: I know your sitting down... Because you have raged against me... I will put my hook in your nose and my bit in your mouth, and... turn you back on the way by which you came: Again, compare 10.12–15. Sennacherib boasted about his conquest of many nations, but now God proclaims that it is He who is Lord over *all* nations, not only of Israel and Judah. He has used the Assyrians to fulfill His purpose, but He will punish the boastful conqueror as a herdsman drives his cattle or a rider his horse (compare 30.27,28 and Ezekiel 38.3,4).

37.30–32: And this shall be the sign for you... out of Jerusalem shall go

forth a remnant...a band of survivors. The zeal of the Lord will accomplish this: These verses are addressed to Hezekiah. As in earlier messages, a sign is given; this time not a name, but the gradual establishment of prosperity for the 'remnant' of God's people. Since the sign will not be completed for three years, it is not so much a direct promise that the siege will be lifted, as a general reassurance that God has not forgotten them (for 'zeal' compare 9.7).

37.33–35: He shall not come into this city...I will defend this city...for my own sake and for the sake of my servant David: A continuation of the 'promise', explicitly stating that Jerusalem, the Mountain of the Lord, will be saved.

37.36–38: The angel of the LORD went forth, and slew 185,000 of the Assyrians; and...early in the morning, behold, these were all dead: See 2 Kings 7; 2 Chron. 32; and compare 10.15,16. Certain epidemics were often regarded (as they sometimes still are) as direct interventions by God. The Greek historian Herodotus, writing in the 4th century BC, mentions that the Assyrian camp was overrun by 'mice', and some scholars have suggested that if these were in fact rats, there might have been an epidemic of bubonic plague. Whatever actually happened, it must have been in some way strange and inexplicable, to account for the later belief that Zion could never be captured.

37.37,38: Then Sennacherib departed...and as he was worshipping in the house of Nisroch his god, his sons slew him with the sword: Little is known of the later years of Sennacherib's reign, and there is no firm evidence as to how he died, though the Babylonian Chronicle confirms that he was killed by his son, and some historians think that this was planned by a Babylonian conspiracy. At all events the people of Jerusalem regarded his failure to capture their city, for whatever reason, to be due to the miraculous intervention of God on the side of His people.

SENNACHERIB'S ARGUMENTS

As pointed out in the Introduction to chapters 36 and 37, there is a difference of emphasis as between the two accounts. In the first, Sennacherib presents Hezekiah with two different sorts of reason why Jerusalem should surrender: first the political and practical reasons, and secondly what we might call the theological reasons.

According to the passages in 2 Kings which are not reproduced in the Book of Isaiah, Hezekiah had rebelled against Assyrian rule, and as an act of defiance had put an end to the Assyrian religious practices which Ahab as a vassal of Assyria had been forced to introduce, and removed the Assyrian cult objects from the Temple. But as Sennacherib's army advanced into Judah, capturing city after city, Hezekiah tried to buy him off. He offered whatever tribute Sennacherib might ask in return for his withdrawal from the siege of Jerusalem.

'The surviving remnant shall again take root and bear fruit...for out of Jerusalem shall go forth a band of survivors. The zeal of the Lord of hosts will accomplish this' (37.31, 32).

After revolution and earthquake in Nicaragua, farmers receive title-deeds to land of their own, and schoolgirls smile at an inscription declaring the people's 'great hope and faith' in the reconstruction of their city.

Who is or are the 'surviving remnant' of God's people today?

And that is where the story in the Book of Isaiah begins.

Sennacherib was not satisfied, but continued to press for total surrender of the city. Hezekiah was expecting help from Egypt, but Pharaoh's promises could not be relied on. Anyway, Egypt was no match for the Assyrians. And even if the Egyptians did provide horses and chariots, Hezekiah had no trained horsemen capable of using them (31.5,6,8,9).

These were the practical, political arguments. Sennacherib may have intended them as propaganda to discourage Hezekiah and weaken his resolve. Or the writer or editor may himself have been convinced, out of bitter experience, that it was dangerous to get involved with either side in the continuing struggle between Assyria and Egypt which Palestine had suffered for so long. Either way, Isaiah would surely have agreed with them (see 7.1–9; 30.3,5,7). But he would have agreed for different reasons. And at first sight it seems that Sennacherib resorted to theological arguments also: 'If you say, "we rely on the Lord", haven't you just been removing many of the altars and shrines where He was worshipped, so how can you expect Him to help you?' In fact, Sennacherib went on, 'The Lord Himself has sent me. And Assyria has overcome the gods of all nations, including Israel, so why should your God be any different?'

These were the theological arguments, and here too it seems likely that Isaiah would have agreed. The story shows Hezekiah as an outstanding example of a pious, god-fearing king, brave enough to resist the pagan power of Assyria in the name of the God of Israel. But then this seems to conflict with what we hear from Isaiah in chapters 1—35, where he continually denounced the kings and other leaders in Judah for their injustice, corruption, and disobedience to God.

As we have seen, according to 2 Kings 18.14–16, conveniently omitted here, Hezekiah had already once come to terms with Sennacherib. Was he now standing out as an act of allegiance and obedience to the Lord? Or did he simply share the conviction, like Ahaz and the ruling class in Judah whom Isaiah had accused and threatened, that serving the political and military interests of the nation was the same as serving God Himself.

THE 'GOD IS WITH US' IDEA

The conviction that 'God is with us' had grown out of the Israelites' continuing experience of God's care and steadfast love for them. But it had gradually turned into an ideology – a sort of slogan, which Isaiah and other prophets had repeatedly warned the people against taking for granted (see interpretation of 2.6–19, and also 7.14; 8.8,10; Hos. 10; Micah 3.1–4).

In the first account, the words of Isaiah suggest that God turned back

Sennacherib 'by the way that he came' (37.34) as a punishment for his arrogance and blasphemy. This is confirmed in the second account. But here Isaiah also seems to be saying that God saved Jerusalem on this occasion because of Hezekiah's virtue: 'Because you have prayed to me' (37.21).

In the second account, (37.9–33), the emphasis on the theological argument is very much stronger. There is no mention of Hezekiah's hope of help from Egypt apart from a passing reference to the Nile in Sennacherib's boasting about the places Assyria had destroyed. The promise that God will save His people, though only a remnant, is repeated.

But the chief ground of Hezekiah's prayer in 37.16–20 is that Sennacherib's claim to have destroyed other gods is not merely boasting but blasphemy, because the God of Israel alone is the living God; the gods of the nations were no gods at all. His plea is that God should save Jerusalem 'so that all the kingdoms of the earth may know that thou alone art the Lord' (37.20).

So it follows that the main theme of the long oracle against Sennacherib in 37.22–29 is that God Himself has planned Assyria's triumphs and also the punishment and downfall of Sennacherib himself because of his arrogance and blasphemy: 'have you not heard that I determined it long ago?... what I now bring to pass' (37.26–29).

One noticeable result of this emphasis is that other writers, both during and after the Exile, as well as Isaiah and earlier prophets, continually reminded the people that their suffering was the direct consequence of sin. But in chapters 36—39 there is no prophetic accusation against Hezekiah or the people of Judah themselves, even while blaming the cruelty and greed of their enemies. We can well understand that these later writers were chiefly concerned to comfort and encourage. But there was some danger that this attitude could lead to the same sort of complacency and self-satisfaction which Isaiah himself had denounced.

THE DANGER OF COMPLACENCY

In criticizing this attitude, however, we should recognize that the danger of complacency is something which Christians have to fight against in every age. There is a great difference between the Christian community described in the New Testament and during the period of persecution up to the time of Constantine, on the one hand, and the official state Church in both East and West in the Middle Ages, after the Reformation in Europe, and even today, on the other.

Often it seems to be at the times when the Churches are weak, suffering, and endangered, that they are most active, lively, and strong, rather than when they are safely established, rich, and respectable.

Whatever our own particular beliefs and allegiances, we may see signs of this today in the difference between countries where the older 'traditional' Churches seem to have become static and inward-looking, and those where the new 'prophetic' Churches may be poor and struggling against oppression, but are nevertheless very much alive and growing. The tendency to identify our own ideas with the will and honour of God can lead to self-righteous exclusiveness, and in the end not only to disagreements and divisions but even to segregation, intimidation, and open warfare between one group of Christians and another. Such attitudes are as godless and blasphemous as those which Isaiah denounced in Sennacherib.

STUDY SUGGESTIONS

WORD STUDY

1. Which of the following words would you use to describe the character of Hezekiah?
   mistaken prudent quiet courageous distressed
   disturbed pious cunning confident conceited
   godly humble trustful truthful boastful
   fretful fearful trustworthy
2. Explain the meaning of the following words and phrases as used in chapters 36 and 37.
   (a) the Rabshakeh (b) broken reed
   (c) daughter of Zion (d) wags her head
   (e) hook...bit (f) streams of Egypt
   (g) zeal

REVIEW OF CONTENT

3. What are the chief differences between the two accounts in these chapters, as regards:
   (a) Sennacherib's messages to Hezekiah?
   (b) Hezekiah's response to Sennacherib's messages?
   (c) the relationship between Hezekiah and Isaiah?
   (d) Isaiah's response to Hezekiah's message?
   (e) the reasons given for Sennacherib's lifting the siege of Jerusalem?
4. What is the probable meaning of the statement that 'the angel of the Lord slew 185,000 in the camp of the Assyrians'?
5. How would you summarize the main themes of each of the two accounts?

BIBLE STUDY

6. Re-read 37.16–20,32b,35, and the notes and interpretation on these passages. Then read Isaiah 40.18–28; 41.2–4,21–29; 43.8–15; 48.9–17; Ezek. 36.22–23. If you have TEF Study Guide No. 16, also read the interpretation and notes on these Isaiah passages. What do we learn from these passages about the God of Israel, His nature, His will, and the demands He makes? And what do we learn about Israel and Judah? What are the chief differences, in general and in detail, between the results of your study under this Question, and the results of your studies under Questions 7 and 8 for 36.1—37.7?

7. Compare God's message to Sennacherib in 37.23–29 with His message to Cyrus in 45.2–7. What was God's purpose, according to each passage, and what is the important theological idea underlying both passages?

APPLICATION, OPINION, AND RESEARCH

8. For most of his lifetime Isaiah disagreed with the belief held by many of his fellow-countrymen, that 'God is with us whatever we do.' What different viewpoint on the subject do we find in 28.14–18; 29.1–4; 30.1–5; 31.1–3; 37.3,4,16–20? What is the viewpoint of people today on this subject? What is your own viewpoint?

9. It has been said that Isaiah made people feel 'insecure'. Did he mean to do so, and if so, why? In what ways and for what reason did Isaiah's hearers and the readers of chapter 37 become so obsessed with their longing for security that they deceived themselves on the subject?

10. How far and in what ways do people's attitudes to security and freedom affect their relationships with other people, and their tolerance of other ideas than their own? Give examples to support your answer.

11. 'It is when Churches seem weak, suffering, and endangered that they are most lively, active, and strong, rather than when they are safely established and "respectable".' How far and in what ways is this statement true of your own Church? If a Church is 'safe and respectable', but inactive and static, what, if anything, can be done to enliven it?

38.1—39.8
Hezekiah's Sickness and Recovery

INTRODUCTION

As with chapters 36 and 37, we list the parallel passages side by side with those from 2 Kings 20 from which they were taken. We should also remember that whilst the aim in compiling 2 Kings was primarily historical, in Isaiah it was to emphasize the prophet's importance, and the virtues of Hezekiah. As we saw, the account in Isaiah 36,37 omitted a passage in 2 Kings which showed Hezekiah as ready to compromise with the enemy. Here in chapter 38 a change in the order of the contents seems to emphasize Isaiah's power of prediction; and a psalm of resignation, petition, and thanksgiving for recovery is inserted as an illustration of Hezekiah's piety.

OUTLINE

Chapter 38 describes Hezekiah's illness and cure and includes the psalm. Chapter 39 tells the story of the embassy from Babylon to whom Hezekiah showed off his treasury and armaments.

ISAIAH	2 KINGS	
38.1	(20.1)	Hezekiah becomes sick. Isaiah's first oracle.
38.2,2	(20.2,3)	Hezekiah's prayer.
38.4–6	(20.4–6)	Isaiah's second oracle.
38.7,8	(20.9–11)	Isaiah's prediction of a 'sign', and its happening.
38.9		Heading to the psalm.
38.10–13		Lament: Death is near.
38.14,15		Complaint, followed by resignation to God's will.
38.16		Petition for life and health.
38.17		Confession of sin.
38.18,19		Declaration of faith.
38.20		Expression of hope and promise of thanksgiving.
38.21	(20.7)	Isaiah prescribes a poultice for Hezekiah.
38.22	(20.8)	Hezekiah asks 'What is the sign?'
39.1	(20.12)	Envoys from Babylon visit Hezekiah.
39.2	(20.13)	Hezekiah boasts of his wealth.

39.3,4	(20.14,15)	Isaiah questions Hezekiah about the embassy.
39.5–7	(20.16–18)	Isaiah predicts that Babylon will seize all Hezekiah's possessions and even take his descendants into captivity.
39.8	(20.19)	Hezekiah does not care.

NOTES AND INTERPRETATION

38.1,6: In those days Hezekiah became sick...Thus says the LORD: I will deliver you and this city out of the hand of the king of Assyria: The words 'in those days', together with the position of this story of Hezekiah's sickness in 2 Kings, immediately following the account of Sennacherib's breaking off the siege of Jerusalem, suggest that Hezekiah fell ill during the siege. So does the reference in v. 6 to God's defence and deliverance of the city from the Assyrians. But then in 39.1 we find the time of Hezekiah's illness linked to a diplomatic visit by envoys from Merodach-baladan seeking Hezekiah's aid against Assyria. This almost certainly must have happened some years earlier, either around 703 BC when Merodach-baladan was trying to incite other vassal states to rebel, or earlier still when he was king in Babylon between 722 and 711 BC.

However, without doubting that Hezekiah was once very sick and recovered, we need not take these questions of chronology too seriously. Other points in the story show very clearly that it was told and retold for the specific purpose of showing that Hezekiah was a good and pious king who 'walked before God' in faithfulness, and that unlike his father Ahaz he did listen to Isaiah.

38.1: Set your house in order; for you shall die: That is, give your last orders to your heirs and successors (compare the action of Jacob and David according to Gen. 49.1,29,33; 1 Kings 2.1–3). Other prophets besides Isaiah, too, predicted the deaths of kings, in some cases giving them time to repent (see e.g. 1 Kings 21.19,27–29; 1 Kings 1.3,4,17–37).

38.2: Then Hezekiah...prayed...'Remember now, O LORD, how I have...done what is good in thy sight': The form of this prayer, like that of the 'writing' or psalm in 38.10–20, resembles many of the psalms which are known as 'laments' (or 'complaints') because they express sorrow and repentance or describe the writer's suffering (see e.g. Pss. 26; 88.3–5; 143.1,2,7–10).

38.5,6: Thus says the LORD...I have heard your prayer...I will add fifteen years to your life...I will deliver you and this city: In 2 Kings 20, vv. 5,6 we find details which are omitted in Isaiah, but they do not really add to our understanding of the passage. The reference to 'fifteen years' is puzzling, and scholars have put forward various ideas related to the time references in 2 Kings 18.2 and 13. But, as already noted, the chronology of the period is uncertain, and the fifteen years in question could only be determined if we knew exactly either when Hezekiah's sickness occurred, or when he died.

38.7: This is the sign to you from the LORD: As noted in the outline above, in 2 Kings 20 this verse *follows* Hezekiah's request for a sign, as seems logical; whilst here Isaiah *offers* both the prediction of Hezekiah's recovery and the miraculous sign confirming God's promise. And here the verse containing the request, together with Isaiah's diagnosis of the sickness as a 'boil' or abscess and his prescription of a fig poultice, is transferred to the end of the story, after the psalm of lament and thanksgiving said to have been recited by Hezekiah after his recovery.

Scholars consider that this change of order was intentional, so as to give greater importance here to Isaiah's offer of prediction and the miraculous sign described in v. 8, though it could have happened through the mistake of a copyist at some stage. Or Hezekiah's request for a sign may have been given more prominence in the 2 Kings account as a way of suggesting that he took the initiative in 'waiting on the Lord'.

38.7,8: The LORD...has promised...'I will make the shadow cast by the declining sun on the dial of Ahaz turn back ten steps.' So the sun turned back: A rather similar 'nature miracle' is recorded in Josh. 10.12–13a. But there the standing still of the sun is said to have followed a violent storm of hail, which could only fall from thunder clouds. Scholars therefore conclude that the 'halting' of sun and moon probably refers to continuing cloud which made the pursuit of the Amorites easier than in blazing sunshine, and that Josh. 10.13b was added by a later writer who wanted to emphasize the help attributed to the Lord.

Here in Isaiah, the Hebrew of v. 8 is uncertain. But the idea of the sun standing still to mark important events is common in the folklore of many countries, and much stress is laid in Deuteronomy and other Old Testament books on the 'signs and wonders' which the Lord sent prophets 'like Moses' to do (see e.g. Deut. 18.15–18; 29.2–4; Neh. 9.9,10; Ps. 135.8–10). Prophets and other 'wise men' often used seemingly 'miraculous' natural events as signs that their predictions were reliable, and Isaiah may have done so in counselling Hezekiah about his illness. We should, however, remember the legendary nature of the stories in these chapters, and the evident intention of their compiler to emphasize Isaiah's reputation as a major prophet, truly a spokesman for the Lord and fully capable of performing such a sign (see also Isa. 7.10–14).

38.9: A writing of Hezekiah: The Hebrew word translated 'writing' is unclear, but is thought to be the same as '*Miktam*'. This appears as a heading to certain psalms, e.g. Pss. 16; 56; 60, which were used for reciting in expiation of sin (rather like the 'penance' Christians are directed to recite after making their confession to a priest in some

Churches). So it does not mean that Hezekiah actually wrote the psalm. Compare this heading with for example Pss. 51; 54; 57, which were often used in this way by people who wanted suitable words to express their feelings in particular situations (e.g. 2 Sam. 22.2–31 is Ps. 18; Jonah 2.1–9 and Luke 1.46–55 are other examples).

38.10: In the noontide of my days: That is, in the middle of my life (compare Ps. 102.24).

To the gates of Sheol: For this and v. 18, 'Sheol cannot thank thee', see note on 5.14, and compare such psalms as 6.5–7. The Israelites were concerned only with life on earth, not existence after death in a shadowy world of which they knew little.

38.12: My dwelling is...removed from me like a shepherd's tent...like a weaver he cuts me off from the loom...bring me to an end...he breaks all my bones: Again in vv. 12 and 13 the Hebrew is uncertain and obscure. But in many psalms the references to sickness, death, or harsh treatment are so confused that it is not always possible to discover exactly what the user of the lament was suffering from. In v. 21 (as in 2 Kings 27) Hezekiah's trouble is plainly diagnosed as 'the boil', but we do not need to take the descriptions in the psalm literally. The important point here is that Hezekiah realized his suffering was not caused by some mysterious enemy, but was willed by God for some reason which he did not understand but accepted as God's will.

38.14,16: My eyes are weary with looking upward...O restore me to health: Compare Psalm 88.1–3,9. In both cases the writer is describing the desperate prayer of those who feel themselves near to death. If Hezekiah was in fact suffering from boils or ulcers, the cause might well have been anxiety about the Assyrian advance, or even a sense of guilt following his attempt to buy off Sennacherib. Many of the 'complaint' psalms show that their writers understood that spiritual, physical, and social problems can all cause 'bitterness' (v. 17), and thus lead to bodily sickness also – something which western medical science has only recently come to recognize.

38.17: It was for my welfare that I had great bitterness...but thou hast cast all my sins behind thy back: See also 43.25; 44.22; Jer. 18.23. All these passages are thought to refer to a rite in which sins were written down and then the writing was destroyed. This was thought to be a means of 'justification' and a return to righteousness for the sinner, rather like the carrying away of the people's sins by the 'scapegoat', as described in Lev. 16.22.

38.19: The living...thank thee, as I do this day; the father makes known to the children thy faithfulness: Compare 37.20 and note. Often when people have come through a time of suffering, they feel that God must be praised for His steadfast love and care, not only for themselves, but in the future; and those who come after them look back on the event with thanksgiving. It is upon such events as this that Biblical tradition is founded. We could say that this is how the Bible itself came into being, as a record of such events as when God created the earth, called Abraham, delivered His people from slavery, gave them the Torah, the land, the prophets, Jesus, the apostles, the Church....

38.20: The LORD will save me: Compare e.g. Pss. 5.11,12; 10.17,18. Many Psalms of lament ended with an expression of hope and confidence that the writer would recover from his illness, and be saved.

38.21,22: Isaiah had said...take a cake of figs and apply it to the boil...Hezekiah had said, 'What is the sign?': See note on v. 7 above. The use of '*had* said', i.e. the past pluperfect tense, here clearly shows that the event described in these verses belonged to an earlier stage in the story, as positioned in 2 Kings 20.

The theological understanding of the writers of the Books of Kings and Chronicles was that piety saves and wickedness brings disaster. This is clearly shown in these chapters of Isaiah which describe the salvation of the 'good' king Hezekiah. Examples of punishment for the wicked appear in the oracles of judgement addressed to King David (2 Sam. 12.1–12), and to King Ahab (1 Kings 21.17–24), both of whom, however, afterwards repented. And a detailed explanation of these ideas is given in 2 Kings 17.7–23, which describes the 'wickedness' which brought disaster upon the people of the Northern Kingdom, and the end of Israel as a separate nation after their defeat and deportation at the hands of the Assyrians.

This is why Hezekiah found it difficult to understand why he should experience sickness, and the expectation of death, at an age when a person would normally expect many more years of life and health. Untimely illness and death were understood as punishments for those who failed to live according to God's law. So when a 'good' person fell ill, it was regarded as 'injustice' (see e.g. Job 9.3–24; Ps. 73.1–14). No rational explanation could be found for this experience, and people could only agree with the words of Hezekiah's psalm: 'What can I say? For he [i.e. the Lord] has spoken to me and he himself has done it' (Isa. 38.15 and see Job 42.1–6; Ps. 73.16–28).

Hezekiah's request for a sign and the emphasis in this chapter on Isaiah's readiness to give it are perhaps a further indication of this way of thinking, which is in fact quite close to the ideas which many people hold today. Of course, we know very much more now about the causes of illness and accidental death, and obviously many innocent people suffer and die through no fault of their own. But the belief is still very widespread that people 'get what they deserve', and that if they do not, they are entitled to some sort of reassurance or 'sign' that God is still in control of His universe. For Christians, however, the sufferings of the prophets themselves, and the example of Jesus's life and teaching, should be enough to convince them that true piety and prophetic vision are not like this at all (see e.g. Luke 13.1–5; John 9.1–4).

39.1: At that time Merodach-baladan...sent envoys with a present to Hezekiah, for he heard that he had been sick: See Introduction and notes on 38.1,6. Merodach-baladan was ruler of a small state in Mesopotamia, who rebelled against the Assyrians and became king in Babylon between 722 and 711 BC, was ousted by Sargon, and rebelled again around 705. It was probably about that time that he sent envoys to seek Hezekiah's aid against Sennacherib. The reference to Hezekiah's sickness as occasion for the embassy may have been inserted by the editor simply as a link.

39.2: Hezekiah welcomed them; and he showed them his treasure house...his whole armoury, all that was found in his storehouses: We cannot tell whether Hezekiah was seriously demonstrating his military and economic strength to a potential ally, or merely showing off.

39.3: Then Isaiah came to Hezekiah and said, 'What did these men say? And whence did they come?': This verse suggests that Isaiah dealt with Hezekiah in a rather superior manner, and he seems to have been nearly as impatient with Hezekiah's foolishness, as he had been with Ahaz's stubbornness many years earlier. This time, the prophet would of course have been a much older man than the king.

39.5,6: Hear the word of the LORD of Hosts: Behold, the days are coming, when all that is in your house shall be carried away to Babylon...and some of your own sons shall be taken away: This 'prediction' seems to show very clearly that the passage was written at a later time. Isaiah's own message in such a situation would almost certainly have been one of much stronger accusation and threat, such as 30.1–6,15.

39.8: Then said Hezekiah, 'The word of the LORD which you have spoken is good; there will be peace and security in my days': Surprisingly, this verse seems to show Hezekiah in a much less favourable light – a sad picture of a much respected king here concerned only with his own happiness and peace of mind. It is difficult to know how far we should take this chapter seriously, because its author so clearly seems to have distorted what actually happened, in order to fit his own ideas about Isaiah's concerns, and the reason for Hezekiah's boasting to the envoys.

Hezekiah during his lifetime was regarded as a good and pious king; but it seems that his piety was not altogether wholehearted. Of course, like any human being, he had faults as well as good qualities. But extreme piety can sometimes become 'religiosity' (see pp. 19, 20), or even be a cloak for selfishness. We can find examples in our own time, of this sort of false religion, as well as Hezekiah's attitude described in these chapters and in 2 Kings. Some people, for example, make a business or commercial enterprise of religion, and use it as a way of exploiting other people. Others use it as a substitute for ordinary social relationships. And for others still it is chiefly a means of escaping from the realities of everyday life. In some it can be a serious mystical search for absolute transcendance, but it can also be simply one way of 'getting high', rather like drinking too much alcohol or taking drugs. But all these are very far removed from the 'Word become flesh', or the 'pure' religion which is the expression of that Word, as described in James 1.27 and as seen in the lives of such people as Martin Luther King, Albert Schweitzer, Desmond Tutu, Mother Theresa, Oscar Romero, and many, many others like them.

STUDY SUGGESTIONS

WORD STUDY

1. Explain the meaning of each of the following symbolic expressions. (You may find it helpful to start by reading the following passages: Gen. 17.1; Job 16.7–9; Jonah 2.2–9; Ps. 107.17–22; Isa. 59.9–11; Matt. 16.18; 2 Cor. 5.1.)

   Set your house in order (38.1).

   How I have walked before thee (38.3).

   The gates of Sheol (38.19).

   My dwelling is plucked up and removed from me like a shepherd's tent (38.12).

   Like a swallow I clamour (38.14).

   Like a lion he breaks all my bones (38.13).

   Thou hast held back my life from the pit of destruction (38.17).

   If you can, suggest traditional sayings or customs in your own language, or in any other language you know, which express comparable ideas to any of those listed.

REVIEW OF CONTENT

2. According to 38.1 Isaiah prophesied that Hezekiah was going to die. What made him change his mind?

3. 'Isaiah seems to have treated Hezekiah in a rather superior manner.' In which verses in chapters 38 and 39 do we find evidence for this statement?

4. What made Hezekiah 'weep bitterly'? What reason did he give for hoping that God would spare him?

5. In what chief ways is the sign described in 38.7,8 like and unlike the signs described in chapters 7 and 8?

6. Why should Merodach-baladan's envoys have wanted to see Hezekiah's stores and weapons, and why should Isaiah have considered Hezekiah foolish to have showed them?

BIBLE STUDY

7. Read again the Outline for Hezekiah's psalm (38.10–20), and then try to analyse Psalm 22 in the same way, looking for such characteristics as complaint, thanksgiving, accusation, petition, promise, confession, etc.

8. Read again the notes and interpretation on 38.7 concerning the word and idea of the 'sign', and then study the following passages: Matt. 12.38–42; John 2.18–22; 6.30–33; 1 Cor. 1.22–25 and also James 2.14–26.

   (a) What do we learn from these passages about the danger of demanding evidence or 'proof' for religious 'truths', and the parallel danger of claiming truth for any religious idea without such proof?

   (b) Why is it foolish to try to prove that God exists, and equally foolish to claim the opposite?

APPLICATION, OPINION, AND RESEARCH

9. 'Psalms were often used by people who wanted words to express their feelings of sorrow or repentance or suffering' (p. 243). Are psalms or other traditional songs or sayings used by individuals or groups in your country at times of distress or mourning? What effect does this have on people? And what happens when such traditional customs are forbidden by religious or political authorities?

10. 'Extreme piety can sometimes... be a cloak for selfishness' (p. 245). Find out as much as you can about the lives and actions of some of the great religious heroes and heroines, Christian or otherwise, of the past or of today. Then read Isa. 1.10–26 and Jer. 7.1–11, and say how far you think the 'religion' of these people was 'pure', and in what ways, if at all, it was selfish or 'escapist'.

11. According to 39.8, Hezekiah showed that he did not care what happened in the future, even to his own family, so long as there would be peace and security in his lifetime. Give examples of some of the ways in which people today show this same attitude of not caring what may happen after they are dead.

Key to Study Suggestions

Introduction

1. See p. 1, para. 1, lines 2, 3, para. 2, and para. 3, last 3 lines.
2. See p. 1, last 3 paras and p. 2, paras 1 and 2.
3. See p. 2, para. 3. **4.** See p. 2, para. 6. **5.** See p. 3, para. 1.
6. (a) See p. 4, lines 1–19. (b) See p. 4, lines 20–30.
  (c) See again the passages listed for (a) and (b), and p. 6, para. 4.
7. See p. 5, numbered paras 1, 2, and 3.
8. See pp. 3, 4, and 5, and p. 6, para. 1. **9.** See p. 6, para. 4.

1.1–9

1. (a) Separated from. (b) Be closely related to.
  (c) See p. 12, note on 1.5. (d) Disregarded. (e) Foreigners.
2. (a) See p. 10, note on 1.1, lines 6–8.
  (b) E.g. 1 Sam. 3.1: 'word of the Lord'; Dan. 7.1–2: 'dream'; 2 Cor.
  12.1: 'revelation'. (NB: As the contexts show, where 'divination' is the
  doublet, the meaning of 'vision' is usually *not* the same as in Isa. 1.1.)
3. See p. 1, para. 5 and p. 10, para. (b). **4.** See p. 12, para. 2.
5. See p. 12, para. 4, p. 13 last para., and p. 14, lines 1–16.
6. See p. 12, note on 1.5. **7.** See p. 13, paras 2 and 3.
8. See p. 12, paras 5 and 6. **9.** Based on p. 14, para. 2.
10. Based on p. 12, lines 7–12 and note on 1.4, and p. 14, para. 3.
11. See p. 13, para. 4.

1.10–20

1. See (a) p. 18, para. 3; (b) p. 18, para. 6; (c) p. 19, para. 4;
  (d) p. 20, last line and p. 21, lines 1–3.
2. Idolatry, detestable, abhorrent. See p. 18, lines 8–12 and p. 20, para. 2.
3. (a) See p. 17, lines 9 and 8 from foot.
  (b) See p. 18, lines 8–10 and p. 20, para. 4, lines 1–3.
4. See p. 18, lines 1–6, including additional Bible passages suggested.
5. See p. 19, last para. and p. 20, paras 1–3.
6. (a) See p. 18, last 3 lines and p. 19, lines 1 and 2;
  (b) See p. 19, lines 17–19.
7. (a) See p. 20, lines 13–15; (b) See p. 20, lines 7–13.
8. See p. 19, para. 7.
9. Compare your answers with p. 20, last 14 lines and p. 21, lines 1–7.
10. Compare your answer with the Outline on p. 17.

1.21—2.5

1. See (a) p. 23, last 2 lines and p. 24, lines 1–3; (b) p. 24, note on 1.23.
2. See p. 23, lines 9–3 from foot and p. 24, note on 1.24, lines 4–8.
3. Ransomed, rescued.
4. (a) See p. 23, last line and p. 24, lines 1 and 2.
  (b) See p. 24, note on 1.22.23.

5. See p. 2, para. 5 and p. 5, numbered para. 1.
6. See p. 25, note on 1.29.   **7.** See p. 25, numbered paras 1, 2, and 3.
8. See p. 29, para. 4 and last 4 lines, and p. 30 last para.
9. See p. 25, note on 2.1. In John 1.1 'Word' means Jesus Himself (see also John 14.6,7).
10. See p. 26, para. 4 and p. 29, para. 2.

2.6—22

1. See p. 33, last line; p. 34; and p. 35, paras 1–5.
2. See p. 33, note on 2.9,10.   **3.** See p. 33, note on 2.7.
4. See p. 33, note on 2.7.
5. See p. 32, summary of vv. 6–8 in Outline, and see p. 36, para. 3.
6. See p. 35, note on 2.19 and p. 36, line 1.
7. Based on p. 33, notes on 2.9, 10.

3.1—4.1

1. See p. 40, first 2 paras: support, sustenance, provision.
2. (a) See other translations: perhaps attitudes, character, behaviour.
(b) See note on 3.14;   (c) See note on 3.26.
3. See p. 40 to end of note on 3.8, especially para. 4.
4. See p. 40, note on 3.6,7.   **5.** See p. 41, notes on 3.14a,15.
6. See p. 41, note on 3.16,17 and p. 43, para. 3.
7. See p. 39, note on 3.1.
9. See p. 19, notes on 1.17,18; p. 26, note on 2.4, and p. 41, note on 3.13.
All 3 passages are in the language of the law-courts.

4.2—5.7

1. See p. 46, note on 4.2, lines 4–end, and compare other translations.
2. See p. 46, note on 4.2,3.   **3.** See p. 45, lines 4,3 from foot.
4. See p. 46, lines 6–2 from foot, and p. 47, lines 5–11 and numbered para. 2.
5. See p. 47, lines 1–4, numbered para. 3, and p. 48, lines 1 and 2.
6. See p. 48, note on 5.1, third para.
7. See 5.2b, 5.4b, 5.7b, and p. 49, lines 6–21.

5.8—23

1. See pp. 52, 53, note on 5.8–10, first para.   **2.** See p. 53, lines 1–4.
3. See p. 54, para. 4 (also p. 56, and p. 57, paras 1–4).
4. See p. 53, para. 2, and p. 56, para. 1.
5. See p. 54, note on 5.22, and p. 57, para. 5.   **6.** See p. 53, note on 5.13.
7. See p. 53, note on 5.14, and p. 58, lines 1–14.

Special Note 1

1. See p. 1, last para., and p. 60, last para.
2. (a) See p. 2, para. 1;   (b) See p. 2, para. 3;
(c) See p. 60, Special Note para. 1.
3. See p. 60, Special Note para. 3.
4. See p. 60, Special Note para. 2, last 3 lines.
5. See p. 61, para. 4.   **6.** See p. 61, para. 3.   **7.** See p. 61, para. 4.
8. See p. 61, last 2 lines and p. 62, lines 1–4.   **9.** See p. 61, para. 5.
10. See p. 62, lines 6–13.

6.1–13

1. See pp. 64 and 65, note on 6.1,5: I beheld, I perceived, I had a vision of, I recognized.
2. See p. 66, note on 6.5, line 4.
3. Imminent (d); immanent (a); eminent (c); emanent (b).
4. See p. 1, last 3 paras, and p. 2, paras 1 and 2.
5. See p. 65, note on 6.1.   **6.** See p. 66, note on 6.5, lines 5–8.
7. See p. 67, lines 8–10.
8. See p. 67, para. 4, numbered para. 1, and p. 68, numbered paras 3 and 4.
11. See especially: Jacob: Gen. 28.10–22; 32.1–32; 35.1–15. David: 1 Sam. 16.1–13. Matthew: Matt. 9.9–13; Luke 27.32. Paul: Acts 8.1–3; 9.1–30.
14. Based on p. 67, numbered para. 1, and p. 68, numbered para. 2.

7.1–9

1. (a) See p. 73, note on 7.2, lines 1 and 2;   (b) See note on 7.2, lines 3 and 4.
2. See p. 73, note on 7.3,4, line 2.
3. See p. 73, Outline, lines 2–4 and note on 7.1.
4. (a) See p. 73, note on 7.3,4, lines 1 and 2 and p. 75, para. 3.
   (b) See p. 73, note on 7.3,4, lines 6–9.
5. See p. 74, note on 7.4, lines 5–8.
6. (a) See p. 74, note on 7.4, lines 1–3 and last 2 lines, and p. 75, paras 1–3.
11. Based on p. 75 last para and p. 76.

7.10–25

1. See p. 78, note on 7.11, para. 1.
2. See p. 78, last 6 lines and p. 79, line 1, and p. 80, last 3 lines.
3. See p. 79, lines 1–3.   **4.** See p. 80, lines 20–35.
5. See pp. 78 and 79, note on 7.13 and p. 79, note on 7.15,22, lines 4–10.
6. See p. 79, lines 5–11 and p. 80, lines 20–27.
10. Based on p. 79, note on 7.14, lines 3–10.

8.1–22(23)

1. See p. 84, note on 8.16,17 and p. 85, para. 1.
2. (a) See p. 83, notes on 8.1 and 8.1–3.   (b) See p. 83, note on 8.2.
3. See 7.15–17 and p. 79, note on 8.4.
4. (a) See p. 83, notes on 8.6,7, and also p. 80, notes on 7.20.
   (b) See again pp. 79 and 80, notes on 7.15,22 and p. 83, note on 8.7, the River.
5. See p. 84, note on 8.11,12, lines 1–5.
6. See p. 84, note on 8.11,12, last 4 lines, and follow up references given.
7. See p. 84, note on 8.19, para. 1 and p. 85, para. 2.

9.1–7

1. (a) See p. 90, note on 9.2–4;   (b) See p. 90, lines 8–11;   (c) See p. 90, last 5 lines;   (d) See p. 91, note on 9.7, lines 1–4.
2. See p. 90, note on 9.6,7, last 4 lines and p. 92, para. 5.
3. See p. 90, lines 1–4.
4. See p. 90, note on 9.4:   (a) lines 1–4;   (b) lines 3–6.

5. (a) See p. 90, note on 9.6,7.

(b) See p. 91, last 2 paras, and p. 92, first 2 paras.

6. See p. 92, paras 2, 3, and 4.

9.8—10.4 and 5.24–30

1. (a) See p. 95, note on 9.8;   (b) Compare 2 Sam. 17.12; Prov. 23.5; and Isa. 34.14.

2. Based on p. 97 last 6 lines and p. 98, first para. and numbered paras 1–3. God's anger is burning, fierce, and slow.

3. For most of the words given the clue is in the doublets or twin-words, i.e. arrogance = pride; adversaries = enemies; devour = snatch, steal, or consume; spoil = prey on, plunder, loot; spare = have mercy on; decree = law, regulation, pass sentence.

4. See Note on p. 59/60 and p. 94, Introduction to Outline.

5. See p. 95, note on 9.9.10.   **6.** See p. 97, note on 10.1.

7. See p. 95, note on 9.14.

8. See p. 95, note on 9.12, and follow up references given.

9. See p. 97, notes on 10.1.

10.5–34

1. E.g. The 'Lord of hosts' (of armies) will eventually destroy the 'stout warriors' of Assyria; the 'light of Israel' will burn up the 'forests and fruitful land'; the 'Holy One of Israel' will support those who 'lean upon' their Lord, and comfort ('be not afraid') the surviving remnant who continue to have faith in Him.

2. (a) See p. 101, note on 5.6, and follow up references given.

(b) See p. 101, also 8.1–4 and notes on these verses, p. 83.

(c) See p. 101, note on 10.9.10, and p. 102, para. 7.

(d) See p. 102, note on 10.33,34.

3. See p. 100, Outline of 10.5–14, and p. 101, notes on 10.15.

4. See p. 101, notes on 10.9,10 and 10.11.

5. See p. 100, Outline of 10.5–14, and p. 102, para 8, lines 3 and 4.

6. See 10.12–19, 24–27 and p. 101, note on 10.15, second para.

7. E.g. in 10.15 (a wood-cutter), in 10.17 (a fire, a flame).

8. See p. 101, last 4 lines, note on 10.20–23, p. 102, lines 1–12, and p. 103, section headed 'The idea of the remnant'.

11.1—12.6

1. (a) Righteousness: goodness, godliness, integrity;

(b) Equity: fairness, impartiality, correctness;

(c) Faithfulness: fidelity, trustworthiness, changelessness.

2. (c).

3. Based on p. 106, last 3 lines, note on 11.11 and the references given.

4. See p. 106, note on 11.2.   **5.** See p. 106, note on 11.3–5.

6. See p. 106, last line, p. 107, lines 1–6, and p. 108, fifth para., lines 1 and 2.

7. (a) See p. 107, note on 11.16, and p. 108, para. 3.

(b) See again p. 97, last para., and p. 98 first para. and numbered paras 1–3.

(c) See p. 197, note on 12.3, and last 2 paras; p. 108, first 4 paras and last line, and p. 110, lines 1–6.

8. Look again at p. 33, last line, p. 34, and p. 35, lines 1–21.

Special Note 2

1. See p. 112, para. 1 of Special Note, lines 1–8.
2. See p. 112, para. 1 of Special Note, lines 8–12 and para. 2.
3. See p. 113, paras 3, 4, 5, and 6.   **4.** See p. 114, para. 1.
5. See p. 114, para. 2 and para. 1, lines 1–5.

13.1—17.14

1. Apocalyptic: See again p. 3, last 2 lines, p. 4, lines 1–13, and look at p. 137.
   Apostasy: See p. 119 and p. 120, note on 17.9–7,11.
   Idolatry: See p. 2, para. 3; p. 33, note on 2.8; p. 35, notes on 3.12–14 and 2.18; and pp. 36 and 37, section on Idolatry.
   Apostleship: Consider the work of those to whom the title 'apostle' is usually given, i.e. the disciples of Jesus, Paul and Barnabas, and those who have been first to carry the gospel into far lands.
2. (a)(m)(o) See 14.29 and p. 116, lines 3–5;   (b)(o) See 17.1–3;   (c)(o) See 17.1–3;   (d)(k)(n) See p. 116, note on 13.17,19;   (e)(i) See p. 5, numbered para. 2;   (f)(l) See p. 120, note on 17.9;   (g)(o) See pp. 118 and 119, note on 15.5;   (h)(o) See 14.6 and p. 117, note on 14.4b–6.
3. (a) 13.9; p. 116, notes on 13.6,9–12,20;   (b) and (c) 13.11;   (d) See p. 116, notes on 13.6,9–12,20;   (e) 14.4–11: See p. 117, note on 14.4a;   (f) See p. 117, notes on 14.12–14 and 14.18–20;   (g) See note on 14.24–27;   (h) 16.7: See p. 115, note on 15.5;   (i) and (j) 17.3–6: See p. 119, notes on 17.1,3,4 and 17.2;   (k) 14.31: See p. 118, notes on 14.29,31,32;   (l) 17.11: See pp. 119 and 120, note on 17.7–9,11;   (m) See p. 120, notes on 17.10 and 17.12,13.
4. See pp. 116 and 117, note on 14.1,2.
5. See p. 120, last 2 paras, and p. 121, lines 1–5.

18.1—21.17

1. (a) See p. 95, note on 9.14.
   (b) See p. 194, note on 19.1, and pp. 47, last 2 lines and 48, lines 1 and 2.
   (c) See pp. 127, last line and 128, lines 1–3, and p. 107, lines 4–6.
   (d) See p. 119, note on 16.14, lines 1 and 2.
2. See 28.16 and p. 125, lines 12 and 13.
3. (a) See p. 80, note on 7.20, and p. 83, note on 8.6,7, lines 4–7.
   (b) See p. 123, lines 12–9 from foot.
4. See p. 123, last 7 lines, p. 124, lines 1–6, and p. 125, lines 1–6 and 13–19.
5. See 21.1–10 and p. 128, note on 21.2,3.
6. Based on 21.13–16 and p. 129, lines 1–9.
7. See p. 125, last line, and p. 127, lines 1–3.

22.1—23.18

1. (a) See p. 131, note on 22.1,2.
   (b) See p. 131, Outline of 22.1–14, note on 22.1,5, lines 1–8, and p. 13, note on 1.8.
   (c) See p. 24, note on 1.25 and p. 95, note on 9.12.
   (d) See p. 80, note on 7.20.
2. See p. 23, note on 1.21 and p. 135, note on 23.17,18.
3. See p. 131, note on 22.1,5, lines 1–5.   **4.** See p. 131, note on 22.1,2.
5. See 22.8b–11,12–14 and pp. 132 and 133 notes on 22.12–14 and 22.13.

6. See p. 133, note on 22.16–19.
7. (a) See p. 134, note on 23.13,14 and p. 135, notes on 23.15,16 and 23.17,18.   (b) See p. 134, note on 23.8.

24.1—25.12
1. (a)(j);   (b)(i);   (c)(h);   (d)(g);   (e)(l);   (f)(k).
2. See p. 140, note on 24.13 and p. 119, note on 17.3.
3. See p. 138 and 139, note on 24.2.
4. See p. 139, note on 24.5, first para.
5. See p. 139, note on 24.5, second para.   **6.** See p. 141, note on 24.23.
7. See p. 141, note on 24.21, lines 1–8.
8. (a) See p. 140, note on 24.10–12.
(b) See p. 141, note on 24.21, paras 2 and 3 and note on 24.21,22.
(c) See p. 138, note on 24.1, p. 139, note on 24.5, paras 1 and 2, and p. 140, note on 24.17–20, especially lines 5–3 from foot.
(d) See p. 140, last 2 lines, p. 141, line 1, and look at Gen. 7.11b.
9. See 25.2 line 3 and 25.5 line 2; 25.3 line 1; 25.3 line 4; 25.4 line 7; 25.5 last line.

26.1—27.13
1. (a)(l);   (b)(g);   (c)(j);   (d)(h);   (e)(i);   (f)(k).
2. (a) The twin-words 'stronghold', 'shelter', and 'cloud' help to explain it in ch. 25.
(b) The twin-words 'dead' and 'dust' help to explain it in ch. 26.
3. See p. 137, paras 3 and 4; p. 141, note on 24.21; p. 145, note on 26,1.2; p. 146, note on 26.5; p. 149, note on 27,1; p. 150, note on 27. 12, 13, lines 7–3 from foot.
4. (a) See p. 146, note on 26.5, also p. 35, note on 2.12–14.
(b) See p. 147, note on 26.19; the clue is in the twin-words 'the dead' and 'the shades'.
(c) See p. 150, note on 27.10,11.   (d) See p. 150, note on 27.12.
5. See p. 140, note on 24.7–9 and p. 142, note on 25.6.
6. See p. 48, notes on 5.1 and 5.2, p. 49, note on 5.6 and p. 149, note on 27.2–4.
7. See p. 149, note on 27.4,5.   **8.** See p. 150, notes on 27.12 and 27.13.
9. See p. 142, note on 25.6, lines 4–12.

28.1–29
1. (a) See p. 154, note on 28.1,3;   (b) See pp. 155 and 156, note on 28,14,15, and p. 156, note on 27.17b,18;   (c) See p. 156, note on 21.16; (d) See p. 156, note on 28.21,22;   (e) See p. 154, Outline of 28.7,8; (f) See p. 156, notes on 28.16 and 28.17 and compare p. 125, note on 19.11,13, first para.;   (g) See p. 155, note on 28.11–13, lines 1–10.
2. See p. 155, note on 28.11–13, lines 7–14.
3. See pp. 153 and 154, Outline and then p. 154, notes on 28.2; 28.5,6; p. 155, notes on 28.7; 28.9,10, lines 1–5 and 28.11,13; pp. 155 and 156, note on 28.14,15, lines 1–6; p. 156, note on 28.23–29 and p. 157, para. 4.
4. See p. 155, note on 28.7.   **5.** See p. 155 and p. 156, note on 28.14,15.
6. (a) See p. 154, Outline of 28.7,8;   (b) See p. 154, Outline of 28.9–13, and p. 155, note on 28.11,13;   (c) See pp. 155 and 156, note on 28.14,15, and p. 157, para. 4.

7. See p. 156, note on 28.21.
8. See p. 156, note on 28.23–29, and p. 157, para. 1.
14. Based on p. 158, especially last para.

29.1–14

1. (a)(h); (b)(j); (c)(g); (d)(f); (e)(i).
2. See p. 165, note on 29.11.
3. See p. 162, note on 29.1–3, also p. 17, Outline of 1.11–15, and p. 18, note on 1.13.
4. See p. 161, note on 29.1, and p. 162, note on 29.1–3.
5. See pp. 162 and 163, note on 29.8. **6.** See p. 165, last para.
7. See p. 165, note on 29.13,14 and following para.
8. See p. 165, note on 29.11, especially last 4 lines.

29.15–24

1. (a)(h); (b)(i) See p. 169, note on 29.24; (c)(f) See p. 168, note on 29.20 and p. 169, second para.; (d)(g) See 29.13; (e)(j).
2. Based on p. 168, note on 29,18,19, lines 6–13.
3. See p. 167, last 8 lines and p. 168, paras 1–3.
4. See p. 168, note on 29.18,19, especially lines 1–5, and pp. 66 and 67, notes on 6.9 and 6.10.
5. See p. 168, note on 29.20,21, and p. 41, note on 3.26
6. See p. 169, note on 29.24 and following paras, and p. 170.
7. (i) See p. 168, and p. 169, notes on 29.18,19 and 29.20,21.
(iii) Based on p. 2 and p. 4, section headed 'The Prophets', and p. 5, third and fourth paras and numbered paras 1 and 2.
8. Based on p. 169, lines 10–2 from foot.
10. (a) See especially 29.9–16,20,21,24.

30.1–17

1. (a)(i); (b)(j); (c)(l); (d)(n); (e)(h); (f)(k) See p. 173, note on 30.8; (g)(m) See p. 174, note on 30.15.
2. (a) See p. 33, note on 2.7; p. 131, note on 22.5–7; and p. 176, line 10.
(b) See p. 174, note on 30.17.
3. (a), (b), and (d) See p. 172, notes on 30.1,2; 30.3 and 30.4.
(c) See pp. 155 and 156, notes on 28.11–13 and 28.14,15.
4. See p. 173, note on 30.7. **5.** See p. 173, note on 30.10.
6. See p. 173, note on 30.11 and follow up references given.
7. See pp. 173 and 174, notes on 30.12 and 30.13.
8. See p. 174, note on 30.15.
9. See p. 173, note on 30.8, p. 175, para. 2, p. 83, notes on 8.1 and 8.2, p. 84, note on 8.16,12, and p. 85, para. 1.
10. (i) See p. 175, para. 2, last 4 lines and paras 3 and 4.
11. (a) See p. 173, note on 30.12. **12.** (e) See p. 174, note on 30.15.

30.18–33

1. (a)(k); (b)(i); (c)(h); (d)(j); (e)(l); (f)(g).
2. (a) and (b) See p. 179, lines 4–7.
3. See p. 178, note on 30.18 and p. 179, lines 1–4.
4. (a) Based on 30.23–26, 29. (b) Based on 30.27,28,30–33.
5. See p. 182, last 3 paras and follow up the references given.

6. See p. 179, note on 30.22 and follow up the references given.
7. See p. 179, note on 30.20,21.
8. See p. 179, note on 30.26, and p. 181, lines 1–3.
10. Based on p. 179, note on 30.26.
11. Based on p. 182, last para. and p. 183, paras 1 and 2, and p. 184, para. 2.

31.1–9

1. (a) See p. 186, lines 7–5 from foot.
   (b) See 31.4,5; p. 188, lines 5, 6, and 15–19, and p. 190, lines 12–14.
   (c) See p. 190, lines 8–10.
2. (a) and (b) Compare the two passages and also pp. 186 and 187, notes on 31. 1; 31.2; and 31.3 with p. 172, notes on 30.1,2 and 30.3.
3. See p. 187, lines 8–10.
4. (a) See p. 187, note on 31.4,5 and p. 188, paras 1–4.
   (b) See p. 188, note on 31.6,7, lines 1–9.
5. See p. 95, Outline of 5.26–30; p. 97, notes on 5.26 and 5.30; p. 82, last 3 lines; p. 83, lines 1 and 2; p. 116, Outline of 15.1—16.14; and pp. 187 and 188, note on 31.4,5.
6. (i) Based on p. 187, note on 31.3.
7. See p. 181, note on 30.29, and p. 190, note on 31.9.

32.1–20

1. See p. 197, para. 5 and also p. 74, note on 7.4; p. 123, last 2 lines and p. 124, lines 1–3; p. 174, note on 30.15.
2. See p. 194, note on 32.6,7.
3. (a) See p. 193, note on 32.3;   (b) See p. 193, note on 32.4 and p. 194, para. 2;   (c) See p. 197, note on 32.15.
4. See p. 41, note on 3.16,17 and p. 43, para. 3, and p. 196, paras 1–4.
5. See especially 32.15–20, p. 197, note on 3.19, and p. 198, paras (a) and (b).

33.1–34

1. (a) See p. 200, note on 33.2, also p. 95, note on 9.12 and p. 181, notes on 30.30,31.   (b) See p. 200, note on 33.3,4;   (c) See p. 201, note on 33.5,6;   (d) See p. 202, note on 33.12;   (e) See p. 202, note on 33.16;   (f) See p. 203, note on 33.18,19.
2. See p. 199, Introduction: p. 201, lines 4,5; p. 201, note on 30.10; p. 202, note on 30.14.
3. See pp. 200 and 201, notes on 33.1 and 33.5,6.
4. Compare p. 200, note on 33.1 and p. 201, note on 33.5,6.
5. See p. 201, note on 33.9.
6. See p. 201, note on 33.11,12 and p. 202, note on 33.13.
7. See 33.14,15 and p. 202, note on 33.14.
8. See p. 203, note on 33.18,19.   **9.** See p. 203, note on 33.20,21.

34.1–17

1. (a) See p. 141, note on 24.31;   (b) See p. 209, note on 34.9;   (c) and (d) See p. 210, note on 34.13.
2. See p. 209, note on 34.11, lines 6–9.
3. See p. 207, Introduction, especially para. 3.

4. See p. 209, note on 34.5,6.
5. See p. 210, 3 final paras and p. 211, paras 1–4.
7. Based on p. 210, note on 34.16.

35.1–10
1. (a)(i); (b)(k); (c)(g); (d)(h); (e)(l); (f)(j).
2. See p. 214, note on 35.4: retribution, pay-back, compensation, reparation.
3. See p. 207, Introduction, paras 1 and 2; p. 214, para. 2 and note on 35.3,4; and p. 215, note on 35.9,10.
4. See pp. 213 and 214, note on 35.1,2, and p. 201, note on 33.9.
5. See p. 214, notes on 35.3,4,5,6; p. 215, para. 4 and p. 217, paras 2–4.
6. See pp. 214 and 215, note on 35.9,10.
8. Based on p. 214, note on 35.8 and the references given.

Special Note 3
1. See p. 219, Special Note 3, para. 1 and p. 222, paras 2–5.
2. (a)(l); (b)(k); (c)(m); (d)(j); (e)(n); (f)(i); (g)(h).

36.1—37.7
1. See p. 230, lines 5,6.
2. See p. 225, para. 4, last 3 lines and para. 5, lines 4 and 5; p. 228, note on 36.10, last 3 lines. Perhaps all except tolerant, decrepit, and considerate.
3. (a) See p. 227, note on 36.7 and following para, and p. 228, lines 1 and 2.
(b) See p. 229, note on 36.18,19, and p. 101, notes on 10.9,10 and 10.11.
4. See p. 228, note on 36.11.
5. See 36.16,17 and pp. 228, 229, note on 36.14–16.
6. (a) See 37.4; (b) See 37.7 and pp. 229 and 230, note on 37.6,7.

37.8–38
1. See p. 236, paras 3 and 4. Perhaps it is only safe to say that he was prudent, quiet, courageous, pious, confident, humble, and trustful.
2. (a) See p. 226, note on 36.2. (b) See p. 36.6 and p. 227, note on 25.4,6; (c) See p. 13, note on 1.8; (d) See p. 233, note on 37.22; (e) See p. 233, note on 37.28,29; (f) See p. 124, note on 19.5, first sentence and p. 233, note on 37.25; (g) See p. 234, lines 1–7 and p. 91, note on 9.7.
3. (a) See e.g. p. 231, last 7 lines, p. 232, lines 1–3 and note on 37.9,10.
(b) Compare 36.21—37.4 with 37.14–20; and p. 229, notes on 36.21,22 and 37.1,2,3 with pp. 232 and 233, note on 37.14,15.
(c) and (d) Compare 37.1–7 with 37.14–35, and pp. 229 and 230 notes on 37,1,2,3,6 and 7 with pp. 232 and 233 notes on 37.14,15 and 37.21;
(e) Compare 37.5–8 and 37.33–37, and pp. 229 and 230, note on 37.6,7 with p. 234, notes on 37.33–35 and 37.36–38.
4. See p. 234, note on 37.36–38.
5. Based on pp. 234–236, section headed 'Sennacherib's Arguments', and pp. 236 and 237, section headed 'The "God is with us" Idea'.
7. Based on p. 237, paras 4 and 5.

38.1—39.8

1. (a) See p. 241, note on 38.1;   (b) Compare 2.2,5 and 9.2 and see
   p. 241, note on 38.2;   (c) See p. 53, note on 5.14;   (d) See p. 243,
   note on 38.12;   (e) and (f) See p. 243, note on 38.12 (and 13): the clue
   is in the rest of the verse, especially line 2: 'I moan like a dove'.
   2. See p. 38.2–6.   **3.** See p. 245, note on 39.3.
   4. See 38.1–3 and p. 241, note on 38.2.
   5. Compare 38.22 with 7.10–12 and see p. 229, note on 37.1,2, and p. 242,
   notes on 38.7 and 38.8.
   6. See p. 245, notes on 39.1,2,3,5,6.

Index

This index includes only the more important references to God, Isaiah himself, Ahaz, Hezekiah and Sennacherib, and to Judah, Israel, Assyria, Babylon and Egypt, because these names occur with great frequency throughout the Guide. Bold-type references indicate the pages where a theme or subject is studied in detail.